Beyond Boundaries

Beyond Boundaries

C.L.R. James and Postnational Studies

Edited by
Christopher Gair

LONDON • ANN ARBOR, MI

First published 2006 by Pluto Press
345 Archway Road, London N6 5AA
and 839 Greene Street, Ann Arbor, MI 48106

www.plutobooks.com

Copyright © Christopher Gair 2006

The right of the individual contributors to be identified as the authors
of this work has been asserted by them in accordance with the Copyright,
Designs and Patents Act 1988.

British Library Cataloguing in Publication Data
A catalogue record for this book is available from the British Library

ISBN   0 7453 2343 X hardback
ISBN   0 7453 2342 1 paperback

Library of Congress Cataloging in Publication Data applied for

10   9   8   7   6   5   4   3   2   1

Designed and produced for Pluto Press by
Chase Publishing Services Ltd, Fortescue, Sidmouth, EX10 9QG, England
Typeset from disk by Stanford DTP Services, Northampton, England
Printed and bound in the European Union by
Antony Rowe Ltd, Chippenham and Eastbourne, England

Contents

Introduction: C.L.R. James and Postnational Studies   1
Christopher Gair

1. C.L.R. James, Genre and Cultural Politics   13
   Nicole King

2. 'Summer of Hummer': C.L.R. James, *American Civilization*, and the (Necro)Political Crisis   39
   Eric Porter

3. C.L.R. James, *Moby-Dick*, and the Emergence of Transnational American Studies   59
   Donald E. Pease

4. Beyond Boundaries: Cricket, Herman Melville, and C.L.R. James's Cold War   89
   Christopher Gair

5. The Odd Couple: C.L.R. James, Hannah Arendt and the Return of Politics in the Cold War   108
   Richard King

6. C.L.R. James's *American Civilization*   128
   Bill Schwarz

7. C.L.R. James and the Politics of the Subject, Culture and Desire   157
   Anthony Bogues

8. C.L.R. James, Critical Humanist   175
   Brian Alleyne

Contributors   197
Index   198

Introduction:
C.L.R James and Postnational Studies
Christopher Gair

Recent decades have witnessed a crisis within what could once less self-consciously be labelled 'American Studies'. The cultural revolutions of the late 1960s inflicted an apparently fatal blow on the hegemony of the myth–symbol school, and initiated what Donald E. Pease has termed the 'critical nationalism' of the 1970s. In place of a metanarrative of American history corroborating American exceptionalism which (to draw once more on Pease) 'engaged a prototypical American self (*American Adam*), in a quest romance (*Errand into the Wilderness*) to liberate "our" native land (*Virgin Land*) from "foreign" encroachment (*The Power of Blackness*)',[1] the pre-eminent scholars of the 1970s constructed what quickly became known as multiculturalist accounts of American history. Now-canonical texts such as Richard Slotkin's *Regeneration Through Violence* and Annette Kolodny's *The Lay of the Land* rewrote the metanarrative in terms of 'Indian removal, frontier violence, government theft, land devastation, class cruelty, racial brutality, and misogyny'.[2] Alongside the rejoinder to the idea that (almost) all great American literature had been written by a group of white men living in New England and New York, whose artistry represented what R.W.B. Lewis once approvingly called the 'lively and creative dialogue' that 'may be said to *be* the culture'[3] (original emphasis), these newer studies also challenged the modernist valorisation of high over popular culture. Thus, intellectual historians such as Slotkin, Kolodny, Alan Trachtenberg and Ann Douglas sought to re-imagine the texts of the established American literary canon, as well as both listening to other voices silenced by the dominant discourse of the nineteenth century *and* reawakening the once widely disseminated sounds of dime novels and sentimental fictions marginalised by the first generations of American Studies specialists.

Despite finding much to applaud in this kind of multiculturalism, many scholars have, in the past decade or more, been anxious to extend, if not break, the paradigm. The contributors to *Cultures of United States Imperialism* (1993), co-edited by Pease with Amy Kaplan, all articulate a general disquiet about the insularity of American Studies throughout its history. Thus, while the move from uni- to multi-vocal accounts of US culture *has* resulted in a paradigm shift, that shift still, as Kaplan argues, 'analyzes American society and culture in terms of internal difference and conflicts', and thus sustains the fiction of an America defined as a 'discrete identity'. While the turn from high to popular culture broadened the scope of the discipline, too many of the newer works (though certainly not those cited above) were, as Paul Giles notes

> Ebullient celebrations of supposedly representative American icons – the dating rituals, the popular romances, the baseball memorabilia – [which took] delight in their own intellectual unpretentiousness and, above all, in the fact that the items under consideration were homespun rather than European.[4]

In another essay, Giles has pointed to a further, related danger associated with this kind of American Studies: in the mid twentieth century, the integration of several different discourses into an interdisciplinary totality was

> seen implicitly as a correlative to the assimilation of immigrant and regional differences in the consensual bosom of mainstream liberal culture, so that American Studies in the 1950s became a patriotic subject in methodology as well as in thematic content.[5]

By extending the discipline to incorporate the study of writings by, for example, women, immigrants, or ethnic communities, multicultural American Studies (whatever the ideological position of particular scholars) perpetuated a notion of national exceptionalism, the ability, in Whitman's words, to 'contain multitudes' within an enclosed national space. Although the leading multiculturalists were ideologically remote from the first generation of Americanists, their interventions did not challenge the notion of nation itself.

Kaplan posits an alternative approach, in her case 'relating ... internal categories of gender, race, and ethnicity to the global dynamics of empire-building'. Thus, in a refutation of earlier American Studies methodologies, she explains that

> *Cultures of United States Imperialism* explores how such diverse identities cohere, fragment, and change in relation to one another and to ideologies

of nationhood through the crucible of international power relations, and how, conversely, imperialism as a political or economic process abroad is inseparable from the social relations and cultural discourses of race, gender, ethnicity, and class at home.[6]

One of the clearest ways in which this methodology departs from the key texts of earlier American Studies is in the desire to oversee the works of even the canonical American authors of the 'American Renaissance', such as Herman Melville, not in terms of national myths, but rather as the product of international exchange. And, for this reason, it is unsurprising that several scholars (including those whose work is gathered in this collection) have recently attempted to situate C.L.R. James as a pioneering practitioner of postnational American Studies. James serves a dual purpose here: not only does his understanding of American (and other) 'national' cultures depart radically from the readings cited by Pease as the founding documents of American Studies, it also provides an account that moves outside the geographical and disciplinary boundaries of national multiculturalism in ways that go beyond the first wave of postnational American Studies exemplified by *Cultures of United States Imperialism*.

Given James's life history, this seems almost inevitable. As Sylvia Wynter has described him,

> James was a Negro yet British, a colonial native yet culturally a part of the public school code, attached to the cause of the proletariat yet a member of the middle class, a Marxian yet a Puritan, an intellectual who plays cricket, of African descent yet Western, a Trotskyist and Pan-Africanist, a Marxist yet a supporter of black studies, a West-Indian majority black yet an American minority black.[7]

James's understanding of Melville and, in particular, of *Moby-Dick* in *Mariners, Renegades and Castaways*, serves as the best known example of his groundbreaking approach. The book both challenges the American Studies readings of Melville published by Richard Chase and F.O. Matthiessen in the 1940s, and acts as a defence of James's own claims (ultimately unsuccessful) for US citizenship. Whereas Chase had read *Moby-Dick* in terms that 'posited Ahab's monomania as the signifier of the totalitarian Other in opposition to which Ishmael's Americanness was defined, elaborated upon and defended', and had constructed an understanding of American Studies around this opposition, James sees Ishmael as an 'intellectual Ahab', a further harbinger of an American security state that, far from representing freedom, 'had put into place the totalitarian rule that it purported to oppose',[8] and which had detained James on Ellis Island, where he wrote much of his book.

Clearly, James's reading of *Moby-Dick* (even in this cursory summary) imagines a text very different from the one which was commonly understood in American Studies for generations following Chase, and a widespread critical appreciation of it could have resulted in the development of a radically different academic discipline. Upon publication, and subsequently, however, *Mariners, Renegades and Castaways* was largely ignored, for both political and theoretical reasons: although James sent his book to every Congressman, feeling that it would prove his suitability for citizenship, his reading is clearly at odds with those which champion American individualism and freedom in their representations of Ishmael. It therefore received little coverage in the academic community during the Cold War, and was rarely even mentioned in the bibliographic essays on Melville compiled from the 1950s to 1970s. More recently, James's focus on the crew of the *Pequod* as the true heroes of the novel has brought charges of wilful critical misinterpretation. William E. Cain, for example, has accused him of 'bringing to light and affirming not what the text contains, but, rather, his vivid reimagination of it'.[9] Similarly, the Marxist critic Paul Buhle, in a reading that posits James as little different from the hegemonic scholars he appeared to oppose, censures James for the political and cultural naivety of *Mariners*, suggesting that James 'more nearly approached an apologia for social life under capitalism than at any other time before or since', a point specifically and convincingly refuted by Pease, who points out that James's criticisms of the communists with whom he shared a cell on Ellis Island do not constitute a defence of capitalism.[10]

When we turn to James's own thoughts about his work, it becomes clear that what he is attempting is a social critique that cannot be reduced to a form constrained by, or privileging, this or that national perspective. James's understanding of the complex postnational exchanges operating in his work is elucidated most clearly in a 1963 letter to V.S. Naipaul, in which he explains his thoughts on *Beyond a Boundary*. In a pattern that could also be used to describe the construction of *Mariners, Renegades and Castaways*, he suggests that:

1. The book is West Indian through and through, particularly in the early chapters on my family, my education and the portraits of West Indian cricketers of the previous generation, some of them unknown.
2. But the book is very British. Not only the language but on page after page the (often unconscious) literary references, the turn of phrase, the mental and moral outlook ...
3. But that does not end it, not at all. That is only the beginning. I believe that, originating as we are within the British structure, but living under such different social conditions, we have a lot to say about the British civilization itself which we see more sharply than they themselves.[11]

James recognises the multiple national identities at work within his book, and appreciates that its power resides in the extent to which it is irreducible to any one nationalising narrative. Although he can identify the West Indian and the British components of its construction, he appreciates that this is 'only the beginning', and believes that, even as author, he is unable fully to recognise or control the 'often unconscious' fusion of outlooks from different cultures. In addition to the narrative of origins laid out here, it would also be possible to read the numerous American cultural referents included in *Beyond a Boundary*, and to suggest that its composition was made possible by James's long stay in the United States – an unusual background for a book on cricket. But, in *Mariners, Renegades and Castaways*, the process functions in a different direction, with James extending his postnational approach to offer a reading of American culture seen 'more sharply' than by many of his American contemporaries.

Even in his early works, written largely before he moved to England, James displayed an interest in subjects that would return in his study of Melville. On the opening page of *The Life of Captain Cipriani* (1932), he notes that, 'During the last eighteen years, [Cipriani] has been engaged in a series of struggles against the bad manners, the injustice, the tyranny, and the treachery of Crown Colony Government',[12] a summary that sounds strikingly similar in both factual detail and moral indignation to James's account of his own relations with American bureaucracy in 1952. Likewise, *Minty Alley* (1936) is an early example of James's interest in the interrelationship between the lone intellectual and the working classes, constructed within a local community viewed trans-locally – a theme that recurs not only in *Mariners*, but also in *American Civilization* (1993), the monumentally wide-ranging study of United States culture that James drafted in 1950, but which he never completed. In *Minty Alley*, Haynes, a middle-class, bookish young man whose prospects are severely curtailed by the death of his mother, moves from the family house to lodgings at Number 2, Minty Alley, in order to 'save some money and do something'.[13] As the novel progresses, he gradually becomes more involved in the lives of the other occupants of the house, and experiences a sexual awakening through Maisie, the niece of Mrs. Rouse, the long-suffering mistress of the property. But, like the Ishmael of James's later reading of *Moby-Dick*, the directionless Haynes is never able fully to integrate himself into this working-class community, and fails to save it. By the end of the novel, that community is fragmented by a combination of local and transnational forces: Maisie has moved to the United States, Mrs. Rouse's unfaithful long-term lover is dead, and she has fallen out with almost everyone who lived in the house, and, finally, has moved out herself and sold the property. The concluding paragraph of the book sees Haynes, now back with Ella, his mother's servant, and apparently reintegrated into the middle classes, stopping outside Number 2, and noting its own gentrification. In place of what had once seemed an organically whole working-class environment, 'Husband and wife and three children lived there and one of the children was sitting at the piano playing a familiar tune from Henry's music-book.'[14]

Although *Minty Alley* is an essential marker of the subsequent trajectory of James's intellectual project, there are aspects of it that are profoundly unsatisfactory. In particular, his representation of the working class as almost entirely female and domestic (although, of course, Number 2 is also a place of work) renders events, in James's treatment of them, rather trivial. The community is destroyed from within by a series of petty squabbles, rather than being portrayed as actively participating in a class struggle, and James appears to see no meaningful role for women in such struggle. By turning to cricket, and later to the all-male world of the *Pequod*, he was able to avoid engaging with this 'problem' in future. Although, late in life, he did express regret at his earlier failure to understand the importance of women's role in potential world revolution,[15] James's major works of the 1930s to 1950s depict essential human struggles as being played out in male environments.

Postnational (American) Studies has become paradigmatic in the years since the collapse of the Soviet Union and the end of the Cold War. In many ways, this is unsurprising: Cold War rhetoric imagined national communities defined by ideological consensus within relatively straightforward binary oppositions between good and evil, or freedom and control. Power was easy to locate both domestically (in government and the official apparatus of the state) and in the political centres, Washington and Moscow. The nation tended to be viewed as a whole – in which a doctrine of 'freedom' generated endless possibilities for internal difference – because to regard it in any other way was to appear 'un-American'. After the Cold War, such binaries are unpersuasive or simply irrelevant: trans- or multinational corporations cannot be accurately associated with individual nations, since production, consumption, advertising, taxation policy and so on function across national boundaries in ways that make such association redundant. Religious ideologies have re-emerged as essential shapers of transnational communities whose identification with hegemonic nationalism is often ephemeral. Unlike during the Cold War, the 'enemy' has no apparent centre; instead, it is subdivided into a potentially infinite number of cells acting more or less independently. Likewise, even hegemonic discourse appeals increasingly in language designed to elicit the support of a disparate collection of interest groups – albeit often couched within a flag-waving appeal to Americanness – rather than taking a shared sense of national character for granted. Thus, as Eric Porter points out in his essay in this volume, the most recent presidential election in the United States was fought by the right on a 'god, gays and guns' platform that appealed to many voters apparently otherwise deeply divided by race, class and geography.

This raises the questions: Why James? Why now? The vast majority of his work was conceived and executed in the time between the rise of totalitarianism in the 1930s and latter days of the Cold War. He died before the collapse of the Soviet Union and the occurrence of indices of the New World Order such as the Gulf War of 1990–91. He was, therefore, writing of a world very different from our own: What, for example, would the author of *American Civilization* have made of accounts of the torture and abuse of prisoners at Guantanamo Bay, or that of *Beyond a Boundary* of cricket-loving suicide bombers in London in 2005?

It is not necessary to go quite so far as James himself in his adoption of Melville as the quintessential American writer of the 1950s to provide answers to these questions, and the essays collected in this volume make clear how significant James's thinking can be to considerations of the early twenty-first century. For Nicole King, in 'C.L.R. James, Genre and Cultural Politics', James's play, *Touissant*

L'Overture (1936) acts as a prototype of the postnational in its creolised subversion of hegemonic systems. Although she does not make the point explicitly, King sees the play as a kind of anticipation of what James would later ask of Melville in *Mariners, Renegades and Castaways*, in that it vocalises the Saint-Domingue slaves in a manner that was absent from *The Black Jacobins* (1938). Even James (in later life) seems to have regarded the play as a relatively minor element of his oeuvre, but King suggests that that it is effective in revealing the 'subaltern voices and bodies of the [Saint-Domingue] Revolution' in a manner absent from *The Black Jacobins*.

In 'Summer of Hummer', Eric Porter uses a reading of *American Civilization* to assess the impact of the increasingly close relationship between militarism and consumerism on national and transnational social groups. For Porter, James's insistence on the 'centrality of minoritarian subjects' to US history, and on the interconnectivity of revolutionary political programmes and scholarly investigations of American culture, serves both as a refutation of the paradigmatic American Studies methodology of the 1950s and as a model for what future American Studies could become. Like most of the other contributors to this volume, Porter also engages with the shortcomings of James's approach to US society, pointing out that James's forecasts about the empowerment of unions were wide of the mark, and highlighting his failure (in *American Civilization*) to engage with US economic and cultural imperialism.

Donald E. Pease and Christopher Gair both focus on *Mariners, Renegades and Castaways* as a model for future versions of postnational American Studies. Highlighting the paradoxical position that James experienced as a detainee on Ellis Island – due to be deported under the terms of the McCarran–Walter Act, yet unable to challenge that act without appearing to demonstrate an example of the very behaviour of which he was accused – Pease argues that James produced a reading of Melville that exposed the state's agency in bringing the ideals of US democracy under threat. For Pease, James provides an interpretation of *Moby-Dick* that 'turned the national mythology inside out', establishing links between US foreign policy and the kind of internal colonisation in evidence on Ellis Island. Thus, *Mariners, Renegades and Castaways* serves as the 'outline of a postnational fable', generating a reconceptualisation of the United States as a 'geo-social space on the move across and between nations'.

Gair adopts a similar stance, but argues that the roots of James's ideas stretched back at least to the early 1930s, when he arrived in England and started to think about totalitarianism. For Gair, the links between the various strands of James's thought – cricket, Melville, totalitarianism, national and postnational identities – are inseparable. Whereas most American Americanists tend to focus on James's writings about the United States, Gair explores the links between James's thoughts on the 'bodyline' conflict that shook cricketing relations between England and Australia in 1932–33 and his attempts to gain US citizenship by appeal to values that he learned on the playing fields of Trinidad. In both cases, it is the gap between institutional rhetoric and practice that enables James to expose the ways in which colonial subjects are marginalised when they attempt to utilise the discourse that has been instilled in them by hegemonic authorities.

In the end, Richard King's 'odd couple' – James and Hannah Arendt – are better matched than would initially seem to be the case. By looking at the pair's shared interest in the origins of political activity in fifth-century Athens, at their understanding of the relationship between totalitarianism and the crisis of modernity, and at their mutual recognition of the 1956 Hungarian Revolution, King challenges the overly narrow approaches to both James and Arendt. For King, the result is that both thinkers can be appreciated within wider fields than is usually the case – by reading James alongside Arendt, his work appears more significant in mainstream Western thought; by reading Arendt alongside James, her writings come to 'illuminate the politics of totalitarian domination *and* participatory freedom outside the narrow confines of the European tradition'.

Like Gair, Bill Schwarz also looks at the links between James's American writings and his work on cricket. Given the nature of this book's insistence on James's postnational credentials, Schwarz's deconstruction of the gap between the 'English' and the 'American' James is invaluable. Likewise, his assessment of *Beyond a Boundary* as a text that 'could not have been imagined into existence without the work of great theoretical labour sustained in the United States' is long overdue. Schwarz (again like Gair) asks the question: What connection could there be between Melville and cricket? For Schwarz, that connection provides evidence of James's ability to think beyond Trotskyism, with the theoretical work that James conducted in the United States on the battle between civilisation and barbarism resurfacing in *Beyond a Boundary*.

All the essays in this collection, either implicitly or explicitly, make the point that it is impossible to think postnationally without considering the role of the United States. Although, as with *Beyond a Boundary*, James often wrote in ways that did not overtly address America, its emergence as both political superpower and disseminator of an increasingly globalised popular culture is traceable throughout his writings. For Tony Bogues, as for Schwarz, the centrality of the United States as hegemonic force proved to be particularly dramatic for James, since (as he famously pronounced) he knew so little about the country before his arrival in 1938. Thus, it is perhaps unsurprising that James's thought underwent such radical transformation during the 1940s. Bogues is surely correct to argue that the period between the late 1940s and the publication of *Beyond a Boundary* in 1963 was 'extraordinarily fertile' for James. Nevertheless, Bogues emphasises how, although James's residence in America produced a growing insistence on the primacy of the human need to express creativity, the James of *American Civilization* was blind to the manner in which American imperial power increasingly curtailed the possibilities of the human. But in an optimistic ending, Bogues suggests that, with *Beyond a Boundary*, James imagines the creation of counterhegemonic ways of life whose struggle against domination can provide useful ideas in the ongoing struggle against the imperial power of America.

In the final essay in this book, 'C.L.R. James, Critical Humanist', Brian Alleyne uses James's 'hybrid approach to culture and politics' to argue that the humanist project has been abandoned prematurely. In a wide-ranging approach, Alleyne reads James's novel *Minty Alley* as a fictional anthropology or ethnography that was crucial to the formation of his early political consciousness. Making parallels between James's career and that of Angela Davis in the United States, Alleyne notes how both adapted early traditional educations in Western thought to their praxis as radical Black activists. One of the consequences of this is that neither would consider any kind of essentialised Black identity in their attempts to transform society. Alleyne's assertion that James was a 'complicated amalgam of influences ... a *bricoleur*' who combined 'seemingly disparate elements to construct a conception of history and culture' could well serve as an epigraph for this book. The hybridity integral to James's work was a *refutation* of both the paradigmatic American Studies of the time and the British imperial education that he had acquired in Trinidad, but this is not to say that it was a *rejection* of these practices. The same could be said of James's later ongoing engagement with Marxism and Trotskyism. It is now for the next generation of postnationalism scholars to attempt to adopt James's hybridity and, as he hoped would be the case with *Beyond a Boundary*, see the world 'more sharply' than has been the case within earlier paradigms.

A book of essays is always a collaborative exercise and, in addition to the contributors themselves, whose insights about James and patience with their editor's succession of queries went well beyond the call of duty, several people deserve special thanks. At Birmingham, I am particularly indebted to Ali Fisher, Conrad James, Scott Lucas and Paul Woolf, all of whom discussed the ideas contained here. In addition, I am grateful to David Castle at Pluto, and to the anonymous readers whose ideas helped turn a loose proposal into what I hope is a coherent book. Bill Boelhower, Bill Brown, Ralph Dumain, Dennis Dworkin, Aliki Varvogli and Jay Williams all made invaluable suggestions. Finally, this book is dedicated to the late Jim Murray, whose enthusiastic response to my first attempts to shape my ideas about James and postnationalism was one of the major inspirations for this project.

NOTES

1. Donald E. Pease, 'New Perspectives on US Culture and Imperialism', in *Cultures of United States Imperialism*, ed. Amy Kaplan and Donald E. Pease (Durham, NC and London: Duke UP, 1993), pp. 23–4. That the leading practitioners of myth–symbol criticism were aware of this disciplinary crisis is indicated by Leo Marx's 'American Studies – A Defense of an Unscientific Method', *New Literary History* 1 (1969), pp. 75–90.
2. Pease, 'New Perspectives', p. 25.
3. R.W.B. Lewis, *The American Adam: Innocence, Tragedy and Tradition in the Nineteenth Century* (Chicago: University of Chicago Press, 1955), p. 2.
4. Paul Giles, 'Reconstructing American Studies: Postnational Paradoxes, Comparative Perspectives', *Journal of American Studies* 28:3 (1994), pp. 335–58, esp. p. 349.
5. Paul Giles, 'Transnationalism and Classic American Literature', *PMLA* 118:1 (2003), pp. 62–77, esp. p. 64.
6. Amy Kaplan, '"Left Alone with America": The Absence of Empire in the Study of American Culture', in *Cultures of United States Imperialism*, pp. 15, 16.
7. Quoted in 'C.L.R. James's *Mariners, Renegades and Castaways and the World We Live In*', Pease's introduction to C.L.R. James, *Mariners, Renegades and Castaways: the Story of Herman Melville and the World We Live In* (Hanover, NH: University Press of New England, 2001), p. x.
8. Donald Pease, 'James, *Moby-Dick*, and the Emergence of Postnational American Studies', in this volume.
9. Quoted in Donald E. Pease, 'Doing Justice to C.L.R. James's *Mariners, Renegades, and Castaways*', *Boundary 2* 27:2 (2000), pp. 1–19, esp. p. 2.

10. Paul Buhle, *C.L.R. James: The Artist as Revolutionary* (London and New York: Verso, 1988, p. 110; Pease, 'C.L.R. James's *Mariners, Renegades and Castaways*', p. xv.
11. C.L.R. James, *Cricket*, edited by Anna Grimshaw (London: Allison and Busby, 1986), p. 116.
12. C.L.R. James, *The Life of Captain Cipriani: An Account of British Government in the West Indies* (Nelson: Coulton, 1932), p. 1.
13. C.L.R. James, *Minty Alley* (University Press of Mississippi, 1997), p. 23.
14. *Minty Alley*, p. 244.
15. See Buhle, *C.L.R. James*, pp. 156–7, for an account of James's embrace of writers such as Toni Morrison, Ntozake Shange, and Alice Walker in the early 1980s. 'James the lifetime reader of literature saw in the evocation of Black women's daily lives ... the promise of revolutionary possibility undiminished, indeed raised by the consciousness of gender.'

1
C.L.R. James, Genre and Cultural Politics
Nicole King

In 1971 C.L.R. James gave three lectures in Atlanta, Georgia on the subject of *The Black Jacobins: Toussaint L'Ouverture and the San Domingo Revolution* (1938). The lectures cover the context of the famous history's creation, place it into conversation with W.E.B. Du Bois's *Black Reconstruction* (1936), and reveal some of James's ideas on what he might do differently, if he had the writing to do all over again nearly 40 years after the original publication. At no point in these three June lectures does James mention his play, *Toussaint L'Ouverture*, the composition and production of which preceded the publication of *Jacobins* by two years, and which drew on the same extensive research he used for the history. In the third and final lecture, 'How I Would Re-write *The Black Jacobins*', James states, 'I would write descriptions in which the black slaves themselves, or people very close to them, describe what they're doing and how they felt about the work that they were forced to carry on.'[1] In fact, James never did revise *The Black Jacobins*, although he added an extensive appendix in 1963. The play has a separate history.

Toussaint L'Ouverture was originally staged in London in March 1936, with Paul Robeson, who was then a well known star of the stage and screen, in the lead role. Three decades later, in 1967, James revised the play; it was staged for a second time in 1968, was finally published for the first time in 1976, and has enjoyed a smattering of productions, some quite warmly received, since the 1970s. At no point, however – then or now – has the play ever received the same attention or critical evaluation that the history has. Perhaps, as James himself suggests through omission in 1971, the play does not stay in the imagination the way that the history does; indeed, *that* is a text which has never been out of print since 1938. But then, his 1967 revision of the play and the renewed interest in it stand in contradiction to such an assessment. Nevertheless, lacking the distinguished reception accorded to the history, the play would have been widely unknown to his Atlanta audience, and bringing it into the frame would certainly have complicated the narrative line of his three lectures. For, while the story told of the Saint-Domingue Revolution is not radically different in either work, the *manner* in which that story is told is quite distinct, because of the ways that James chooses to activate the genres of history and drama. Ironically, what James might have done differently in the history suggests he needn't have looked much further than his very own play. For certain scripted moments in the play do give voice to the ex-slaves, and allow them to present their own interpretation of the convulsive events of the Revolution. In its ability to present these voices, the play has an immediate advantage over the history: ritual, music and dance, as well as stage effects, are all mobilised in the service of revealing the subaltern voices and bodies of the Revolution.

The formal qualities of the play present provocative contrasts with the history. Thus, when read together, a more complex narrative of the events of the Saint-Domingue Revolution emerges, a narrative that more closely approximates the one James imagined in his 1971 comments about *Black Jacobins*. Thus, taking our lead from James himself, the story of the play's narrative is what concerns us here: it is a compelling, creolised text. The drama's meta-narrative is an enactment of creolisation as it encompasses original and rewritten text, different stagings in multiple locations and timeframes which span from anticolonial movements to postnational moments. The generic dynamism and fluidity that attend to theatrical productions are key components of *Toussaint L'Ouverture*'s inhabitation of creolisation. As a play staged in the 1930s, and then the 1960s–1990s its creative force and contexts are about C.L.R. James and his cultural/political vision on one level, but at the same time extend out and beyond him. For too long James's play has been pushed aside before being recognised for what it can reveal about James, and about arguments now understood as central to cultural and postcolonial studies. A consideration, then, of the internal and external creolised contexts of *Toussaint L'Ouverture* makes visible how James and his dramatic medium bring to the surface non-national dimensions of putatively national histories, literatures and politics.

The fact that we do not study *Toussaint L'Ouverture* sharply recalls the genealogical link between critical literary practices and the formation of national identity at the beginning of the twentieth century. In the Anglophone Caribbean, for example, the development of national literatures paralleled the push for self-determination and independence. Texts were evaluated and became canonical according to a rubric that prioritised a particular kind of unity and coherence, and recognised such traits as essential to a successful literary work (ironically proving just how thorough the colonisation process had been). In the pages that follow, I argue that both despite and because of the considerable obscurity of *Toussaint L'Ouverture* (renamed *The Black Jacobins* in 1967), and its so-called aesthetic failures, it demands our attention. The very contextualisation that James provides for the history in his 1971 lectures is necessary for this play, produced at the fulcrum of pan-Africanism, and emblematic of much of what that multinational political formation and ideology strove to achieve. The continued relevance of the drama as a dynamic mechanism within varied spaces of local and transnational politics is signalled by the renewed interest in the play that occurred in the latter decades of the twentieth century. Asserting creolisation as a habitus – one used variously to denote a coming into being, the lived experience and practice of individuals – while also serving as an explanatory mechanism for large-scale social structures, societies and histories, my reading of the play argues for a keener appreciation of the play and the work it continues to accomplish.[2] An analysis of how James and Robeson came to the point of collaboration, the production history of the play, the unfolding historical contexts of the play – especially as related to Marxism and Communism – and the specific representation of vodou within the play, constitute my presentation of a creolised aesthetics for reading *Toussaint L'Ouverture*.[3] A focus on vodou is a notable critical reward of revisiting and revising the ways that the play has been valued and evaluated; the representation of vodou in the play is the primary mechanism James has at his disposal for showing how the slaves and ex-slaves of Saint-Domingue felt about the convulsive events of the Revolution. Such re-viewing and contextualization of the play is complicated considerably by the fact that *only* the revised 1967 version of the play survives. But perhaps it is fitting that the present analysis of the play, within a creolisation framework, cannot rely upon a straightforward comparison of revision to original, and instead must treat the available text as an obscured, only partially discernable palimpsest through which to assess a series of interventions and consequences.

PARADIGMS OF CREOLISATION

Considering *Toussaint L'Ouverture* in a creolisation framework helps to account for its adaptations, its ongoing nature and its interest in subverting hegemonic systems, in the same way that a postnational perspective exceeds the boundaries and conservatism of the nation-state. Creolisation according to Kamau Brathwaite's model, works in two key ways: first 'the basis of culture lies in the folk'[4] who continually perform a sort of 'marronage', which allows them continually to adapt, subvert and influence the hegemonic system in which they exist – this is the practice of creolisation. Second, creolisation is itself ongoing and ceaseless. These two characteristics situate Brathwaite's theories as analytic models aligned, if not synonymous, with the basic tenets of what has come to be known as cultural studies. In the sense that we might view Brathwaite's Caribbean as a text, he locates that text 'across a range of competing moments of inscription, representation and struggle'. Creolisation, I would argue, like cultural studies, 'seeks to keep in equilibrium the different moments of cultural production, textual production, and the "production in use" of consumption'.[5] Thus, in Brathwaite's famous geographical metaphor, 'the unity is submarine';[6] such competing moments of inscription, representation, and struggle can be understood historically and physically, where the Caribbean archipelago is simultaneously a series of islands and an underwater mountain range, alternately terra firma and volcanically explosive.

In James's play, the past speaks in specific paradigms of creolisation. Worked through Stuart Hall's use of concepts of identity and diaspora, the past as it emerges from *Toussaint L'Ouverture* is not a 'simple, factual past', but rather one that addresses us and is 'constructed through memory, fantasy, narrative and myth'.[7] The other side of history, the notion that history and its telling are less stable than we may have imagined, is conveyed in James's play through the scenes of vodou gatherings and ceremonies. Furthermore, James's basic intention to give life to the dramatic personae of Toussaint, Dessalines and others alongside the dramatic events of the Revolution, is partnered with a desire to represent black diaspora politics within the specific political context of pan-African activity in 1930s London. What is fascinating, and ultimately perhaps most useful, about the play is that it gives voice to what Hall calls 'unstable points of identification', as transmitted by both the leaders and the masses, the individual and the collective players. The active realisation of selfhood, nationhood and community within *Toussaint L'Ouverture* is anchored in a collective desire to overthrow slavery; and yet discontinuous visions of Haiti emerge from its various constituencies. Such simultaneous unity and discord, singular and collective visions of black empowerment – the ever-present ethos of creolisation – are the core message, perhaps, that *Toussaint L'Ouverture* has delivered to political activists since the 1930s. I advocate reading James's dramatic and historical works on the Haitian Revolution together, and as creolised texts. Creolisation, used to read *Toussaint L'Ouverture*, allows for a consideration of transnational and differing blacknesses that encompass James and Robeson, Toussaint and Dessalines. Creolisation, then, is both a reason for and a mechanism used to recognise multiplicity and diversity within representations of blackness.

As a catalysing event that affected the new world and the old, the Haitian Revolution provides a site to which scholars continually turn. Since many of James's well regarded texts from the 1930s and 1940s are overshadowed by *The Black Jacobins*, it is not surprising that the play leads a rather obscure existence, that it was out of print for decades, and that reviewers in different eras found it to be disappointingly static. When, however, we leave aside considerations of the play as entertainment, or as commercial success, and instead examine the circumstances of its production for what they reveal about intellectual contexts, and engage the play's significations in high and low culture as a technique employed by James to explore and identify the meaning and legacy of the Haitian Revolution in not just one or two but multiple time frames, we have a cultural object before us that resoundingly exceeds its aesthetic shortcomings.

By reading the play through a creolist model, and thereby conducting a three-dimensional analysis that emphasises content, context and place, as well as players, this frequently ignored play suddenly yields a wealth of information and a diverse perspective on subjects such as the convergence of politics and practice in 1930s pan-Africanism, and the representation and lived experience of black, male, transnational, hybridised subjects. Resistance, creolisation, and nation-building all converge within James's play. Although unequal and incommensurate states of action, they are nevertheless, related phenomena, and they become activated within *Toussaint L'Ouverture*. A new nationhood and people are perceptible in the play. With characteristic optimism, James heralds their emergence in his appendix to *The Black Jacobins* when he speaks of nearly independent West Indian peoples and nations 'bringing themselves' to the world stage, newcomers as nations but not as players, and thus able to offer a wealth of experience to help shape modernity further. The cumulative effect of *Toussaint L'Ouverture* – its multiple significations of creolisation – can be read in a similarly optimistic fashion, and the partnership of Robeson as leading man and James as playwright is perhaps the most appropriate place to begin. Each man finds his way to the play through his modern experiences of race, nation, culture, and political struggle.

DRAMATIS PERSONAE: ROBESON AND JAMES

There was an affinity of outlook between Robeson and James that made *Toussaint L'Ouverture*, with its one-two punch of speaking out against imperialism and bringing attention to a major black historical figure, an ideal joint venture for the two men. With its tale of the rise and fall of Toussaint and the triumph of black rebels in Saint-Domingue over their slave masters and colonial rulers, James's play reflects his engagement with revolutionary Marxism, pan-Africanism and anticolonial struggle, and was informed by the communities of political activists he circulated among in England.[8] James's political objective and method in staging the play was the explicit 'juxtaposition of personality and events' used 'to highlight some of the broader historical and political themes raised by the Saint-Domingue revolution', and among these were, as James himself stated, the specific anticolonial and anti-fascist Abyssinian resistance to the invasion by Mussolini's forces.[9] Moreover, the occasion to dramatise the Haitian Revolution was simultaneously seen as an invitation to audiences to remember, or simply to learn of, the long history of black revolutionary activity that took place between the Abyssinian crisis of the twentieth century and the Haitian Revolution of the eighteenth century. In its conception and various productions, then, the play was defined through radical politics. That James, a quickly matured Trotskyite, and Paul Robeson, a far more orthodox advocate of communism, came together in 1936 to work on *Toussaint L'Ouverture* was perhaps predictable, given the significant overlap between each man's political perspective and orientation within socialism, pan-Africanism, and anticolonialism; but those very political affiliations also set specific limits on their collaboration.

Both men experienced the early 1930s as a period of special political education, and England provided each of them with exposure to pan-Africanism and the organised left. Speaking of his personal consciousness as a black person of the diaspora, Robeson wrote, 'It was in London, in the years that I lived among the people of the British Isles and traveled back and forth to many other lands, that my outlook on world affairs was formed.' Indeed, it was in England, his home from 1927 to 1938, that Robeson 'discovered Africa' and came to consider himself 'an African'.[10] Such sentiments and experiences stood in sharp contrast to life and the racial outlook in Jim Crow America. What Bill Schwarz has called Robeson's 'political faith in the vernacular' was developed during this period of the 1930s, as he made the transition from being a very specifically commercial artist into also being a champion of vernacular artforms and working-class struggle.[11] This shift was helped along by Robeson's visits to the Soviet Union in 1934, 1936 and 1937, and his developing sympathy for Soviet communism as a vehicle to end the oppression of working people around the globe. For Robeson, who first entered the Soviet Union by train, via Hitler's Germany, 'Nazi fascism and Soviet communism became opposite, symbolic representations of evil and good'.[12] James, having grown up in the very different milieu of British colonial Trinidad, entered formal politics in England more rapidly, and much further to the left, than Robeson.[13] As has been widely discussed, in England James's acculturation within Trotskyism was prompt, and built upon his interest in working-class politics and peasant life in his native Trinidad.[14] These interests found expression in two texts he wrote before arriving in England, and published soon thereafter: a biographical study, *The Life of Captain Cipriani* (1932), and a novel, *Minty Alley* (1936), and these works set the stage, so to speak, for his Haiti texts.

The 1930s, in England and elsewhere, saw the waning of Garveyism and the upsurge of a new anti-imperialist pan-Africanism. Totalitarianism, too, was on the rise with Stalin, Hitler, Mussolini, and Franco in power, while worldwide economic depression helped feed such reactionary politics, on the one hand, and kept the poor hungry, on the other. James and Robeson chose political paths – Trotskyism and Communism, respectively – that diverged radically in ideology, but came together at key junctures: anti-imperialism, black self-determination and working-class struggle. Many years later, in 1970, when Robeson, post-McCarthyist persecution, was a ghost of the charismatic person he had been, James recalled the vision they had shared:

> Paul committed himself completely to the communist doctrine that only a world revolution could save society from the evils of imperialism and capitalism, in general. And, in particular, only such a revolution could assist the Black people of the United States to gain freedom and equality, and assist the white people in the United States in making America a place where all

men, Black and white, could live in peace. That Paul believed completely and without reservation. In the thirties and forties I believed the same.[15]

Yet Robeson's alignment with Stalinist Russia dictated that he and James would hold distinct views on how such world revolution could be achieved. As James writes in the same piece, he and Robeson had no further artistic or political collaborations after the play's brief run. James suggests that this was due in large part to their differing approaches to Marxism: 'At that time Paul was headed towards Moscow and I, as a trotskyist [sic], was most definitely anti-Moscow. We knew about each other and never quarreled, but the idea of doing the play [commercially] faded into nothing.'[16] Thus, despite a shared commitment to working-class struggle, anti-imperialism and the liberation of black people globally – all of which makes their interest in the events and leaders of the Haitian Revolution eminently understandable – it was also a unique, unlikely, and very brief association between James and Robeson, marking off the 1936 production of *Toussaint L'Ouverture* as singular. While Buhle considers 'the necessary attenuation' of their divergent political perspectives in order to work together on *Toussaint L'Ouverture* as rather commonplace within 'the sphere of anti-colonialism' at the time, I would add that James and Robeson had deeper, longstanding desires to present the Haitian Revolution in one form or another that perhaps made their political '*détente*' in 1936 a foregone conclusion.[17]

Although in some ways *Toussaint L'Ouverture* was a likely vehicle for collaboration, since James and Robeson each had, in the 1930s, a growing sense of political commitment to black and working-class struggle, it is even more intriguing that *Toussaint L'Ouverture* and the Haitian Revolution would have animated each man long before they were notable figures in the public domain, long before they traveled to England, long before the Abyssinian crisis. James's authorship of the play and Robeson's decision to accept the lead role are part of larger, parallel goals held by the two men. In hindsight, it seems Robeson was destined to accept the part, as much for what it was about as for how he would evolve as a political figure standing up against fascism in America in the 1940s and 1950s. Before and after *Toussaint L'Ouverture*, Robeson had been searching and would continue to search for what Duberman describes as 'socially significant' roles to balance the more popular roles and vehicles that were his bread and butter as an entertainer.[18] In fact, the large sums of money he was able to make from his concert tours and big-budget (commercial) films facilitated both his search for and acceptance of more meaningful and/or experimental roles.[19] *Toussaint L'Ouverture* fell into the latter category, and in order to appear in it Robeson accelerated his work on the Hollywood version of *Showboat* (for which he was paid $40,000 – an extraordinary sum, especially during the Depression): 'The shoot was condensed into a two-month period so Robeson could get back to London for rehearsals of C.L.R. James's play.'[20] But, additionally, a full decade earlier, in 1926, Robeson told a journalist he 'dreamed' of a 'great play about Haiti, a play about Negroes, written by a Negro, and acted by Negroes ... of a moving drama that will have none of the themes that offer targets for race supremacy advocates'.[21]

Robeson's detailed yearning underscores the artistic, intellectual and political void that James and Robeson, each in his own way, was motivated to fill in their work together in 1936. A footnote buried in Duberman's expansive biography deserves repeating here for the light it sheds on the paucity of 'socially significant' roles Robeson was actually able to find, as well as the challenge of staging the Saint-Domingue events. Both before and after the collaboration with James, Robeson and his wife Essie looked at numerous scripts about Toussaint and Saint-Domingue:

> Robeson continued to consider material about the Haitian Revolution as a vehicle. A year after the James play, Essie wrote an aspiring writer that they had read fifty books and some hundred plays and scenarios about Christophe, Dessalines, and Toussaint. 'All have been strangely disappointing save one, which we actually did produce here in London at a special experimental theatre. Even that didn't prove good enough. We feel the history and characters are too good to spoil in a poor play, and so we are continuing to read manuscripts.'[22]

The Robesons knew their history, and were as interested in the post-revolutionary leadership by Dessalines and Christophe, as well as the failure of that leadership, as part of the dramatic and political significance of the Haitian material. Indeed, according to Duberman and James, despite *Toussaint L'Ouverture*'s short run of just three performances, Robeson found the play to be an important 'experience'.[23]

James, too, was concerned with projects that would provide a different, previously neglected representation of history, especially in the New World. *The Black Jacobins* and *A History of Negro Revolt* (1938) continued that work after the production of *Toussaint L'Ouverture*.[24]

In *Beyond A Boundary*, James remembers that in the aftermath of publishing 'The Case for West Indian Self-Government' (1933) in England, and its 'grand success' in the West Indies,

> West Indian history now began to assume a new importance. Stuck away in the back of my head for years was the project of writing a biography of Toussaint L'Ouverture – the leader of the revolt of the slaves in the French colony of San Domingo. The revolt and the successful establishment of the state of Haiti is the most outstanding event in the history of the West Indies.[25]

What is significant here is that the Haitian Revolution and Toussaint L'Ouverture had long resided in James's consciousness, as in Robeson's, in the particular context of uplift and self-determination.[26] By the time he wrote and staged *Toussaint L'Ouverture* in 1936, he would have acquired an education in Marxism and socialism, and be more advanced in his own interpretations of these political philosophies than Robeson.

In addition to the trajectories that led James and Robeson to the same theatrical stage in 1936, there was Abyssinia. Abyssinia, later renamed Ethiopia, was a vivid example of European imperialism and African self-determination in the 1930s, and the nodal point of various pan-African activities and organisations. In response to the invasion of this sovereign African nation by Italy, James helped form the International African Friends of Abyssinia (IAFA) in August 1935, and served as its chairman.[27] This work, comments Hill, 'marked James's baptism in the headwaters of the modern Pan-African movement'.[28] The IAFA counted among its members George Padmore, Jomo Kenyatta and Amy Ashwood Garvey. 'Soon after the Ethiopian crisis subsided ... members regrouped and formed the International African Service Bureau (IASB) with Padmore at the helm', writes Robin D.G. Kelley.[29] James participated in this latter organisation as editor of its journal, *International African Opinion*, for a good part of 1938.[30] Within the same London context, in 1933 Robeson enrolled at London University's School of Oriental Studies to study African languages, and began to immerse himself more fully in African culture.[31]

Thus, *Toussaint L'Ouverture* brought together two budding black transnational spokespersons from different strata of a socialist orientation, a collaboration that did each man a great service. Indeed, despite the play's short run and poor reviews, both James and Robeson understood their work together as highly significant, and as the fulfillment of longstanding individual aspirations. Robert Hill goes so far as to suggest that the most important thing about their work together, for James, was the very fact that the acquaintance with Robeson developed.[32] The play functioned, then, as a meeting point for men who would eventually be credited in distinct realms for advancing complex notions of black subjectivity. We can also infer that each learned a great deal from the other's perspective. We might view their collaboration, and the way in which the play is embedded in the historical context of the Abyssinian crisis, as the practice of creolisation. James and Robeson working together, pan-African organizations in London, a drama bringing Haitian politics to the fore in London theatre – all of these factors overlap within the zone of counter-politics and poetics. They give voice to acts that subvert, adapt to, and influence Europe-driven politics, history and aesthetics.

THE PLAY'S THE THING:
PRODUCTIONS, AESTHETICS, JUDGEMENTS

The 'special experimental theatre' Essie Robeson mentions above is not insignificant in the larger narrative of *Toussaint L'Ouverture*. The very venue at which *Toussaint L'Ouverture* was staged in 1936 underscores the play's radical credentials, and how it was therefore not appropriate for a more mainstream theatre. Indeed, the significance of the James/Robeson collaboration is amplified by considerations of the institutional structures of the play's production. The first aspect to be considered in this regard is the production company, the Stage Society, which was responsible for contracting the Westminster Theatre in London and producing *Toussaint L'Ouverture* on successive Sundays in March 1936.[33] Formed in 1899 and active until 1939, the Stage Society had a two-fold mission: it chose to mount small productions of plays deemed artistically worthy but otherwise unlikely to generate the big profit necessary for a commercial, West End venue. At the same time, it strove to 'introduce to the English public the best plays of contemporary foreign dramatists'.[34] Towards this latter goal, the Stage Society credits itself for the earliest British production of plays by Maugham, Chekhov, O'Neill and others, while George Bernard Shaw, a prominent progressive in addition to being an acclaimed playwright, 'admitted that but for the Stage Society he would have forsaken dramatic writing'.[35] As an organisation committed to new playwrights and their work, the Stage Society's decision to produce

Toussaint L'Ouverture is clearly in keeping with its overall mission. The details of exactly how the play came to be produced are scarce, but this much is known: the deal was either sealed by or predicated upon Robeson playing the lead. As Hill and Duberman agree, 'persons who read the script were inspired to attempt a production of it if Paul Robeson could be interested in accepting the title role of Toussaint'.[36] In three acts, *Toussaint L'Ouverture* tells the story of Saint-Domingue's twelve years' struggle against slavery, colonisation, and imperialism. Against the backdrop of Abyssinia falling to Italy in 1935, James provides a very particular view of the Haitian revolution for consumption: as one scholar has observed, the play

> does not put forward any 'negritude' sentiments, nor does it concentrate on celebrating the military feats of slaves ... The playwright approaches his Haitian characters as a critical investigator whose concern is to reveal and examine the strengths *and* weaknesses of the revolution's black leadership.[37]

The play, on the one hand, venerates the fact, and actions leading to, black self-determination in Saint-Domingue, yet simultaneously presents a clear-eyed critique of that revolutionary action. In telling the story of the Revolution's leadership – principally Toussaint and Dessalines, but also Christophe and Moise – James conveys the ways in which independence was achieved through a mixture of military acumen, charismatic leadership, and raw brutality, which then set the stage for post-revolutionary 'despotic regimes'. In brief, Toussaint's ascent is rapid: he assumes leadership of the Revolution soon after joining the slave uprising already underway in 1791 through various alliances with the Spanish, French, and English. As a result of charisma and brilliant strategy, he eventually becomes governor of the French colony. But, unable to sustain his leadership because of his strong allegiance to France in contradiction with the people's (and his generals') desire for independence, Toussaint is eventually betrayed and captured by Napoleon's agents. The play concludes with the crowning of Dessalines as Emperor in 1804. When Dessalines and Christophe – each a general under Toussaint – became Emperor and King of Haiti, respectively, their reigns became infamous for terror, bloodshed and totalitarianism: 'white masters were exchanged for black ones; slavery though abolished in name, persisted; and the dream of liberty, equality and fraternity was dissipated'.[38]

One aspect of James's goal in writing the play (and later the history) can thus be understood as a desire to represent the intricacy of black leadership and subjectivity alongside a black revolutionary tradition. In the historical context of the 1930s, such a perspective could do the double work of both galvanising resistance to European imperialism and signalling a political self-awareness. For the leaders James focuses on in the play and history embody, as Sander notes, 'four contrasting approaches to the ideal and objectives of the liberation struggle'.[39] Speaking of this Marxist method he applied to *The Black Jacobins*, James reveals truths applicable to his play as well:

> I tried to show that black people were able to make historical progress, they were able to show how a revolution was made, they were able to produce the men who could lead a revolution and write new pages in the book of history.[40]

Despite an overall concern with demonstrating historical progress, in the play James's affinities clearly lie with the leadership of Toussaint (indeed, his personality and actions dominate the drama, as the original title suggests). Yet James does not soften the edges of his portrait of Toussaint, and includes his flaws and miscalculations while continuously juxtaposing his style with that of Dessalines. As in *The Black Jacobins*, the dramatic narrative places blame for 'the disastrous outcome of the revolution on the decline of Toussaint's power as a leader, which creates weaknesses in the Haitian line of command that are easily exploited by Dessalines'.[41]

The Black Jacobins and Haiti's revolutionary history have been studied widely enough that these facts, and this understanding of James's treatment of it, are generally acknowledged and agreed upon. The play, as I have stated, is usually not included in such acknowledgements or studies, partly because of its obscurity but also because, when it is known, the consensus has been that it is not a very good play. The contemporary reviews from 1936 identify the play's principle structural weakness – correctly, I think – as an over-reliance on the description of these events; action and nuanced interaction between characters is too scarce to bring the historical events compellingly to life. The revised version, as a text at least, does not seem to fare much better. For instance, in a 1968 correspondence with James, Arnold Wesker, a successful London playwright, gives the following assessment:

Your canvas is enormous and I was fascinated to read the way you handled it ... But there is a spark which is missing from the whole work. Forgive me but there does seem to be something wooden about the play. The construction is dramatic; the dialogue carries the story and the dialectic of what you want to say, but when all the component parts are put together, it doesn't work.[42]

I would argue that, for the James scholar and for the post-millennial student of nationalism and post-nationalism, the value of the play is beyond whether or not it 'works', and instead has to do with where and how it is contextualised in the historical moment of the 1930s, and among the other activities of James and his associates, as in the IASB, as well as its production history in later decades. The discursive achievement of the play is something quite apart from its poor performance in 1936, and its status of neglected sibling to James's more famous efforts.

Significantly, the neglect of the play has reinforced the way it is perceived as lacking intellectual, historical or dramatic value relative to other works by James. On the occasion of its second and most prominent inclusion in an anthology, *The C.L.R. James Reader* (1992), edited by Anna Grimshaw, the 1967 revised version of the play is roundly blamed by one reviewer as the most egregious of the volume's faults, both because it is a poor play and because of what it supposedly does not say about James. The commentary illuminates the nearly untenable position (and positioning) of the play as a subject of scholarship to which James is central:

> [I]t seems that any perspicacious reading of *The C.L.R. James Reader* leaves James looking more like a cultural critic than the political thinker, philosopher, and revolutionary organizer that he was, which in my opinion, is what gives James his claim on our scholarly attention ... [*The Reader*] lacks so much that is vitally James, so much of the James that grabs our attention and rivets our intellectual concerns ... Yet the real problem of the volume ... centers around Grimshaw's use of the play *The Black Jacobins*, with which James's involvement was minimal if not absent.[43]

According to this view, the play's lack of aesthetic value violently interferes with its political and historical value in relation to the playwright. The reviewer goes on to make further provocative claims (plausible but unsubstantiated), including the notion that James himself did not revise the play in 1967, that there are key differences of 'tone and content' between the two versions, and that 'the 1967 version is highly unrepresentative of James's intellectual position and his power as a dramatist in 1936'.[44] Most disturbing to the reviewer are not these concerns about authorship, but rather the sheer space that the play takes up in the anthology, as if it is not worthy of the pages upon which it is printed.[45] In short, the key problem is that the play is not a great play of James's making, and Grimshaw's error in including it is that it heralds the first slide down a slippery slope of aberrant categorisation: 'It is the first barrage in an attempt to transform James from political activist to cultural critic', exclaims the reviewer.

With the republication of the play in a text called *The C.L.R James Reader*, the concern that Grimshaw is 'skewing' James as a literary person and as a cultural studies thinker, to the detriment of a true appreciation of his political and economic work as an organiser and theorist, is not insignificant. Since the categorising of James has moved on considerably since the 1990s, while gaining needed nuance, the time has come to consider the play outside of formalist/ aesthetic literary frames of greatness and value; and further, not just as a text among other Jamesian texts that are more or less brilliant, but rather as an event in a specific time and place. The obscurity of the play, prior to Grimshaw's inclusion of it in the *Reader*, means other realms of knowledge and understanding of James are also obscured. A reluctance or refusal to engage the play obscures the event of the Robeson collaboration; it closes off the opportunity to appreciate the various locations and dimensions of black political and cultural activities in London in the 1930s – activities that included stage productions as well as leafleting on street corners. It forecloses an opportunity to appreciate (and criticise) James's approach to revolutionary activity and representation: the play is also of a piece with James's short fiction and novel, in terms of both what it has to say about 'the masses' and how that message is conveyed dramatically. Robin D.G. Kelley marks these interrelationships among James's early works quite effectively:

> [W]hat is unique is James's claim that revolutionary mass movements take forms that are often cultural and religious rather than explicitly political. He forces the reader to re-examine these seemingly odd movements with new eyes, to take the beliefs and superstitions of Africans and African descendants seriously ... his first and only novel *Minty Alley*, and his 1936 play about Toussaint L'Ouverture, demonstrate an amazing sensitivity to the power of religion and culture as major social and political forces in life.[46]

Kelley's comments crucially attend to what is useful about reading James in an integrated and creolised, rather than compartmentalised, fashion. James steadfastly believes that one can write politically minded texts that use religion and culture, and that one should do so, because of what it teaches us about 'the masses and the supernatural forces that moved them'. Kelley asserts that these representations by James reveal his 'incredible faith in the masses', and I agree.[47]

It remains, then, to respond to the questions of the play's aesthetic value, and thus its significance within James's oeuvre: to do so we must turn first to the play's use of vodou and, second, to productions of the play after 1967. We have no data on who was in the audience for the three performances of *Toussaint L'Ouverture* in 1936. Thus, we cannot know whether, as James hoped, the audiences were afterwards inspired by Robeson's performance as Toussaint to support Abyssinia's resistance to Italy's invasion. That is, we cannot know if the original staging produced the effects envisioned by James. We can speculate, however, that the reviews that appeared in five major London newspapers captured the attention of their readerships, who in turn may have recognised a connection between the drama and contemporary events unfolding between Southern Europe and Northern Africa.[48] Speculation is unnecessary, however, when we examine the later-twentieth-century productions in which neither James nor Robeson were involved. Notices of at least two such productions (to be discussed momentarily) reveal how *Toussaint L'Ouverture* was staged and directed in such a way as to have exactly the intended effect of forging political action through a consciousness of a historical memory, and a historical continuum, of revolutionary black activity.

THE REVOLUTIONARY EPISTEMOLOGY OF VODOU[49]

Toussaint L'Ouverture was (and remains) a significant text for the particular emphasis it gives to the cultural and spiritual forces of vodou, beyond the obvious fact that vodou is itself a creolised, syncretic cultural formation. Such an emphasis was surely a key component of James's effort as playwright to provide a road map for pan-African and anticolonial political activity in general. Such an effort is discernable in two key areas: the play's use of and representation of vodou expand our understanding of the masses' involvement in the revolutionary thinking and way of being, and the carefully choreographed vodou scenes are the principal device

James has at his disposal to show, rather than narrate, the ultimately fatal distance that comes to separate the leaders of the Revolution from the people.

The incorporation of vodou in *Toussaint L'Ouverture* presents an alternate and yet parallel ontology and epistemology to the political–historical frame of the play. A long vodou ceremony in the first act is central to James's overall project of telling the story of the Haitian Revolution. But even as this story is recounted, the vodou images and references announce what is not 'knowable' in the way that battles and personnel are recorded in military and government records, and accessible in institutional archives.[50] Rather, the vodou images and references signal to the audience or reader what has to be imagined and re-presented (as VéVé Clark uses that term) in James's new telling of history.[51] The total effect of vodou as a mechanism in *Toussaint L'Ouverture* (as in *The Black Jacobins*) is how it becomes a vehicle for telling an under-told or 'lost' history, while suggesting other such narratives yet to emerge.[52] These potential, yet-to-be-recovered histories are exactly what James recognises he has failed adequately to midwife in his third Atlanta lecture. He knows such narratives are there, and in 1936 or 1967 (we cannot know if it was at both times) he used the structural apparatus of his play – vodou ceremonies on-stage or alluded to off-stage – to bring such narratives to the fore. What comes through – on the printed page, at least – is how these vodou scenes, which articulate how the masses feel and attempt to direct the leaders, are to be understood as legitimate, valuable and necessary components of the other politics happening on battlefields and at summit talks.[53] James's creolising work here is his focus on culture as a specific politics, while also demystifying vodou. Joy Mahabir provocatively states that such juxtaposition and demystification are precipitated in part by the standpoint brought to bear on vodou:

> While the popular North American desire is always for the inner, mystical secrets of vodou, in the Caribbean these are taken for granted: the hidden code of vodou is, unexpectedly, not its ritual and sacred aspect but its secular one: its important historical and social role; its marriage of spiritual and worldly praxis.[54]

The scene I focus upon here (Act III: i) reveals exactly how vodou operates as the nodal point around which the actions and dilemmas of the play provocatively and irresolutely revolve. The scene ends with Dessalines declaring: 'In France they write plays. But listen, listen. That is San Domingo. We can't write plays about voodoo!'[55] The comment culminates a scene where Dessalines not only plots to betray Toussaint to the French (with the help of Christophe and others), but also discusses the role of vodou in the Saint-Domingue he and Christophe want to bring into being once Toussaint is moved off the island. This Saint-Domingue is a nation that Dessalines envisions as politically independent and culturally sophisticated. Before the comment about writing plays, Dessalines and Christophe have an exchange about their opinions regarding vodou in the specific context of independence and nation-building: Dessalines has just given an order to troops waiting nearby to stop their audible 'vodou drumming'.

> CHRISTOPHE: Why have you stopped the drumming? When Toussaint was Governor, he gave those instructions, but those days are over.
> DESSALINES: When it came to governing the country, Toussaint was always right.
> CHRISTOPHE: But General Leclerc and all the French generals say that the people can drum and dance voodoo as they like. Madame Leclerc is absolutely fascinated by voodoo. As a matter of fact, in the old days, they say, you were a great voodoo dancer yourself, General Dessalines.
> DESSALINES: After one time is another. For instance, now you are for voodoo and you have always been against it ... you were always very stern in putting it down; and if I remember, you would shoot voodoo dancers almost at sight. I heard you say that voodoo prevented the population from becoming good citizens and Christians and warning about liberty and equality and the whole set of principles that come from France. (*Reader*, p. 102)

In describing Christophe's changing sentiments, Dessalines betrays his own. The way in which Saint-Domingue, and thereafter Haiti, are situated between modernity – 'the whole set of principles that come from France' – and its opposite is bewildering, even as it is empowering to the leadership. Thus Dessalines, in recognising his shifting position as a rebel, an officer and soon-to-be leader, also recognises the fluidity of strategy and policy, without perhaps knowing exactly the best means for choosing the right one at the right time. Hence his declaration that one cannot write plays about 'voodoo' is in direct response to his wife, Marie-Jeanne, quoting on his request lines from *Iphegenie* (a work by French playwright Racine), and his announcement to her that he is going to become the supreme leader of the colony and soon-to-be sovereign nation. Hearing his favorite lines, 'My strength returned, once more I knew my will/I loved him then and now I love him still' (*Reader*, 106), Dessalines is emboldened to carry out his military coup: by the very next scene Dessalines has accomplished his task, and prepares to be crowned Emperor.

Understanding 'voodoo' as a synecdoche for Haiti, indeed, James does manage to write, produce, and eventually publish a play about 'voodoo' that helps to transform our understanding of the prevalent revolutionary epistemology employed by the Saint-Domingue rebels, even as it illuminates for audiences in the 1930s, as it would now, the complex interrelationships of culture, religion, belief structures and history that propelled the Saint-Domingue slaves to seize their freedom and independence. The ability to write plays about 'voodoo' is the ability to write plays about Haiti – to bring Haiti into the historical record for others, beyond the moment of the Revolution, to discern and potentially to learn from. Laurent Dubois helpfully elaborates upon this notion of understanding Haiti within modernity, as have David Geggus and Michel Rolphe-Trouillot before him:

> [T]hroughout the last two centuries, whereas the French Revolution has become a symbol of the advent of modernity, the Haitian Revolution and Haiti itself have become symbols of political backwardness rooted in African superstition. Instead of being proof of the failure of the colonial venture, Haiti has been recast as its justification. The highly developed plantation economy and the radical political revolution that emerged from it have been primitivized, masked by the powerful image of a backward country practicing 'Voodoo' in the absence of a guiding European influence. Through a trick of historical silencing, Haiti has been abolished from the West.[56]

Vodou is the device James uses to break the silence while exposing the trick. He achieves this by weaving reputedly 'high' European culture (Racine and later Mozart are named in the play) with so-called 'low' New World syncretic forms of culture, such as vodou ceremonies, drumming and dancing. In broad creolist strokes he alters the very texture of the historical record by showing how tightly politics, culture and spirituality are braided together in the Haitian revolutionary narrative.

PLATFORMS OF DISSENT

Despite these fascinating aspects of *Toussaint L'Ouverture*, its descent into obscurity at the close of the 1936 production was rapid, and was further consolidated when *The Black Jacobins* was published in 1938. As mentioned above, James and Robeson went in separate directions, never to collaborate again. But the handful of post-1967 productions of the play suggest that new directors saw merit in the script, and felt there were ways to overcome its faults of dialogue and characterisation.[57] The first production of the play after it was revised in 1967 took place at the University of Ibadan in 1968, and was directed by Dexter Lyndersay. It is noteworthy because the play was deliberately staged to be in conversation with the real-time events of Nigeria's civil war and recent independence, echoing the circumstances of Haiti in the nineteenth century and prefigured by the Abyssinian context of the 1936 London production.[58]

In James's home country of Trinidad, a 'highly successful' three-week revival of the play was mounted in 1993 by the Theatre Arts Faculty at the University of The West Indies at St. Augustine'.[59] The production utilised a technique called 'Immediate Theatre Involvement', aimed at combating 'the tremendous apathy and even aversion to the discussion of the problems of Haiti' in the same year.[60] Accordingly, the production included scenes of 'Haitian villagers waving slogans such as "Bring back Aristide" and "Down with the Ton Ton Macoutes" and being clubbed down by Haitian secret police thugs'.[61] The Nigerian and Trinidadian productions each carried forward James's original goal of inspiring political action through an accessible cultural medium. In many ways *Toussaint L'Ouverture* is a characteristic James text in its ambition to combine individual and collective voices. The story of Toussaint and the populace he tried to lead constitute one of James's many attempts to balance an articulation of individual will with the mobilisation of a political struggle. The creative medium of theatre, and the drama of vodou imagery, are the forces James marshals to create an intelligible text that is simultaneously a cultural and political event. Indeed, the representation of vodou and the collaboration with the talented Robeson momentarily breathe life into the black Jacobins of Saint-Domingue. Yet the aesthetic failure and critical neglect suffered by *Toussaint L'Ouverture* only highlight the predicament of bringing together history and politics in this play.

James is unable to sustain the formidable task of presenting the lives of Toussaint, Dessalines, and the Saint-Domingue rebels as a performance: eventually the voice of the historian subsumes the voice of the playwright, resulting in what Arnold Wesker called 'wooden' characters. It is my contention that what James attempted in 1936 was left unfinished, and in truth was unfinishable. Picked up by others in 1968 and 1993, the evidence of the play and its players being pushed and pulled along a historical continuum is plainly visible. Such bridges across time and place, continents and nations – never exactly the same anywhere, never only about Haiti – are how I understand *Toussaint L'Ouverture* to be orbiting as a creolised, postnational text. Brathwaite reminds us that, central to creolisation as he defines it, regardless of how it has circulated as a term, is its unfinished, mercurial character. Indeed creolisation is nurtured through 'a historical continuum of movement and interruption'.[62] The circumstances of the play's always limited run, the mutual influence between the playwright and the leading actor, and the play's specific engagement with the politics of culture, collectively gesture towards a methodology of creolisation.

In conclusion, it is instructive to return to Robeson and to the syntax of vodou – two of the 'submarine' treasures of the heretofore-buried play. Robeson's thirst for meaningful roles was only deepened by *Toussaint L'Ouverture*, and would intensify, to his fateful detriment, after his collaboration with James. The career-ending denial of Robeson's right to travel outside the continental United States, which began in 1951, was due to the fact that Robeson

> had chosen the 'wrong' kind of culture – he explicitly conjoined politics and performance, expanding his repertoire beyond show tunes and spirituals to include an international array of working people's songs, and transforming his stage into a platform for political dissent.[63]

While Robeson's political education and development would begin in earnest after he appeared in *Toussaint L'Ouverture*, the foundational work of being able to create political art, to 'conjoin politics and performance', was tested in James's play. Subsequently Robeson would be both hailed and persecuted for using his performances of national folksongs to foster 'transnational formations of a Leninist tradition'.[64] Such circles of influence capture the creolisation effect of James's text(s). When we pay close attention to James's deployment of vodou in *Toussaint L'Ouverture*, our ability to assess the drama's aesthetic value is released from the choke-chain of formalism in a way not dissimilar to that in which the play opens up into multiple registers when we understand how it productively signifies across time and space. As Joan Dayan writes, 'the history told by these [vodou] traditions defies our notions of identity and contradiction.

A person can be two or more things, simultaneously. A word can be double, two-sided, and duplicitous.'[65] It is both playful and wise to read *Toussaint L'Ouverture* as duplicitous. As a play it blossoms or wilts according to one's methodological approach; it carries the aims and echoes of other James endeavors, even as it appears to some to be an anomaly. It promises one thing and delivers another: it delivers fragments but cannot sate our desire for unity. Instead it pushes us closer to an understanding of unity – whether within a text, the form of a nation-state, or a single individual – as impossible, and asserts revolutionary change as necessarily ceaseless and ongoing.

NOTES

I am indebted to Neda Atanasoski, Jinah Kim, and librarian Robert Melton for their research assistance as I prepared this chapter, and I would like to thank Kandice Chuh, Chris Gair, and Brett St Louis for their comments on earlier drafts.

1. C.L.R. James, 'How I would Re-write *The Black Jacobins*', *Small Axe* 8 (September 2000), p. 99.
2. As far as this author has been able to determine, the 1936 play was never published. The revised version, re-titled *The Black Jacobins*, is the version on which all sustained scholarship has been based, and, again as far as I have been able to determine, the version which all other productions, other than the 1936 premiere, have utilised. I will be discussing specifics of the 1936 production and also commenting on the 1967 text. Thus, for ease of reading I will refer to both versions as *Toussaint L'Ouverture* in order to distinguish them from James's history *The Black Jacobins: Toussaint L'Ouverture and the San Domingo Revolution* (1938).
3. Throughout this essay I use the spelling *vodou* as is generally accepted (for example see David Geggus and Joan Dayan) and for the purposes of consistency. Any exceptions, such as *voodoo*, appear in this text only within or in reference to a direct quotation.
4. Kamau Brathwaite, *Contradictory Omens: Cultural Diversity and Integration in the Caribbean* (Mona: Savacou Publications, 1974), p. 64.
5. Jon Story (ed.), *What is Cultural Studies?* (London: Arnold, 1996), p. 2.
6. Brathwaite, *Contradictory Omens*, p. 64.
7. Stuart Hall, 'Cultural Identity and Disapora', in Jonathan Rutherford (ed.) *Identity: Community, Culture, Difference* (London: Lawrence and Wishart, 1990), p. 226.
8. Robin D.G. Kelley, 'Introduction', in C.L.R. James, *A History of Pan-African Revolt* (Chicago: Charles H. Kerr, 1995), p. 3. The book was originally published in 1938 under the title *A History of Negro Revolt*.
9. Anna Grimshaw, 'Introduction: C.L.R. James: A Revolutionary Vision for the Twentieth Century', in *The C.L.R. James Reader* (Oxford, UK and Cambridge, USA: Blackwell, 1992), p. 6.
10. Paul Robeson, *Here I Stand* (Boston: Beacon Press, 1988), pp. 32–3.

11. Bill Schwarz, 'Black Metropolis, White England' in Mica Nava and Alan O'Shea (eds) *Modern Times: Reflections on a Century of English Modernity* (London: Routledge, 1996), p. 184. Schwarz asserts a key contradiction within Robeson: principally that while 'he condemned the commercialization of black culture' he was himself a commercial artist, no less than 'the most prominent black entertainer performing for white audiences'. Robeson's 'political faith in the vernacular', Schwarz suggests, is 'what held these conflicting demands in place' for Robeson as he began to become more of a public figure within politics as well as entertainment. For our purposes, such a 'faith' offers evidence, as will be discussed more fully below, of the affinity Robeson would immediately have felt for James's drama about Toussaint L'Ouverture.
12. Martin Bauml Duberman, *Paul Robeson* (New York: Alfred A. Knopf, 1988), p. 191.
13. James would almost immediately be attracted to Trotskyism upon arrival in the UK in 1932 – a predictable attraction since, as a member of the Labour Party in England, he was often drawn to its leftmost tendencies. See Anthony Bogues, *Caliban's Freedom: The Early Political Thought of C.L.R. James* (London: Pluto, 1997), p. 28.
14. See Bogues, *Caliban's Freedom*; Paul Buhle *C.L.R. James: The Artist as Revolutionary* (London: Verso, 1988); Kent Worcester, *C.L.R. James: A Political Biography* (Albany: State University of New York, 1996); Aldon Lynn Nielsen, *C.L.R. James: A Critical Introduction* (Jackson: University Press of Mississippi, 1997).
15. C.L.R. James, 'Paul Robeson: Black Star', in *Spheres of Existence* (London: Allison and Busby, 1980) 261–2.
16. Ibid., p. 259.
17. Buhle, *C.L.R. James*, p. 57.
18. Duberman, *Paul Robeson*, p. 194.
19. The play, originally titled *Black Majesty*, was twice also a potential film, both before and after the Stage Society production. Duberman reports that film director John Whale, along with Jerome Kern and Oscar Hammerstein II, 'became excited about the script after Robeson showed it to them, and they immediately bought the film rights' (p. 196). Kern wrote to Robeson that Hammerstein thought the film 'must be done on a very large scale or not at all' (p. 196). In the end it wasn't done, as interest amongst the Hollywood set waned. Prior to James's play, Soviet Lettish director Sergei Eisenstein planned a film about Toussaint's life, also starring Robeson, and even shot some test scenes with him, but the project was never completed (Iain Fraser Grigor, 'Scotland and Haiti: The Mystery of Duncan Stewart' Scotland's Transatlantic Relations Project Archive www.star.ac.uk/Archive/Papers/Grigor_DuncanStewart.pdf, 2005).
20. Duberman, *Paul Robeson*, p. 196.
21. Ibid., p. 105.
22. Ibid., p. 634, footnote 32.
23. Ibid., p. 197.
24. James's collaboration with Robeson not only parallels his other working relationships of the 1930s, with Learie Constantine, the IASB, and so on,

but also foreshadows his collaborative publications of the 1940s and 1950s, such as *State Capitalism and World Revolution* (1956, with Raya Dunayevskaya and Grace Lee) and *The Invading Socialist Society* (1947, also with Dunayevskaya and Lee).
25. C.L.R. James, *Beyond A Boundary* (Durham: Duke University Press, 1997), p. 119.
26. According to Reinhard Sander, James's earliest published comments on Toussaint L'Ouverture 'appeared in an article in *The Beacon* entitled "The Intelligence of the Negro: A Few Words with Dr. Harland", in which he attacked Dr. Harland's article on the intellectual inferiority of the negro race'. The article appeared in July 1931. Sander asserts that James 'was among the first West Indian writers to draw attention to Toussaint's exceptional stature'. Reinhard Sander, 'C.L.R. James and the Haitian Revolution', *World Literature in English*, 26: 2 (1986), pp. 277–8.
27. Kelley, 'Introduction', p. 10.
28. Robert A. Hill, 'In England, 1932–1938' in Paul Buhle (ed.), *C.L.R. James: His Life and Work* (London: Allison and Busby, 1986), p. 68.
29. Buhle explains how this new organisation, the IASB, was formed out of frustration with the League of Nations, which was reluctant 'to take serious moves against Mussolini' (p. 55). With a small constituency and small membership, which Buhle estimates at 'perhaps thirty', the IASB nevertheless had a grand mission, as articulated in its journal: it pledged to 'assist by all means in [our] power the unco-ordinated struggles of Africans and people of African descent against oppression which they suffer in every country' (quoted in Buhle, *Artist*, p. 56)
30. Kelley, 'Introduction', p. 11.
31. Duberman, *Paul Robeson*, p. 169.
32. Hill, 'In England', p. 73.
33. Duberman, *Paul Robeson*, p. 197.
34. Emanuel Wax, 'Note on the Stage Society', in *Drama n.s.*:15 (1936/1937), p. 120. (Published by the Drama League).
35. Wax, 'Note on the Stage Society', p. 121.
36. Hill, 'In England', p. 73.
37. Sander, 'C.L.R. James', p. 279. Sander provides an excellent close reading of the play, especially in conversation with *The Black Jacobins* and in relation to the actual historical figures the play attempts to represent.
38. Ibid.
39. Sander, 'C.L.R. James', p. 279.
40. C.L.R. James, '*The Black Jacobins* and *Black Reconstruction*: A Comparative Analysis', 15 June 1971, *Small Axe* 8 (September 2000), p. 85.
41. Sander, 'C.L.R. James', p. 280.
42. Grimshaw, *Reader*, p. 418, footnote 1.
43. Selwyn Cudjoe, 'C.L.R. James Misbound', *Transition: An International Review*, 58 (Oxford University Press, n.d.), 126–7.
44. Cudjoe, 'C.L.R. James Misbound', p. 127. A project beyond the scope of this essay is to peruse the James Papers for a copy of the 1936 playscript (if it survives), and then to make a thorough comparison with the published text.
45. Ibid.

46. Kelley, 'Introduction', p. 15.
47. Kelley, 'Introduction', p. 16. It is important to add here that Kelley speculates as to whether James chose to include representations of belief and superstitions 'independently', or if W.E.B. Du Bois's *Black Reconstruction* influenced him in this respect.
48. The five London reviews were as follows: 'Wordsworth', *Sunday Times*, 1 March 1936; 'Careful', *Observer*, 22 March 1936; untitled, *Daily Herald*, 17 March 1936; untitled, *The Times*, 17 March 1936; untitled *Evening Standard*, 17 March 1936.
49. I borrow this phrasing from Joy A.I. Mahabir's text, *Miraculous Weapons: Revolutionary Ideology in Caribbean Culture* (New York: Peter Lang, 2003).
50. See Joan Dayan, *Haiti, History and the Gods* (Berkeley: University of California Press, 1995).
51. See VéVé Clark, 'Haiti's Tragic Overture: (Mis)Representations of the Haitian Revolution in World Drama (1796–1975)' in James A.W. Heffernan (ed.), *Representing the French Revolution: Literature, Historiography, and Art* (Hanover: University Press of New England, 1992), pp. 237–61.
52. This formulation of emergent narratives as signalled by the subaltern form of vodou is borrowed from Esther Margaret Lezra's theorisation of the monstrous as outlined in her Ph.D. dissertation, 'Looking for Monsters: Mechanisms of History, Mechanisms of Power' (Literature 2005, UC San Diego). See especially the Introduction and Chapter 4, 'Solitude Past, Present and Future: Remembering the Monstrous: Facing Effacement'.
53. Although space does not permit a thorough discussion of this point here, several researchers have noted how vodou allows for, even requires, the presence of women who, in contrast, are wholly absent from *The Black Jacobins*, and are frequently absent in non-fiction studies of the Saint-Domingue Revolution. Thus, as James provides a forum where spiritual belief systems are valued as a component of revolutionary political praxis, female characters are given an – admittedly limited – voice with which to speak and act (see Cora Kaplan, 'Black Heroes/White Writers: Toussaint L'Ouverture and the Literary Imagination', *History Workshop Journal* 46, Autumn 1988, pp. 33–62; see also Kelley 'Introduction', and Sander, 'C.L.R. James').
54. Joy A.I. Mahabir, *Miraculous Weapons*, p. 82.
55. Grimshaw, 'Introduction', p. 106.
56. Laurent Dubois, 'The Citizen's Trance: The Haitian Revolution and the Motor of History', in Brigit Meyer and Peter Pels (eds), *Magic and Modernity: Interfaces of Revelation and Concealment* (Stanford, CA: Stanford University Press, 2003), pp. 107–8
57. Gordon Collier has compiled an impressive survey of the representations of the Haitian Revolution in novels, plays, poetry and essays from around the world. He speculates on the appeal of the Revolution within a remarkably long timeframe, and among a particularly diverse group of writers, many of whom are from the Caribbean. Indeed, Derek Walcott alone has written three plays about the Haitian Revolution.
58. Other productions include one in London staged by Yvonne Brewster at the Riverside Studios in 1986, and a 1971 BBC radio adaptation. See

Gordon Collier, 'The "Noble Ruins" of Art and the Haitian Revolution: Carpentier, Césaire, Glissant, James, O'Neill, Walcott and Others', in *Fusion of Cultures?*, Peter O. Stummer and Christopher Balme (eds) (Ansel Papers 2) (Amsterdam and Atlanta, GA: Rodopi, 1996), pp. 269–328.
59. Collier, p. 288.
60. Ramcharitar, quoted in Collier, p. 288.
61. Ibid, pp. 288–9.
62. Brathwaite, Contradictory Omens, pp. 63–4.
63. Kate Baldwin, *Beyond The Color Line and the Iron Curtain: Reading Encounters Between Black and Red 1922–1963* (Durham: Duke UP, 2002), p. 204.
64. Ibid, p. 211.
65. Dayan, *Haiti*, p. 33.

2
'Summer of Hummer': C.L.R. James, *American Civilization*, and the (Necro)Political Crisis

Eric Porter

I believe in the instinct of humanity to survive and that this is the only way it can survive. The modern world is organizing itself scientifically at such a speed that either it must be ruled in totalitarian fashion or by a new conception of democracy beyond anything we have known.[1]

C.L.R. James, *American Civilization*

During the summer of 2004, my family and I chose Laughlin, Nevada, as our overnight stopping point on a driving trip between Albuquerque and Los Angeles. The break gave us a chance to rendezvous with an old friend on vacation there and also see for the first time this gambling and water-sports oasis situated in the southern Nevada desert along the Colorado River, at the point where California, Nevada, and Arizona meet. I was struck by many things in Laughlin, not the least of which was the sensory overload I experienced upon stepping out of the air-conditioned hotel a few hours after our arrival and into the eerie red light of a sunset, accentuated by the 115-degree temperature and a strong desert wind. It felt, simply, like I was not on planet Earth. While spending the next few hours exploring the casinos lining the river, I was also struck by the very visible publicity for 'Summer of Hummer', a promotion promising to give away a brand new Hummer sports utility vehicle and several lesser prizes to regular visitors to the town's casinos. (The more hours sitting at tables averaging $5 wagers, the more entries one received for the drawing.)

Admittedly, the thought of trading in our Volkswagen and finishing up the drive in a large, bright yellow driving machine had its appeal. But I also wondered about the broader and highly symbolic appeal of this military vehicle qua status symbol, which had recently been in the news because of its ostentatious size and fuel consumption, its visibility in numerous hip hop videos and

California's movie star-turned-governor's car collection, and its well-publicised service to the US military and targeting by rebels in the current Iraq war. What might it mean, I asked myself, stepping back into academic character in the middle of my summer respite, for a multicultural and multiracial group of vacationers in Laughlin, of varying citizenship status, most of whom, it seemed, at least from appearances and conversation, could be considered members of what Robert Perrucci and Earl Wysong call the 'new working class'.[2] What social phenomena enabled the casino public relations people to surmise that this rich symbol of our neoliberal military state – with its continual blurring of the line between profit motive and security, its production of this new working class, and its dependence on the lives and limbs of its sons and daughters for its imperial adventures – would address a set of desires effectively enough to keep people happily losing their money? And, more generally, what roles might such popular manifestations of militarism play in the maintenance of a neoliberal hegemony and/or the interpellation of the vast numbers of working-class subjects who have supported the perpetual state of war in which the United States is involved? Can we see in the commodity dreams associated with such symbols some sort of resistance to the social and economic order? Or, does their popularity suggest we're slouching towards fascism at the beginning of this new millennium?

Although I will not offer a definitive reading of 'Summer of Hummer' in this essay, I will begin to address some of the challenges I think it presents to American Studies as a symbol of the articulation of militarism and consumer desire that is expressed by, and which affects, the life chances of diverse individuals and social groups within and outside the United States. I will do so by offering a reading of C.L.R. James's *American Civilization*. James worked on this text in 1949 and 1950, but never completed it. However, since its publication in its unfinished state in 1993, it has been embraced as an exemplar of mid-century radical cultural criticism, and as a source for creating new analytical paradigms. After briefly summarising the text and situating it within the multiple political and intellectual trajectories and revolutionary goals that defined James's project at mid century, I examine the ways *American Civilization*, as a product of its moment, imagined an alternative American Studies that implicitly challenged the dominant version offered by scholars during the 1950s. Thus, *American Civilization* in important ways anticipated some of the moves that have defined the field through to the present. However, my larger interest is what James's study suggests for the future of American Studies. And here I am concerned with the question of how scholars should respond to a situation in which present-day enactments of US citizenship, consumerism, and other identities, as well as a concomitant primacy of violence (militarism, homicide, surveillance, incarceration, and so on) in popular culture may, in contradictory ways, reflect and serve a US state- and corporate-sponsored 'necropolitics' – following Achille Mbembe – and the permanent state of war during the post-9/11 period. Therefore, in addition to confirming James's importance to American Studies in general, I consider how his attention to violence in the US popular imagination, as part and parcel of a larger 'struggle for happiness' during the political crisis circa 1950, has implications for re-orienting the conceptual and ethical frame animating American Studies during the political crisis facing the world today.

In *American Civilization* James seeks to understand the growing impact of US ideologies and popular culture on the world stage at a moment when the nation was redefining its imperial project as that of a superpower. James identifies within US popular culture, and at least certain manifestations of democratic ideologies, a radical and, indeed, revolutionary project in the face of an emerging totalitarianism, horrifically realised under Hitler and Stalin but also evident in the growing bureaucratisation and routinisation of modern life in the United States and elsewhere. Beginning with a brief treatment of 'key concepts' such as individualism and democracy, he next analyses their articulations within nineteenth-century literature and political writings, with an eye towards what these texts provide to an understanding of the problems and potentials of US society at mid century. James subsequently examines the critical social transformations wrought by Fordism, which provided both the means for self-activity and self-awareness for American labour and the conditions for its further alienation. He then explores popular culture as a site where such contradictions are expressed, and moves into specific analyses of how labour, African-Americans, women and intellectuals respond to and provide insight through their actions into the growing crisis. James concludes by offering the hope that a mass social movement would soon emerge, fundamentally altering the political system in the United States and eventually ushering in 'the thing itself' – in other words, of course, socialism (p. 278).

The title, subject matter, terminology, and method of *American Civilization* should all be understood as exemplifying the intellectual and activist formations of which James was a part, as well as the political moment in which he lived. Although *American Civilization* deploys the exceptionalist rhetoric and nationalist ideology commonly deployed to fight the cultural Cold War, James's reasons for invoking the language and tropes of liberal democracy at this particular moment were complicated. He was clearly interested in reaching and appealing to a popular audience at a moment of growing reaction and anti-left persecution; but he had also been struggling to stay in the United States since coming to the attention of immigration officials in 1947 (he was eventually deported in 1953), and was thus interested in demonstrating his own claim to American civilization.[3]

James was also, of course, writing his way through the broader political crisis apparent to many on the left – at a moment that E.P. Thompson called 'a time of political and theoretical disaster' for the Marxist tradition[4] – and this comes across clearly in *American Civilization*. James's analysis is indeed fundamentally concerned with the very survival of civilization, defined in terms of both the radical democratic society he hoped would evolve and human society more broadly. Yet also evident in the text is not simply the optimism that people have quite often located in James's work, but a commitment to developing out of these theoretical and political crises an understanding of society and a mode of analysis that will meet the challenges posed by the changing order. As Grimshaw and Hart argue, the 'central theme' in this volume is

> the struggle of ordinary people for freedom and happiness, a struggle which he found to be most advanced in America. At the same time James recognized that the forces mobilized to repress these popular energies had never been so developed, or so brazenly employed, as in the twentieth century.[5]

James's aversions to the bureaucratic, administrative, and propagandistic arms of the US and Soviet states alike, as well as his view that the future struggle between labour and capital would be manifested as 'world-wide conflict *between the workers and the bureaucratic-administrative-supervising castes*', were consistent with the analyses of other members of the anti-Stalinist left, such as James Burnham and Max Shachtman. However, unlike some of its more pessimistic commentators, James was buoyed by the self-activity of labour and civil rights agitation in the United States during the 1940s. And like others whom Michael Denning terms 'American

"Western Marxists"', James built upon a Popular Front commitment to understanding the revolutionary potential in cultural activities, even as he remained suspicious of the complicity of the Popular Front with emergent state apparatuses.[6]

James's analysis in *American Civilization* was further distinguished by his immersion in a long history of black radical activism and the specific goals and theoretical projects of the Johnson–Forest Tendency, a small political and intellectual group allied with, although often at odds with, the Trotskyist movement during the 1940s. James's focus on the key role of 'Negroes' in the text can be situated in his longstanding commitment to placing black labour and black political struggle at the centre of the modern world: a project exemplified by the publication in 1938 of both *The Black Jacobins* and *The History of Negro Revolt*. James had also been encouraged by Trotsky to go to the United States to encourage African-Americans to join the revolutionary movement. Early in the 1940s, after travelling through the American South and participating in a sharecroppers' strike in Mississippi, he began to view contemporary African-Americans as being at the centre of revolutionary change. Although for the first half of the decade he continued to argue that race-based political activism could be retrograde, by the time of the publication of his 1947 pamphlet, 'The Revolutionary Answer to the Negro Problem in the USA', he argued not only that race-based struggle was valid, but also that African-Americans were potentially the most revolutionary social formation in US society.[7]

James's critique of totalitarianism in *American Civilization* as a general problem of modernisation, as well as his focus on the revolutionary potential in the 'practical activities' of the proletariat, stem not just from the anti-Stalinist left's general aversion to bureaucratisation, but also from the specific anti-statist and ultimately anti-vanguardist platform that he and his colleagues in the Johnson–Forest Tendency – namely Raya Dunayevskaya, Martin Glaberman, and Grace Lee – had been developing through the 1940s. Such positions would lead James and the Johnson–Forest Tendency through a precarious series of alliances through the 1940s, as they first left the Trotskyist Socialist Worker's Party for the Worker's Party, only to leave that group in 1947 to rejoin the former. In his 1947 essay, 'Dialectical Materialism and the Fate of Humanity', James had developed a flexible and nuanced understanding of human agency and the 'creative powers of masses'. He had also affirmed his growing sense, drawn from Marx's writings, that in the present political crisis humankind was precariously perched at the nexus of socialism and barbarism.[8]

As an expression of both a radical politics and a radical intellectual practice, *American Civilization* has profound implications for rethinking the past, present, and future of American Studies. Although it deploys the language of bourgeois liberalism and provides an exceptionalist account of US history and society, it can be understood as being exceptionalist with a difference. At this moment, witnessing the emergence of the myth–symbol school, *American Civilization* provided a radical alternative – an example of what George Lipsitz terms the '"other" American Studies'[9] – to the Cold War-friendly version of the field.[10] James countered American Studies' homogenising approach to US culture and its service to the US Cold War propaganda machine by insisting on the centrality of minoritarian subjects to the nation's history, by demanding that US society be understood in world-historical terms, by offering a systematic account of totalitarianism across geopolitical borders, by refusing to decouple critical investigations of US culture from a revolutionary programme, and by the very definition of civilisation permeating the text.

James's alternative version of American Studies was in some respects indebted to the established objects and discourse of the field, although it also sought to open up new terrain for investigation. The former approach may be found in James's chapter on nineteenth-century intellectuals in the United States. Like his contemporaries, James identifies in canonical literary texts antecedents to key questions regarding the relation between individualism and democracy. However, unlike many operating within the institutional framework of American Studies at this moment, James refuses the kind of exceptionalist narrative that would service the Cold War state by offering an end-of-ideology denouement and championing a triumphant nation defined against an encroaching totalitarianism without, as well as a radical subversion and messy pluralism within. Like other observers, James locates in Melville's Ahab a prototype for a totalitarian dictator; however, in James's analysis, he is not simply a threat to the heroic individualism of the US nation but rather an outgrowth of US society.[11] He is both the authoritarian bureaucrat threatening democracy from within and an archetype for the violent, amoral character increasingly evident in US popular culture and embraced by a mass audience. His angst ultimately anticipates a life-world where the 'consuming rage with the social and psychological problems of society is eating away at the whole of humanity' (p. 81).

James moves further from the centre of early Cold War American Studies in the discussion of abolitionist politicians that concludes the chapter. If Melville was a 'prophet of destruction', he suggests, the abolitionists were 'advocates of mass revolution' (p. 98). James thus affirms the importance of radical thought to the development of individualism and democracy in the United States – in abolitionism we see a radicalism emerging from the very 'genius of the country' (p. 91) – thereby challenging the myth–symbol school's foreclosing of Marxist analyses of culture. The Johnson–Forest Tendency's agenda is also evident in this assessment of abolitionism. One finds an important radicalism articulated in abolitionist programmes, in James's view, but one does not find the traces of the totalitarianism that has ruined the contemporary Communist Party. Wendell Phillips may have demonstrated 'the same breadth of view, the revolutionary conception of democracy, and political ruthlessness which are associated with what is loosely called Bolshevism', but the CPUSA's attempt to incorporate him into its pantheon of heroes was an unfortunate and ultimately unsuccessful endeavour (pp. 96–7). James's view of abolitionism also articulates his anti-vanguardist politics with his commitment to showcasing black presence and agency in the modern world. Abolitionism starts, James argues, with black resistance to slavery. Black people are at the centre of this social movement; abolitionists are only successful to the extent that they can learn from and articulate the concerns of an established struggle (p. 85–7).

James also seeks to redefine the very concept of citizenship in the text in a way consistent with his revolutionary vision. By civilization, in the words of Grimshaw and Hart, James means a 'progressive tendency of world history as a whole. Its core was the drive to integrate the individual and society; and its creed was a humanist desire for universal freedom and happiness.'[12] This desire would, of course, ultimately be realised through a radical activism challenging the 'barbarism' of totalitarianism, and it was in fact his faith in the potential for such revolutionary activities emanating from the American masses that led him to claim that they were 'the most civilized people on the face of the globe'.[13] Given this definition of civilisation, as well as his interest in the practical activities of American workers, it should be no surprise that the core chapters of James's study are dedicated to labour activism and 'popular arts and modern society'.

Through this definition of citizenship, James provided alternatives to both the elitism of the intellectual history synthesis driving much American Studies scholarship during the 1950s and the highly critical analyses of mass culture coming from the left at mid century, most famously from Theodor Adorno and Max Horkheimer. James was instead deeply interested in popular culture and in its contradictions: the fundamental problems of individualism and democracy embedded within it, its potential role in the emergence of totalitarianism – but also its potential role in the realisation of a utopian society. Although he recognised its regressive propagandistic and ideological functions and the fundamental power imbalance shaping its production, he remained keenly interested in how popular culture, like mass production, provided a space for possibility; and he sought in dialectical fashion to understand the relationship between the two as they provided a stage for future human action. He likewise refused the notion that members of a mass audience were merely passive consumers of a popular culture whose form and content were determined by dominant groups and individuals. Rather, he recognised a culture industry beholden, to some extent at least, to popular desire, a continual struggle over the meanings of popular culture texts, and a self-aware mass audience who brought their own experiences and needs to their readings of these texts.[14]

In addition to offering an alternative to American Studies circa 1950, *American Civilization* also anticipates the field's present. To make this argument, however, requires us to acknowledge some of the shortcomings in James's unfinished assessment of US society. He was simply wrong in some of his forecasts. For example, James was far too optimistic about the growing power of the US labour movement and the radical vision it would inject into the public sphere, and much too pessimistic about what black activists could achieve in the Southern states. He spoke eloquently about the marginal position and thwarted aspirations of women in society, but made a bizarre comment about relations among men representing the pinnacle of American civilization (p. 223). And, as Andrew Ross suggests, James's 'populist definition of "civilization"', his alternative exceptionalism, and his strategic avoidance of Marxian economism, come at a price. Strikingly absent from this book 'by someone considered to be among the century's most acute analysts of colonialism' is an analysis of US economic and cultural imperialism or, for that matter, any engagement with the role of the international or transnational capital, labour, and cultural flows that are increasingly central to American Studies today.[15]

Still, *American Civilization* does in important ways point to the re-mapping of the human geography of American Studies that would take place in subsequent decades. Anticipating the influence of the New Left on American Studies during the 1960s and 1970s, James's focus on labour and a mass audience reflects the commitment among many scholars during these decades to writing American Studies from below, to examining practical activities of work and labour as well as grass-roots social activism. By integrating a discussion of women and African-Americans into the text, he foreshadows the inclusive interventions that feminist and ethnic studies scholars would make during this same period. And his insistence on the critical role that a history of black activism and presence play in understanding the nation, its contested meanings, and its future, presages more recent calls to put ethnic studies at the centre of the field.[16] Moreover, even as his text fails to analyse American imperialism, he still insists that the United States be understood as a world-historical phenomenon. Referring to the objects of his analysis, James wrote: 'All that is American about it is that in the United States these world-wide tendencies and developments have reached their sharpest expression' (p. 224). And within James's own perspective, forged in diasporic movement and conversation, we can also locate the seeds of the comparative and transnational understanding that informs much current scholarship.

James also anticipates and offers a response to some of the fundamental questions and challenges driving American Studies' investigations of the terrain of popular culture in the wake of the influence of critical theory and cultural studies. As noted earlier, James offered an alternative to the dour pessimism and elitist avant-gardism of Adorno and Horkheimer. Yet, as others have pointed out, it would be a mistake to deem James simply a celebrant of popular culture or a harbinger of a Fiskean cultural studies, in which popular culture fundamentally and transparently reflects popular desires and a perpetual and multifaceted struggle against domination. He is better understood as charting a synthesis of sorts between the Frankfurt School positions outlined by Adorno and Horkheimer and that of Benjamin and, in so doing, anticipating the most careful deployments of Gramsci by scholars hoping to understand how popular cultures serve multiple interests, are sites of possibility, but by definition are components in the maintenance of hegemony.[17]

Moreover, James's dialectical method, and specifically his desire to understand how the thwarted ambitions of a mass audience may be found in popular culture, presents us with a challenge for understanding the terrain of popular culture even more deeply, and for re-instilling in our analyses a commitment to political change. For popular culture, in James's mind, ultimately cannot satisfy a mass audience: by definition, it does not allow through its consumption an expression of the individuality and social freedom that this audience desires. Freedom 'is *not* the enjoyment, ownership or use of goods', James wrote elsewhere, 'but self-realization, creativity based upon the incorporation into the individual personality of the whole previous development of humanity. *Freedom is creative* universality – not utility.'[18] But, rather than following Adorno's lead and assuming that members of a popular audience are unwittingly consuming a false sense of individualisation, or taking the opposite approach and blithely claiming that audiences are simply imposing their own resistant interpretations of cultural texts, James's reading offers its own dialectic, concerned in large part with the 'radical negativity' apparent in popular culture. As Neil Larsen puts it, we err in

> our spontaneous assumption that the transgressive 'meanings' of popular culture reside in the latter as their *positive content*. The reality pointed to by James is that, on the contrary, such 'meanings' are not positive presences in popular culture at all, but are the results of an absence, of a negation. They are the product, not of what this culture 'means' ... but of what, in the most determinate sense, it does not mean.

It is this understanding of negativity that, in a sense, best reflects the utopian Marxist–humanist vision informing James's analysis. Cultural forms thus do not merely exist in society as the transparent terrain on which social struggles are undertaken. They are, rather, evidence of the nature of society itself, its contradictions, and its progressive unfolding. 'The aim of critique', Larsen explains,

> ceases to be either the defense or the condemnation of the existing culture as such. Rather, it is to probe the latter's contradictions in such a way as to identify both those aspects of culture that anticipate and advance the movement towards a higher stage of social existence as well as those that act to impede the movement.[19]

American Civilization thus offers a challenge to those accounts of popular culture that would seek as an endpoint the location of forms of resistance that affirm the agency of human subjects within and against various modes of domination. It asks, instead, that we understand how, within the contradictions of popular culture, its apparent imagery and in its negative disavowals, we can find the most profound threats to humanity, as well as the potential for understanding, following Aldon Nielsen's description of James's work in general, 'how the masses of the people form the conditions of possibility for the future'.[20]

So where do James, his dialectical method, his vision, and his commitment to writing through the political crisis circa 1950, leave us when thinking about the *future* of American Studies 50-plus years later? Whenever one shifts the discussion of a historically situated piece of social analysis from anticipating the present to moving the present forward, there is the question of historical specificity and relevance. Although there are potential problems inherent in excavations of social theory written during earlier historical formations, I suggest that James's *American Civilization* remains useful to us in the twenty-first century, as long as we follow Stuart Hall's cautionary instructions directed to late-twentieth-century scholars wanting to employ Gramsci's 'conjunctural' ideas for contemporary social analysis. 'To make more general use of them', Hall argues, 'they have to be delicately dis-interred from their concrete and specific historical embeddedness and transplanted to new soil with considerable care and patience.'[21] Moreover, the very methods James himself employs in the text suggest additional justifications for bringing *American Civilization* to the present for productive purpose. On the one hand, James's own successful applications of nineteenth-century texts to the analysis of post-World War II society invites us to 'dis-inter' and 'transplant' his own work so that it can be read 'in relation to the popular social and artistic movements of today' and thus 'assume a new significance' (p. 37). On the other hand, James's larger intellectual project, committed in its dialectical mode of critique to continually reappraising his own interpretations, and always being aware of the 'emerging social formations that would remake the world', gives further impetus to those hoping to find new uses for his work.[22]

At this present moment, when 'American Civilisation' is being invoked to justify the perpetual state of war that the United States seems intent on bringing ever more to people across the world, as well as an increasingly violent and repressive domestic security apparatus, I want to return to James's concern about an encroaching totalitarianism that developed hand-in-hand with the American masses' engagement with popular culture and their broader 'struggle for happiness'. It is worth dwelling for a moment on the fact that James brings to *American Civilization* the sense of imminent danger and possibility found in his more theoretical writings that preceded it. For even as James advocates a kind of exceptionalism when focusing on the potential for revolutionary action by American workers, he writes against the notion that the United States, by virtue of its status as a 'free society', is an exception to the modern tendency towards totalitarianism. As he states in the introduction to the volume,

> I trace as carefully as I can the forces making for totalitarianism in modern American life. I relate them very carefully to the degradation to human personality under Hitler and under Stalin. I aim at showing that the apparently irrational and stupefying behavior of people in totalitarian states is a product of modern civilization, not merely in terms of the preservation of property and privilege but as a result of deep social and psychological needs of man in modern life. (p. 38)

Of critical importance to James's analysis of this crisis is his focus on mass activity as creating 'the conditions of possibility for the future'. James begins the chapter 'The Struggle for Happiness' by posing an alternative to Lenin's famous vanguardist dilemma, 'What is to be done?' The question facing James at this moment is, instead, 'What is it that the people want?' (p. 166). He goes on to survey factors facing labour in the United States, noting that, despite the reactionary views held by many people, the important things to keep in mind are their 'deep responses to work', which articulate 'sentiments with the most revolutionary implications conceivable' (p. 167). Thus, we have a utopian, revolutionary vision that is notable for locating with the masses the possibility and ultimately the responsibility for responding to the contemporary political crisis and its violent consequences. By invoking this responsibility, James suggests an approach to the analysis of mass activity in the social and cultural spheres that moves beyond reproach and romanticism. Although James's utopian aspirations affirm the best of recent work that locates in such activities a transformative potential, with the responsibility he locates in this social group comes a duty for scholars to enter into critical engagement with those popular ideas and practices that may, whether intentionally or not, abet the political crisis.

Bringing James's 'big picture' account to the present thus encourages us to think about the value and viability of coming full circle, to think once again about what might be gained by theorising cultural production and consumption at the level of the nation – or, in James's terms, 'a totality' – in order to consider the collective effects of our diverse actions at a moment of crisis. We have come to a point in American Studies where we have thought in very smart ways about the complexities of cultural production and politics, occurring as they do in multiple, heterogeneous, and mobile spheres. We have moved over the course of the field's history from isomorphisms of nation and culture to isomorphisms of ethnicity, gender, sexuality, region, class, and culture; to recognitions of movement and indeterminacy within and across social and cultural formations.[23] But we may also want to consider, at this post-nationalist moment, whether it is worthwhile to think in terms of how blocs are forged out of heterogeneity, where a fragmented population, positioned in impossibly complicated ways, with an almost infinite array of affiliations, can operate globally as one, when articulated with and through the exercise of national economic and political power. We have seen in the most recent elections in the United States how diverse working-class and middle-class communities, deeply distanced from one another by geography, race, and the competition for resources, have found common ground over 'god, gays, and guns', and helped consolidate the power of the right. We would do well to consider also how our collective consumption of popular culture engages, challenges, and abets these very same political formations.

Any American Studies of the future interested in the responsibilities and activities of heterogeneous blocs would also do well to emulate seriously James's attention to violence in popular culture, and use this as an imperative for developing new paradigms and ethical frames for academic work. As James examines a mid-century US 'economy and society where individuality, freedom, etc. are in essence lost', it is the sphere of popular culture that 'mirror[s] from year to year the deep social responses and evolution of the American people in relation to the fate which has overtaken the original concepts of freedom, free individuality, free association, etc.' But this mirroring, following his negative critique, takes complicated forms. For popular culture 'expresses the American people today' not only through 'what it is', but also through 'what it is *not*' (p. 118–19). James argues that popular culture is a synthesis of mass desires and dominant ideologies, and thus, 'if only negatively, represent[s] some of the deepest feelings of the masses, but represent[s] them within the common agreement – no serious political or social questions which would cause explosions' (p. 123).

James saw the mass identification with Hollywood stars as representing a necessarily constrained 'perversion', or negative expression, of individuals' thwarted desires for personal freedom and democratic communion. However, it is in the growing violence and sadism of Hollywood cinema and comic books – in particular the gangster and detective genres – where we find the fullest, and for our purposes most relevant, account of what popular culture 'is and what it is not' at that critical moment. Within the synthesis determining the production of these genres, these representations of violence are the negative expression of the loss of freedoms under an encroaching totalitarianism – what James termed 'esthetic compensation' (p. 127) – the symbolism by which state and corporate interests might consolidate more power and generate limitations on freedom, and a positive expression of the violent impulses emanating out of mass frustrations. Such frustrations, he argues, might lead to socialism, but might also serve as popular support for totalitarianism:[24]

> Impotent rage, anger, and frustration which can find expression only in a popular art of blood, destruction, torture, sadism; and an outlet for cheated, defrauded personality in vicarious living through a few striking personalities, these are the basic results in the only field where the masses are not free but at least have some choice in deciding ...

> By carefully observing the trends in modern popular art, and the responses of the people, we can see the tendencies which explode into the monstrous caricatures of human existence which appear under totalitarianism and closely intertwined with the blood and violence and cruelty, now elevated into social forces, is the social substitution of the individual for the mass. (pp. 158, 161)

Achille Mbembe has provocatively argued for a social analysis and an understanding of politics animated less by a 'philosophical discourse of modernity' than by 'other foundational categories that are less abstract and more tactile, such as life and death'. Using the terms 'necropower' and 'necropolitics' as frames of reference, Mbembe seeks to build upon Foucault's notion of 'biopower' to understand the 'practical conditions [under which] the right to kill, to allow to live, or to expose to death [are] exercised'. 'My concern', he states, 'is those figures of sovereignty whose central project is not the struggle for autonomy but *the generalized instrumentalization of human existence and the material destruction of human bodies and populations*' (emphasis in original). Taking issue with the notion of the 'state of exception' that would identify the death camps as the primary and exceptional site where the normal rules of law are suspended, Mbembe argues that such death-making has been fundamental to modernity: to regimes of slavery, colonialism, modern state formations, late-modern colonial occupations, and also quite often to the movements (for example, Marxism) that have sought to counter these regimes. Again and again we find the state of exception deployed as 'the normative basis of the right to kill. In such instances, power (and not necessarily state power) continuously refers and appeals to exception, emergency, and a fictionalized notion of the enemy.'[25]

Mbembe's ultimate aim, beyond improving our understanding of 'the repressed topographies of cruelty' constituting modernity and asking us to rethink the basis of politics, is to show how necropolitics and necropower more generally account for the systematic destruction of people and, following that, the emergence of 'new and unique forms of social existence in which vast populations are subjected to conditions of life conferring upon them the status of *living dead*'.[26] But the analysis also raises critical questions about 'the conditions of life' within those societies, such as the United States, defined by their political commitment both to the exercise of freedom and autonomy in the normative political sense and to their 'material destruction of human bodies and populations' at home and abroad. At an 'exceptional' moment, when collateral damage (that is, mass civilian casualties), torture, and political assassination abroad in the name of security have become acceptable and necessary evils for large segments of the American population, while mass incarceration and military indoctrination seem to be its government's primary and acceptable response to racial and class inequalities at home, one is compelled to think about the dialectic of a normative politics and a necropolitics, as well as about how our collective 'practical activities' respond to, potentially resist, and may perhaps enable the death-making that Mbembe argues is constitutive of our (and especially others') social worlds.

I want to suggest, then, that despite his fundamental concerns with labour and capital, James's emphasis on the violence produced out of the bureaucratisation and routinisation of modern life is not inconsistent with the Foucauldian notions of governmentality and biopower, as employed by Mbembe. Moreover, I believe there is great value in putting Mbembe's concept of necropolitics in dialogue with James's ethical commitment to recognise and respond to the danger in the political crisis of the moment, his concern with the contradictory forms and functions of violence in popular culture and the political uses to which they may be put, and his foregrounding of social responsibility among citizens of the United States for life and death across the globe.

Reading James through Mbembe pushes us towards a more fundamental, visceral, life-and-death understanding of politics, where life for some means death for others in a way that is not always logical, but is always consequential. Such a fusion asks us to think more carefully about the consequences of our cultural and political acts within the United States. Just as James saw in 'church services and singing of the very poor, in the responses to the great Negro bands in the dance-halls and sometimes in the theaters in the Negro districts' a 'modern Americanism, a profoundly social passion of frustration and violence', so too can we understand the life-embracing function of similar acts today within a neoliberal order that brings death to many through the prison industrial complex, failing healthcare system, lack of affordable housing, chronic joblessness, and so on. But we must also begin to investigate how such acts may abet these same social phenomena at home, as well as a host of injustices outside the United States that bring much greater suffering.

Returning to the 'Summer of Hummer' and its symbolic articulation of militarism and consumerism, I believe that the dialectical logic of James's analysis of popular culture in *American Civilization* lends itself to rich possibilities for seeking to understand how this sports utility vehicle may well speak both of thwarted political desire and, in a negative sense at least, of the possible democratic impulses hopefully still alive within the heterogeneous mass in present-day 'American Civilisation'. But it also cautions us to take stock of how such desire may also represent the collective sadism and wilful political choice that enable the necropolitical crisis facing us – whether expressed in colonial occupation, inner city policing, the prison industrial complex, or modern warfare – and helps create the symbols by which those with a greater investment in this crisis (whether economic, ideological, or spiritual) can win our consent for their projects.

American Studies will benefit if scholars choose to embrace James's negative dialectic, and select as their object the popular manifestations of militarism (or other violent phenomena reflecting and abetting the necropolitical order). One can imagine a host of interesting projects analysing the violent symbolism and effect of blockbuster epic films detailing the rise and fall of various empires throughout human history; the glut of 'reality' and dramatic police dramas on television; increasingly violent and militaristic music videos, video games, and toys; and the emergent and no less violent genre of millenarian biopics. These texts could quite productively be examined in the context of the global, neoliberal political–economic order, keeping in mind the multiple, intersecting social formations that come with it. And, following James, we would hopefully understand these texts not merely as vehicles for the dissemination of the dominant ideologies that sustain this order, and for the production of counternarratives that resist it. For within these cultural expressions we can also find a contradictory complex of desires that emerge from, are complicit with, but also imagine (even if only negatively) alternatives to the life- and death-making across the globe that defines this order.

But beyond the relatively specific project of analysing violent imagery and symbolism in popular culture, I also hope that anyone reading *American Civilization* will more generally be inspired by James's response to his political crisis to develop her own ethics around the writing of culture in its various manifestations during the present necropolitical crisis. For James's work – both in its attention to an encroaching totalitarianism and in its firm belief that writing about culture went hand in hand with envisioning an alternative future – suggests the need for an (e)valuation invested not only in locating the good in the ways people achieve their humanity and their subjectivity by resisting the various forms of domination that they face, but invested also in a collective responsibility for writing through the crisis.

Whatever progressive change may happen in the future, James said in the conclusion of his volume, 'the vast majority of Americans ... will have to do it themselves' (p. 276). Following that logic, I want to suggest that the difficult questions that emerge when scholars (both Americans and others) begin to think carefully about US subjects' complicity with violence and militarism can produce an ethical imperative that might animate a variety of kinds of future scholarly projects, as well as other kinds of professional pursuit (teaching, advising, service to community, political work, and so on). James was quite pessimistic about the ability of intellectuals to participate in meaningful social change. Not only was he anti-vanguardist but he also decried the trend of intellectuals moving into the managerial and bureaucratic positions that supported the encroaching totalitarian order. But he still provides us with a model – through his radical vision and his willingness continually to re-think society and his interpretations of it – through which productively to engage our complicity in the most recent manifestations of totalitarianism, through our consumerist and professional pursuits alike, and to use that knowledge to push our work in new directions.

NOTES

1. C.L.R. James, *American Civilization*, edited and introduced by Anna Grimshaw and Keith Hart (Cambridge, MA: Blackwell, 1993), p. 76. Subsequent references to this work are made parenthetically, in the body of the essay.
2. Robert Perrucci and Earl Wysong, *The New Class Society: Goodbye American Dream?*, second edition (Lanham, MD: Rowman and Littlefield Publishers, 2003), p. 28, Table 1.2. According to Perucci and Wysong, this social formation, comprising approximately 75 to 80 per cent of the US population, is defined by a relatively small comfort class at the top (10% of the US workforce), consisting of nurses, civil servants, small business owners, skilled labourers, and certain service-sector workers, as well as by a much larger set of contingent classes, consisting of a large group of low-wage and low-skilled workers (approximately 50 per cent of the American workforce), a very small group of self-employed people (3 to 4 per cent of the workforce), and an excluded class of people moving in and out of the labour force (10 to 15 per cent).
3. Grimshaw and Hart, Introduction to *American Civilization*, p. 19; Andrew Ross, 'Civilization in One Country? The American James', in Grant Farred, ed., *Rethinking C.L.R. James* (Cambridge, MA: Blackwell, 1996), p. 76; Neil Larsen, 'Negativities of the Popular: C.L.R. James and the Limits of "Cultural Studies"', in Farred, *Rethinking C.L.R. James*, p. 9; Michael Denning, *The Cultural Front: The Labouring of American Culture in the Twentieth Century* (London: Verso, 1996), p. 460.
4. Quoted in Cedric J. Robinson, *Black Marxism: The Making of the Black Radical Tradition* (London: Zed Press, 1983), p. 377.
5. Grimshaw and Hart, 'Introduction', p. 1.
6. Denning, *The Cultural Front*, pp. 108–9, 425. Denning lists as members of this group of 'American "Western Marxists"', Sidney Hook, Kenneth Burke, Louis Adamic, Carey McWilliams, Oliver C. Cox, Elizabeth Hawes, Sidney Finkelstein, and James himself.
7. Robin D.G. Kelley, 'The World the Diaspora Made: C.L.R. James and the Politics of History', in Farred, *Rethinking C.L.R. James*, pp. 115–16; Robin D.G. Kelley, *Freedom Dreams: The Black Radical Imagination* (Boston:

Beacon Press, 2002), p. 54; Anthony Bogues, *Caliban's Freedom: The Early Political Thought of C.L.R. James* (London: Pluto Press, 1997), pp. 51–2, 93–4; Robinson, *Black Marxism*, pp. 349–415; Paul Buhle, 'C.L.R. James: Paradoxical Pan-Africanist', in Sidney J. Lemelle and Robin D.G. Kelley, *Imagining Home: Class Culture and Nationalism in the African Diaspora* (London: Verso, 1994), pp. 158–66.

8. Bogues, *Caliban's Freedom*, pp. 53–63, 71, 100–1, 111–12; Robert A. Hill, Literary Executor's Afterword to *American Civilization*, pp. 302–22.
9. George Lipsitz, *American Studies at a Moment of Danger* (Minneapolis: University of Minnesota Press, 2001), pp. 27–8.
10. Examples of this version of American Studies include Daniel Boorstin, *The Genius of American Politics* (Chicago: University of Chicago Press, 1953); Perry Miller, *Errand into the Wilderness* (New York: Harper & Row, 1956); David Potter, *People of Plenty: Economic Abundance and the American Character* (Chicago: University of Chicago Press, 1954); Henry Nash Smith, *Virgin Land: The American West as Symbol and Myth* (Cambridge, MA: Harvard University Press, 1950); R.W.B. Lewis, *The American Adam: Innocence, Tragedy, and Tradition in the Nineteenth Century* (Chicago: University of Chicago Press, 1955).
11. James would, of course, extend this analysis of *Moby-Dick* in his 1953 book *Mariners, Renegades and Castaways*, written largely while he was awaiting his deportation hearing at Ellis Island. For an excellent account of how this text provides an alternative to early American Studies and the field's complicity with the politics of the McCarran-Walter Act, see Donald E. Pease, 'C.L.R. James, *Moby-Dick*, and the Emergence of Transnational American Studies', in this volume.
12. Grimshaw and Hart, 'Introduction', pp. 19–20.
13. Quoted and analysed in Ross, 'Civilization in One Country?', p. 76.
14. Aldon Lynn Nielsen, *C.L.R. James: A Critical Introduction* (Jackson, MS: University Press of Mississippi, 1997), pp. 144, 149–51; Denning, *The Cultural Front*, pp. 46–7, 455, 460–2; Ross, 'Civilization in One Country?', pp. 76–7; Grimshaw and Hart, 'Introduction', p. 15; Bogues, *Caliban's Freedom*, pp. 136–7.
15. Ross, 'Civilization in One Country?', pp. 81–2.
16. For calls to place ethnic studies at the centre of American Studies, see Mary Helen Washington, 'Disturbing the Peace: What Happens to American Studies If You Put African American Studies at the Center?', *American Quarterly* 50: 1 (1998), pp. 1–23; George Sanchez, 'Creating the Multicultural Nation: Advances in Post-Nationalist American Studies in the 1990s', in John Carlos Rowe, *Post-Nationalist American Studies* (Berkeley: The University of California Press, 2000), pp. 40–58.
17. Ross, 'Civilization in One Country?', pp. 78–80; Larsen, 'Negativities of the Popular', pp. 85–100.
18. Davies, *Modern Politics* (Detroit: Bewick Editions, 1973), p. 115.
19. Larsen, 'Negativities of the Popular', pp. 85–100. It is important to note here that Larsen states quite emphatically that James's project is fundamentally opposed to what we know as cultural studies. As he puts it, 'I would like both to anticipate and to preemptively critique the statement that, especially with the republication of James's writing on

North American popular culture ... James belongs, albeit ancestrally, to the thing we now call "Cultural Studies."' See Larsen, pp. 85–6.
20. Nielsen, *C.L.R. James*, p. xxvi.
21. Stuart Hall, 'Gramsci's Relevance for the Study of Race and Ethnicity', reprinted in David Morley and Kuan-Hsing Chen (eds), *Stuart Hall: Critical Dialogues in Cultural Studies* (London: Routledge, 1996), p. 413.
22. Nielsen, *C.L.R. James*, p. xxiv, p. 186.
23. Lipsitz, *American Studies in a Moment of Danger*, pp. 4–5.
24. For excellent discussions of the details of James's argument about popular culture and violence, too detailed to reproduce here, see Ross, 'Civilization in One Country?' and Nielsen, *C.L.R. James*.
25. Achille Mbembe, 'Necropolitics', *Public Culture* 15:1 (2003), pp. 12–16.
26. Ibid., p. 40.

3
C.L.R. James, *Moby-Dick*, and the Emergence of Transnational American Studies

Donald E. Pease

I publish my protest with my book on Melville because, as I have shown, the book as written is part of my experience. It is also a claim before the American people, the best claim I can put forward, that my desire to become a citizen is not a frivolous one.

C.L.R. James, *Mariners, Renegades and Castaways*

On 10 June 1952, men in black suits from the Immigration and Naturalization Service abruptly interrupted C.L.R. James's research for the book he intended to write that summer on Herman Melville and removed him to Ellis Island, where he was detained, awaiting deportation hearings, for the next four months. As warrant for his internment, the state agents cited the McCarran-Walter Act (henceforth referred to as the 'McCarran Act'), which, despite the fact that it was passed two years after James had completed the examinations qualifying him for citizenship, would nevertheless ultimately become the juridical instrument invoked by the state to justify James's detention.[1]

At a time in which the United States was increasingly dependent on Third World labour, the McCarran Act put into place regulations concerning the legal and economic conditions for citizenship that ratified neocolonial distinctions. The bill authorised INS officials to apply different combinations of rules and norms for the purpose of sorting immigrants into economic and political classifications. The taxonomy to which INS officials subordinated their clientele invoked racialised categories that were designed to reflect extant US geopolitical alliances, and to expand US markets at home and abroad.

The phrases whereby the bill distinguished immigrants the state could exclude on political grounds from migrants whose labour it could exploit included within the former category 'any alien who has engaged or has had purpose to engage in activities "prejudicial to the public interest" or "subversive to the national security."'[2] In addition to granting the state the right to expel subversives, the bill also called for a careful screening of persons seeking to reside in the United States, and installed cultural literacy as one of the criteria whereby the state might determine whether or not 'they' were adaptable to the American way of life.

Although the state had kept James under scrutiny from the time of his formal application to become a legal resident in 1938, its designation of him as a subversive brought about a drastic change in his juridical relationship to the category of US citizenship. The temporal flexibility invested in the phrase 'who has engaged or who has had the purpose to engage in activities' subversive to the national security granted the INS powers of retroactive jurisdiction over the entire period of James's US residency.

US citizenship was grounded in the legal fiction by which an individual citizen was construed as both legislator – the 'I' who was the sender of the law – and subject – the 'you' who was its addressee. By way of its derecognition of James's personhood, the state denied him the first-person pronominal powers necessary to support and defend his civil and political liberties. After the state pronounced him a security threat, James's legal subjectivity underwent demotion to the status of 'you'. As its secondary addressee, James was subject to the law's powers of enforcement, but he was no longer recognised as the subject of its norms.[3]

James's loss of the power to speak as 'I' also deauthorised the testifying phrases through which he could convey his claims before a court, and invalidated his interlocutory privileges within the civil society.[4] The state's restriction of his pronominal identifications to the 'you' who must obey the law had also disallowed James membership in the 'we' of 'we the people', whose sovereign will the state was understood to represent. 'You' could never become 'we' because 'you' named the subversive whom the state had refused the rights of dialogue with or as an 'I'.[5]

Jean-Francois Lyotard has proposed the term 'differend' to describe the kind of juridical dilemma in which James was embroiled. Lyotard defines a differend as a 'case of conflict between at least two parties, that cannot be equitably resolved for lack of a rule of judgement applicable to both parties'.[6] Since the damage for which James sought legal remedy originated with the legislation whose rules the courts were required to render applicable to their decisions, the judgment

James sought exceeded the appellate courts' juridical authority. James could not appeal the state's ruling without calling for the repeal of the McCarran Act. But James could neither organise nor participate in a movement calling for the repeal of the McCarran Act without providing the state with an example of the activity for which he was accused. Moreover, any US citizen who came to James's defense was liable to prosecution for collaborating with a subversive.

In an effort to supply a rule of judgement that the courts lacked, James produced an interpretation of *Moby-Dick* underwritten by a juridical standard by which he intended to define the illegality of the McCarran legislation, and to represent as well the wrong against him which the state had perpetrated on McCarran's authority. At the time James published *Mariners, Renegades and Castaways*, Americanist critics had already placed *Moby-Dick* into service as a weapon in the Cold War. In their readings of it as a prototypical national narrative, these critics deployed the United States' opposition to the Soviet Union to justify neocolonialist policies in James's native Trinidad, and elsewhere in the hemisphere. The United States bore the responsibility, as these interpreters argued, to colonise life-worlds – at home and abroad – as an effort to oppose the Soviet Union's anticipated colonisation of them.

In a reading of *Moby-Dick* he had published four years earlier, the literary critic Richard Chase had provided James's usage of the novel with an academic warrant. Chase represented Melville's novel as the foundational fiction of the Cold War state. Chase fostered an allegorical understanding of *Moby-Dick* that posited Ahab's monomania as the signifier of the totalitarian Other in opposition to which Ishmael's Americanness was defined, elaborated upon and defended. While subsequent interpreters would introduce at times ingenious variations upon this theme, the essentialised opposition between Ishmael and Ahab would dominate readings of the novel in the field of American literary studies for the next 50 years.[7]

James believed that Americanist interpretations of *Moby-Dick* like Chase's corroborated the emergency powers of the national security state whose hegemony the field of American literary studies had indirectly legitimated. Engaging himself in the work of constructing a counter-hegemony, James confirmed the prevailing understanding of Ahab as a 'totalitarian type' (p. 16). But after arguing that the security state had put into place the totalitarian rule that it purported to oppose, he also generalised this type to include Ishmael, whom he described as 'an intellectual Ahab', (p. 44) as well as the members of the McCarran Committee, and the administrators of the national security state. As justification for this extension of the applicability of the type, James cited the administrators' individual and collective failure to repeal the state's emergency powers as signs of their complicity with Ahab's totalitarian rule.

In his efforts to delegitimise the state's emergency powers, James discriminated the people that the McCarran legislation presumed to represent, whom he correlated with Ahab's officers, from those who, like Ahab's crew, were its potential victims. James associated the emergency powers of the state with Ahab's transgression of his duly constituted authority, and offered the following contrary proposition as the theme the book allegorised: 'How the society of free individualism would give birth to totalitarianism and be unable to defend itself against it.'[8]

With this correlation of his experience with the INS authorities on Ellis Island with his reading of an exemplary national classic, James had devised a signifying practice that was in one of its aspects a hermeneutic exercise, and in another a juridical appeal. In the process of working on the book while detained on Ellis Island, James fashioned these discrepant facets into a personal memoir through which he was able to come to terms with the ordeal he underwent there.

Stuart Hall has remarked on the juridical dimension of James's Melville book by recasting it as an imaginary conversation with an INS officer:

> As a part of his defense he made a wonderfully Jamesian gesture ... he attempted to present *Mariners, Renegades and Castaways* ... as testimony to the fact that he was a much better American than the Immigration authorities. It was as though he were saying 'You do not understand your greatest artist, Melville, and I do. How can you expel me for un-American activities when I am telling you that next to Shakespeare, here is the greatest use of the English language? It is because you do not understand what your own author is telling you that you can expel me. You should welcome me – not throw me out.'[9]

Hall's account is valuable for its discrimination of the civil liberties to which the state had legally denied James access from the cultural and political practices through which he continued to perform his citizenship. By way of his representation of this exchange between James and an INS officer, Hall has communicated James's belief that US citizenship be understood as the effect of disparate activities within a contested terrain for which the people rather than the state should act as arbiter. Hall has also usefully discerned the compensatory powers of James's interpretation; its capacity to provide imaginary restoration of the civic prerogatives that the state had nullified.

While Hall's imaginary scenario underscores James's having continued to practice a cultural form of US citizenship, however, it overlooks the political and juridical dimensions of James's quandary. Moreover, Hall's depiction of James's Melville book as the symbolic gesture wherein he demonstrated the superiority of his cultural literacy ignores the irrelevance of this script to the state's absolute control over James's social destiny. Had he conducted his reading of *Moby-Dick* simply as evidence of his fluency in the literary idiom reproductive of the state's cultural capital, James would have indirectly legitimated INS policies. James's decision to continue the project that the state had interrupted cannot be ascertained apart from the work's relation to his untenable legal position.

The state's representation of James as a security threat had placed him outside the state's protection. Because he lacked any other form of secure placement, James's writing became for him a resolutely physical exercise. It provided him with a way corporeally to inhabit and keep record of his material presence within a space the state had defined as a geography for the bodily excluded. As he resumed daily the practice of writing, the role of Melville interpreter resubjectivised a Jamesian body otherwise denied any position the state was obliged to recognise. As the means whereby he disputed the state's authority, James's interpretation of Melville also materialised a site that was quite literally external to the state's boundaries.

Unable to argue against the McCarran legislation in his own name, James advanced his interpretation of the authority of figures that he described as the disavowed 'heroes' of *Moby-Dick*. 'It is clear', James explains, what led to their disavowal: 'that Melville intends to make the crew the real heroes of his book, but he is afraid of criticism' (p. 20). James referred one source of Melville's fear to the negative response he anticipated had he narrated the crew's revolt against the *Pequod*'s captain. After 'Ahab had stated that the purpose of the voyage was different from that for which they had signed', James stipulated the rationale for the heroic action that Melville was afraid to narrate: 'the men were entitled to revolt and to take possession of the ship themselves' (p. 14).

James's decision to write about *Moby-Dick* from the standpoint of the figures Melville had felt prohibited from depicting as its heroes required that he position himself in resistance to what had prohibited Melville's freedom of expression. Assuming the stance of the bodily relay required for the transmission of the mariners', renegades' and castaways' discontinued narratives, James thereafter interpreted *Moby-Dick* as if they represented Melville's previously unnarratable intentionality.

In accomplishing the intention that Melville could not, James devised a series of interlocking homologies which respectively correlated: the criticism Melville feared with the violence that the state had directed against James's person; Ahab's exceeding his duly constituted powers with the state's emergency powers; 'mariners, renegades and castaways' with the change in legal status that the national people might undergo should the state decide to deprive them of their rights; and the *Pequod*'s crew with his fellow detainees on Ellis Island. James thereafter triggered the undischarged social energy that lay dormant within this relay with the proposal that the mariners' belated right to legal remedy be construed as a kind of legal precedent for the repeal of the McCarran legislation.

Mariners, Renegades and Castaways put into place a multi-layered strategy. It produced a frame of intelligibility that supplied James with the categories and themes required to challenge the findings of the McCarran legislation, with the pronominal rights of an interpreting 'I', and with an interpretive object through which he could express his grievances against the state. As the continuation of the activity James had undertaken at the time of the state's forcible resettlement, the book was construable as the proximate cause for the state's action, as well as being documentation of the violence the state had exerted against his person. James's interpretation of Melville brought this example of his activities before the court of public opinion, and invited its readers to decide as to the justice of the state's actions.

In an effort to respond to the layered dimensions of James's project, I shall divide the following remarks into sections devoted respectively to a consideration of his engagement with the Cold War state, and of how James's means of engagement implicated the past and the future(s) of American Studies.

TAKING EXCEPTION TO US EXCEPTIONALISM

The Tradition of the oppressed teaches us that 'the state of emergency' in which we live is not the exception but the rule.[10]

Walter Benjamin, 'Theses on the Philosophy of History'

Before its passage into law, the McCarran Act required the public's consent to its construction of subversives as exceptions to the state's democratic norms. McCarran solicited the public's acquiescence with declarations like the following, in which he claimed that the threat immigrants posed to the sovereignty of the national borders had precipitated a state of emergency:

> Our entire immigration system has been so weakened as to make it often impossible for our own country to protect its security in this era of black fifth column infiltration and Cold Warfare with the ruthless masters of the Kremlin. The time has long since passed when we can afford to open our borders indiscriminately to give unstinting hospitality to any person, whose ideological aim is to overthrow our institutions and replace them with the evil oppression of totalitarianism.[11]

Because the McCarran Act's anti-democratic measures openly violated more or less agreed-upon political norms, it exposed a political paradox that, while foundational to the liberal state, was exacerbated throughout the Cold War. Within a liberal democracy it is the citizens who are sovereign. They accord certain powers to the state in return for the protection, education, and administration of a territorially bound national community. Since the state derives its powers from the sovereign will of the citizens, the state's actions can be construed as legitimate only when endowed with the prior consent of the sovereign will of the people. Due to the incompatible registers – the state's and the people's – in which political sovereignty operates, however, no political action can ever fully conform to this condition.[12]

Never fully authorised at the moment of its enactment, a political action always lacks the legitimacy that can only be conferred retroactively with the invocation of standards, norms and rationales 'incompletely thematized and consented to at its inception'. The sovereign will of the people is, on the one hand, presumed to have already been given expression and, on the other, construed to entail a consensual process that must continually be accomplished. The interval in between a political action and the sovereign consent required to legitimate it discloses an 'element of arbitrariness that cannot be eliminated from political life'.[13]

The arbitrariness refers to the temporal lag in between the enactment of a policy like the McCarran Act and the people's recognition of the act as representative of their will. Although McCarran represented the bill's measures as the reflection of the citizenry's already declared consensus, the people the McCarran bill has presumed to represent did not yet exist. The effort to afford the bill the appearance of representing a national consensus led to its affiliation with the discourse of US exceptionalism. In representing the McCarran Act as an execution of the popular will purportedly expressed in that discourse, these legislators proposed that the public be understood to have already granted their consent to that bill's mandates.

US exceptionalism was a political doctrine as well as a regulatory ideal assigned the task of defining, supporting and transmitting the US national identity. Throughout the Cold War, the state invoked the doctrine of exceptionalism to validate its emergency power to produce exceptions to democratic norms. The doctrine of exceptionalism declared exceptional in the US political economy institutions – class antagonism, totalitarian rule, a colonial empire – whose putative absence from the US political economy provided the state with warrant to except exponents of such institutions from the national community.[14]

Scholars in the disciplines of American literature and history presupposed exceptionality as the normative framework guiding their interpretation and transmission of the national culture. The field of American Studies promoted US exceptionalism as the basis for the institutionalisation of the American Studies Association in 1950. 'It was this interest in American Exceptionalism', Janice Radway has recently noted,

> that led to the desire for an interdisciplinary method that would be equal to the notion of American culture conceived as a unified whole, a whole that manifested itself as a distinctive set of properties and themes in all things American, whether individuals, institutions or cultural products.[15]

In the writings of the so-called consensus historians – Arthur Schlesinger, Daniel Boorstin and Louis Hartz – the state discovered the means whereby it could secure retroactive consent for its exceptions. In stipulating the absence from the American past of the class system or the precapitalist colonial formations, which they described as the preconditions for totalitarian communism, these architects of US exceptionalism provided the state with an historical justification for the production of 'unamericans' and for their removal from the US political order. Observing that Tocqueville had found US political society exceptional in lacking the feudal traditions that had precipitated the violent confrontations in France's moment of transition, Louis Hartz advanced the claim that the absence of class conflict from a liberal capitalist order had rendered impossible the emergence of socialism within US territorial borders. 'One of the central characteristics of a nonfeudal society is that it lacks a genuine revolutionary tradition', Hartz noted approvingly. 'And this being the case, it lacks also a tradition of reaction: lacking Robespierre, it lacks Maistre, lacking Sydney, it lacks Charles II.'[16]

Richard Chase indicated the contribution American literature offered to the emergency state when, in the 'Preface' to his Melville book, he explicitly affiliated its 'purpose' with the effort to disassociate the American Studies movement from the political radicalism of its earliest practitioners. Whereas C.L.R. James numbered Frederick Douglass, Lydia Marie Childs, Jose Marti, Randolph Bourne, Richard Wright and Granville Hicks among the precursors to his scholarly project, Chase described that entire lineage as representative of the 'progressive liberalism' whose practices he would except from American literary history. Chase's 'purpose' was

> to contribute a book on Melville to a movement which may be described (once again) as a new liberalism – that newly invigorated secular thought at the dark center of the twentieth century which ... now begins to ransom liberalism from the ruinous sell-outs, failures, and defeats of the thirties. The new liberalism must justify its claims over the old liberalism. It must present a vision of life capable, by a continuous act of imaginative criticism, of avoiding the old mistakes: the facile ideas of progress and 'social realism', the disinclination to examine human motives, the indulgence of wish-fulfilling rhetoric, the belief that historical reality is merely a question of economic or ethical values, the idea that literature should participate directly in the economic liberation of the masses, the equivocal relationship to communist totalitarianism and power politics.[17]

While the 'purpose' Chase describes in this passage would suggest an academic struggle between more or less equivalently empowered academics, the phrasing with which he concludes the passage – 'the equivocal relationship to communist totalitarianism and power politics' – echoes rhetoric that the McCarran legislation had instrumentalised to 'justify' its deportation of scholars like C.L.R. James. The legal apparatus for surveillance that the Cold War state had recently put into place deployed similar language when it purged the American Studies movement of members in political solidarity with the 'progressive tradition' that Chase has repudiated.

In providing the doctrine of US exceptionalism with the coordinated rationalities of literary interpretation and consensus history, the field of American Studies had indirectly legitimated the McCarran legislation. Both disciplines produced what might be called a facilitating retroactivity for the construction of exceptions to the Americanist creed of tolerance for dissent and democratic inclusiveness. In their characterisation of C.L.R. James as a dangerous subversive, the INS depended upon the discourse of exceptionalism as a tacit warrant.

The McCarran bill could be construed as legitimate only if it reflected the prior consent of the people's sovereign will; McCarran and Walter solicited that consent by fashioning the historical absences US historians had added to the master narrative of US exceptionalism into grounds for their exclusion of subversives and aliens. In supplying the illusion that the McCarran Act's exceptions to democratic inclusiveness had already been mandated by the unique conditions of the national history, the discourse of exceptionalism closed the temporal gap between the people that the act presumed to represent and the people constituted out of this legislation.

Instead of authorising the reading of *Moby-Dick* that had declared Ahab's totalitarianism an 'exception' to forms of democratic governance, James proposed that the McCarran Act continued Ahab's form of governance. In his revisionist reading, James focused upon three figures who had not survived the wreck of the *Pequod*. Specifically, James's reading singled out Queequeg, the South Sea Islander, Tashtego, the Gay Head Indian from Massachusetts, and the 'African Giant' Daggoo. In the following passage, James associates the three harpooners with his fellow detainees on Ellis Island.

> This is my final impression. The meanest mariners, renegades and castaways of Melville's day were objectively a new world. But they knew nothing. These know everything. The symbolic mariners and renegades of Melville's book were isolatoes federated by one keel, but only because they had been assembled by penetrating genius. These are federated by nothing. But they are looking for federation. I have heard a young Oriental say that he would fight on either side (in the Cold War) – it didn't matter to him. What he wanted was a good peace no half peace. This peace, however, he added almost as an afterthought, should include complete independence for his own little country. (p. 186)

This passage is remarkable for the example James has supplied of the difference between Melville's 'symbolic mariners' – who knew nothing – and his fellow detainees' knowledge of everything. The anecdote James reports to exemplify such knowledge, however, has removed any meaningful distinction between exactly what these political refugees know and how they put it to the work of negotiating with the Cold War state. Throughout the Cold War, Asian countries acquired significance through their alignment with one or the other of the global hegemons. Both occupying powers conflated Asian countries with the systems of representation through which they administered and controlled their territories.

But with the declaration that 'he would fight on either side (of the Cold War)', the 'young Oriental' has refused the discursive rules requiring that he identify himself as either friend or foe. Rather than agreeing to be constituted out of these categories of identification, he has suspended the Cold War's rules of discursive recognition and disrupted the bipolar logic that the discourse has mandated. Having rendered the codes that would impose it indefinite and insecure, he decodifies their imposed identity. Because he cannot be stably located for or against either of these positions, his ambivalence has opened up a space that is internal to his country but extrinsic to Cold War governmental rule. Having made these opposed ideological systems appear reversible rather than mutually exclusive, his renegade positioning has actively removed the divide between East and West, enabling him an unimpeded transition from one side to the other.

Moreover, in proclaiming his loyalty to a 'good peace' rather than either antagonist, James's interlocutor might be described as having set himself against Cold War rule by way of his identification with a 'higher' rule that is internal to its code. The oppositional logic of the Cold War had presupposed the attainment of a complete peace as at once the grounds for conflict and the condition that should supplant the warfare. But while its protagonists would acknowledge peace as their common goal, the Cold War's bipolar logic had rendered it impossible for an occupied country to obtain any outcome other than a 'half peace'. By aligning his country with the 'good peace' that predated the Cold War, James's fellow ward of the Cold War state has appealed to an element within the code that the code itself has recognised as a 'higher' rule, and empowered with the authority to supplant it.

James's description of his fellow castaway's knowledge also characterises his own project's relation to the state. Having been classified by the state as an exception to democratic norms, James has discovered a way to turn the paradoxical space in which the exception is located to his rhetorical advantage. Giorgio Agamben has analysed the space of the exception with great precision. An exception 'cannot be included in the whole of which it is a member and cannot be a member of the whole in which it is already included'.[18] Included within a liberal democracy, exceptions name what that democracy must exclude to achieve unity and coherence. Because they name the limit to democratic inclusiveness, exceptions also produce what might be described as the illusion of an enveloping border for the members of the national democracy who have not been excluded. As the member that the nation must exclude in order for the state to achieve coherence and unity, exceptions also designate the figures that a state produces when it establishes a historically specific concretisation of the universalising process known as nation-formation.

Exceptions describe what results when a state asserts the distinction between the nation as a universal form and its historically specific particularisation. As a limit internal to the nation, an exception specifies the difference between nationalism as a universal modern norm and a state's historically specific concretisation of that norm. When understood to specify the limits to the universalisation of the nation-form, exceptions invite comparison with contingencies. Understood as non-universalisable social categories, the contingencies of race, class, gender, and ethnicity often provide the state with the raw material for its construction of exceptions.

But the space of the exception is not reducible to these signifiers of the internally excluded. It would also include the rules of law themselves, which by definition cannot be subject to the norms they would regulate, as well as the state of emergency. A liberal democracy is understood to enter a state of emergency when its members are subjected to the extreme conditions of a war or a natural catastrophe. During an emergency, the state's requirement to protect the nation would take precedence over its obligation to acquire the people's consent for its decisions.

By way of the observation that, after Ahab 'stated that the purpose of the voyage was different from that for which they had signed, the men were entitled to revolt and to take possession of the ship themselves' (p. 14), James has fashioned Ahab as the totalitarian exception to a state's emergency powers. He has also described the crew as the democratic exception to Ahab's totalitarian rule. As the internal limit to Ahab's totalitarian governance, the crew hold the place of the rule of law, and, like the 'young Oriental' they are comparably empowered by this 'higher' law to overthrow Ahab's totalitarian order.

It was because they owe 'no allegiance to anybody or anything except the work they have to do and the relations with one another upon which that work depends' (p. 20), that the mariners in *Moby-Dick* produce a discontinuity with the oppressive conditions that prevail under Ahab. Thus reimagined, Melville's castaways enabled James to talk back to the power of the Cold War state through figures who were likewise extrinsic to its forms of governance.

Upon remarking the parallel between Ahab's illegal change of the contract and the emergency powers claimed by the Cold War state, James replaced the Ishmael–Ahab opposition, which establishment Americanists had proposed as the narrative's thematic centre, with the unacknowledged knowledge that the 'meanest mariners, renegades and castaways' constituted exceptions to both forms of totalitarian rule. In drawing upon this subaltern knowledge to focus his reading, James also disclosed the state's interest in its disqualification.

With the observation that while they bore its traces, Queequeg, Tashtego and Daggoo lacked explicit knowledge of their histories, James engendered a creative collaboration between the consciousness of the experiences he underwent on Ellis Island and the unnarrated memory of the harpooners' past. This collaboration produced within James the recollection of the histories of colonial exploitation, Indian removal, and the African slave trade that Melville's fear had disallowed the harpooners. In articulating his knowledge of state power by way of reactivating the memories of these vanished intermediaries, James constructed partial and strictly provisional identifications with the national community.

Refusing compliance with the state's production of exceptions, James characterised dereferentialisation and derecognition as the processes through which the state produced the absences in which the doctrine was grounded, and thereafter restored to Melville's crew the knowledges of class hierarchies, resettled populations and internal colonialism that the doctrine of exceptionalism had disqualified. James proceeded to link these derecognized knowledges with the other versions of subaltern knowledge circulating through Ellis Island. Then James positioned this knowledge in the temporal interval between the McCarran Act and the consent to it that US exceptionalism was understood to have manufactured – after the fact.

Throughout his interpretation of Melville, James exploited the incompatibility between the national citizenry's democratic norms and the state's emergency powers. He did so in order to exacerbate the asymmetrical registers – the state's, the people's – in which national sovereignty operated, and to render it impossible for the discourse of Exceptionalism to close the gap between these two levels. In removing the mask of exceptionalism from the bill's enactments, James demonstrated how McCarran's declaration of a danger to their security had produced the image of a totalised national community that McCarran thereafter claimed to represent. The McCarran Act had in effect granted the state the power to practice violence against the people in the name of preserving the state. Offering his case as proof, James claimed that it was McCarran's emergency measures that posed the real danger to US democracy.

James intended that his reanimation of the democracy's grounding paradox would effect two related political outcomes: the description of the McCarran Act as law-breaking rather than norm-preserving, and the emergence within the social order of the subjects out of whose absences that order had constructed its coherence. In thus reversing the optic of governance from the state to these people, James expounded the ethical proposition that freedom and justice should not be sacrificed in the name of security. This proposition effectively reshaped his interpretation of *Moby-Dick* into a quasi-imperative: You will have properly understood *Moby-Dick* only if you repeal the McCarran legislation.

CALIBAN ON ELLIS ISLAND

Like Caliban, James could use the language he had been taught to push into regions Prospero never knew.[19]
    Sylvia Wynter, 'Beyond the Categories of the Master Conception'

James's interpretation of *Moby-Dick* designated the discourse of exceptionalism and the field of American Studies in which it was produced as interdependent justificatory discourses responsible for the legitimation and normalisation of the state's emergency powers. His efforts to impede their work led him to reconceptualise Ellis Island as an enclave lying between the nation and the state, in which the state exercised a totalising power. In negotiating his right to citizenship from within this space, James elaborated similarities between the emergency state and the colonial state apparatus. James's interpretive work compressed the field of American Studies to the dimensions of the colonial encounter that he staged on Ellis Island, and exposed US history and literature as interlocking systems of state formation.

American Studies transmitted an understanding of national US history and literature that was formative of the autonomous citizen–subject on one level of operation, and with the formation of a collective national identity on another. Under this description of its disciplinary effects, the field of American Studies produced citizens who were accountable to the state and capable of promoting its interests. The vast majority of scholars in the field of American Studies may have understood their belief in US exceptionalism to be far removed from the INS's deportation policies. Through the juxtaposition of his reading of *Moby-Dick* with his transactions with the INS's bureaucratic apparatus, however, James discerned concrete and specific linkages between the two orders. The INS officers may have applied the rules determining the conditions of national belonging, but the tributary discourses of US history and literature supplied the standards, norms and rationales that naturalised them.[20]

Having compressed US citizenship to the dimensions of his encounter with the colonial state apparatus, James re-described the exchange structuring the US symbolic economy during the Cold War as entailing the substitution of the state's actual colonisation of its citizenry's life-worlds for the grand narrative of US exceptionalism developed within the field of American Studies. In revealing Ellis Island as the mediator between the nation and the Cold War state, James referred to the totalising operations there as interchangeable with the totalitarianism and colonialism that the doctrine of US exceptionalism had officially opposed.

In pursuing the analogy between his negotiation with the INS and a colonial encounter, James also established similarities between the imperial state's neo-colonialisation of Third World countries and the administrative state's colonisation of domestic life-worlds. According to James, the Cold War state positioned the national people in a quasi-colonialist structure. It thereby effected a relation of false reciprocity between domestic policies and national security interests that transferred the foreign policy of Americanisation abroad into an instrument for securing domestic solidarity at home.

The contradictory relations that James had thereby delineated between the state and the nation reconfigured Americanisation as an 'event' that sedimented political, social and economic registers within a layered structure that could not be reduced to a symbolic resolution. Interpretively connecting the 'internal colonialism' of the national security apparatus to the structure of colonial relations still in force in his native Trinidad, James's account of his experiences on Ellis Island strategically materialised the site of a post-nation from within an Americanist narrative that had previously been deployed to effect just such an imaginary resolution.[21]

James's 'postcolonial' knowledge of state subjection forced into visibility the foundational violence out of whose disavowal establishment American Studies had been constituted. Interpretations fostered within the field had sought to dissolve the contradictory relations between the nation and the state. The 'end of ideology' thesis put in their place the image of an integrated national identity that would displace historical contingencies and subsume cultural and political differences. In transforming incompatible matters into an imaginary coherence, the national mythology had constructed a fetish of national identity. Deploying Melville to bring into sight the disjunctures between the imaginary wholeness of the national community and the nation's foundational disavowals, James unstitched the imaginary thread suturing the national community to the national security state.

In articulating this 'other' realm (where state power operated unconcealed) to the narrated life-world of the national community, James represented Ellis Island as a colonial enclave within US democracy. Here the state discriminated citizens who belonged to the national community from the Island's inhabitants, whom he represented as wards of a colonial state. In a version of what might be called post-colonial colonialism, citizens were encouraged to disavow knowledge of the state's violation of their democratic norms, and to construe the persons who bore that knowledge as, like James's fellow Islanders, exceptions.

Interpreting *Moby-Dick* by way of a conceptual apparatus that uncovered colonialism and cultural imperialism as unacknowledged elements within the nation's official literary tradition, James represented himself as non-Americanisable in the official terms of that tradition. Writing from the position of the exception between the state and the normalising procedures that would legitimate its powers, James, instead of becoming Americanised or subjectivised in those terms, directed two questions to the architects of the Cold War canon: 1) How does the literary tradition Americanise migrants, refugees and other stateless persons? and 2) What knowledge is foreclosed in the process?

The imagined domestic community through which the state conducted its policy of Americanisation at home and abroad depended on the romance genre for the emplotment of its fantasy. The fantasy involved controlling the globe's ideological map. It was underwritten by an interpretive method produced within the field of American literary studies known as the myth–symbol school. The method derived its authority from endowing its practitioners with the capacity to represent entire cultures as ritual reenactments of this national fantasy. It yoked an anthropological imaginary to ritualistic explications of others' cultural stories, and facilitated exchanges between literary and geopolitical realms that effectively transformed the field of American Studies into an agency of neocolonialism. Its practitioners designed a cultural typology with which to interpret, and thereafter to subsume, other literatures and geopolitical spaces into a universal Americanism.[22]

The myth–symbol school's method of reading enacted the quasi-colonialist project of absorbing the mores and customs of Third World nations into an allegory of nation-formation that represented them as in the process of developing into an American nation. The colonialist component of this project absorbed the rituals of the so-called 'developing nations' into an allegory of nation-formation underwritten by the quest romance. It consigned indigenous forms to the status of 'outmoded rituals'. The disavowal of colonialism globally, and the foreclosure of the tragic nationally, comprised interlinked practices of the national romance.

Instead of reproducing this nationalising mythology, James established concrete linkages between neocolonialism as a US foreign policy and the practices of internal colonisation in evidence on Ellis Island. In thereby reversing the direction of the symbolic economy that the American literary establishment authorised, James brought the Americanist mythos to its limit. He wrote from within a Melvillean life-world that the myth–symbol school had translated into the terms of the national mythology. Then he operationalised his interpretation of Melville as a lever that, in demonstrating how American myths colonised others' life-worlds, turned the national mythology inside-out.

Unlike establishment Americanists, James wrote his commentary from the standpoint of a figure that had become excluded from within US political culture. While James was reading the violence inherent to the reason of state from the perspective of Melville's frame narrative, he was also delineating the complex affiliation between this rationality and the interpretive assumptions that were grounded in it. Insisting on the inherence of acts of state violence to the literary establishment's image of the fulfilled national destiny, James removed *Moby-Dick* from the precincts of modern nationalism and linked its themes and events with his efforts to recover from state violence.

As an artifact within the tradition of modernist symbolism, *Moby-Dick* effected a synecdochal continuity between the present and this image of 'universal totality' it was made to prefigure. The postnational emerged, in James's reading of Melville's text, at and as the interval between the reason of state and the national mythology upon which establishment American literature was 'grounded'. Writing from outside that culture with an insider's knowledge of its workings, James's commentary uncovered in Melville's texts the political unconscious of official literary history: the codes and assumptions informing the structures of exclusion whereby the reason of state had secured its identification with the national mythology. Understood as a structure of containment, the pivot of the national metanarrative turned on the mythology of US exceptionalism.

In James's account of their relationship, the nation's myth of itself ratified the social dynamic intrinsic to domestic Americanisation. He invoked his own experiences on Ellis Island to criticise that dynamic as involving the exception of contingencies – ethnicity, race, gender, sexuality, and locale – which were represented as otherwise than Americanisable. On Ellis Island, James rendered visible the act whereby the state made 'one people out of many'. When he did this, he materialised the nation's internal limit. James, in occupying this always already traversed border between being and becoming American, revealed how far apart the state's violent practices were from the desires of individuals who wanted to organise their societies differently. The anti-exceptionalist strategies James subsequently devised here required that he confront US citizens with the hard facts concerning their disavowed histories.

Promoting such knowledge required that James upset the relay of cultural relations that supported its denial. Two nodal points in this network of relations linked the ethnographic imaginary authorising Melville's descriptions of Tashtego, Queequeg and Daggoo to the criteria informing the deliberations of bureaucrats within the INS. An explanation of the strategies James deployed to disjoin these relays requires an understanding of the circular causality conjoining them.

When resituated within the semiotic field brought into coherence by the INS, the taxonomies of cultural types that the public had learned from interpretations of Melville's narrative were made to signify a ranked hierarchical order.

The INS in turn conscripted the visual perceptions underwriting US citizens' reading practices to reproduce and thereby authorise its categorisations. In visualising 'foreigners' according to INS categories, US citizens linked them to formulations that also evaluated them. Members of other cultures thereafter became servants of INS categories that they could not escape and that seemingly legislated their existence. When they recognised immigrants as functions of distinguishable traits, US citizens practiced what might be called visual imperialism. Visually sorting immigrants according to the INS's taxonomy involved citizens in the imperial practices whereby the US colonised other life-worlds.

But if cultural imperialism constituted a kind of optical unconscious for its citizens' visualisation of cultural otherness, the assimmilationist model through which they comprehended these processes rendered them unable to become conscious of this fact. Assimilation was the form US exceptionalism assumed when it 'naturalised' its citizens' cultural stereotyping. Assimilation actively disavowed the cultural imperialism that immigration policies and visualisation practices reproduced.

Immigrant narratives that represented the US as a haven from colonial and political oppression closed this circle by authorising the mythology of US exceptionalism in which INS policies of exclusion and denationalisation were grounded. Each story that represented the US as a safe haven from colonial oppression abroad eclipsed the history of US colonial relations. The myth of the US as a promised land lacking the history of imperial domination and class oppression which haunted European memory effaced the middle passage narrative of slaves who were brought to the US against their will, and the stories of migrant labourers the state had newly colonised, and of migrants who felt their conditions had worsened.

James thoroughly understood how the negative reference to the state's production of exceptions to the official belief in US exceptionalism regulated the citizenry's optical unconscious. He dedicated himself to the work of representing to US citizens the knowledge that the discourse of exceptionalism could not include without breaking down. But before he could dismantle exceptionalism's hegemony, James was obliged to disrupt the structures supporting the disavowal through which it ruled. James contested these structures most vigorously at Ellis Island, the site of entry into and deportation from the United States.

In his re-description of Ellis Island, James did not altogether replace but complicated competing descriptions of it as a safe haven for political and colonial escapees. In writing there, James represented the emergency state's construction of 'exceptions' to the credo of democratic inclusiveness as productive of a nodal point at which social relations within the domestic life-world intersected with global capitalism and the international division of labour. And he transformed this intersection into the site whereon he imagined an alternative future.

A POSTNATIONAL FABLE OF TRANSNATIONAL AMERICAN STUDIES

To establish his own identity, Caliban, after three centuries, must himself pioneer into regions Caesar never knew.[23]

C.L.R. James, *Beyond a Boundary*

Thus far I have proposed the future field of American Studies as the horizon onto which C.L.R. James projected his interpretation of *Moby-Dick*. Because imagining the future involves trading in counter-factuals, the remainder of this essay should be understood as the outline of a postnational fable – an allegory of the narrative strategies already described, as well as the evocation, at the site of this fable, of a transnational American Studies.

Upon fashioning his brief against the Cold War state as a narrative of the stateless persons who had not survived the wreck of the *Pequod*, James also constructed an uncanny relationship to the time he served on Ellis Island. After linking the chronologically distinct moments of the *Pequod*'s past with his involuntary incarceration, James imagined himself as if recalled into the past by figures whose present memory depended upon the knowledges that James's reading of *Moby-Dick* constructed out of their traces. These Melvillean figures resembled James in their lacking the condition of belonging to any nation. In establishing imaginary relations with them, James produced an extraterritorial site that was extrinsic to any of the themes through which the state assimilated persons to the national geography, and that did not participate in the progressive temporality ascribed responsibility for the development of US history and literature.

In his reading of *Moby-Dick*, James produced a fictive retroactivity whereby he represented the experiences he underwent on Ellis Island as having 'realised' in historical time one of the national futures Melville had imagined a century earlier. Instead of ratifying the continuist and homogeneous time reproduced within US literature and history, James re-described his lived historicity as composed out of interruptive temporalities. Ransacking Melville's narrative for the figures through which he might communicate syncopated times required the representation of the experiences he underwent on Ellis Island as involving a disjoined temporality. *Mariners, Renegades and Castaways* associated James's contemporaneity with what might have become of Melville's past imaginings.

James transformed this temporality into a writing practice that conjoined slightly different orientations towards US citizenship: at once not quite a citizen but also not yet not one, James characteristically split the difference between these dis-positions into the desire for forms of citizenship that, while incompatible with INS categories, were consistent with the relationships that pertained among the mariners, renegades and castaways.

The participants in a transnational social movement, 'mariners, renegades and castaways', did not belong to a national community. The irreducible differences and inequivalent cultural features characterising the 'mariners, renegades and castaways' refused to conform to a state's monocultural taxonomy, and could not be integrated within a nationalising telos. Not yet *not* a US citizen, James produces through their motion the capacity to disidentify with the categories through which he would also practice US citizenship.

Forever between arrival and departure, the elements comprising the composite figure 'mariners, renegades and castaways' perform a process of endless surrogation. Each term names the movement of a 'we' that is responsible for its constitution and that traces the presence within it of an alterity irreducible to an 'I'. In and out of the terminological places through which 'we' pass, the figure 'mariners, renegades and castaways' produces multiple spatial and temporal effects. Each figure would appear to fill the absence in the space evacuated by the preceding figure, and to empty that space in turn. Their goings and comings sound forth disparate absences and distant places that emerge from a past that, in James's bipolar world order, had been territorialised as the 'Third World.'

The temporality that James's writing might be understood to enact in the relationship he adduces between their past and his present is neither the past definite that historians deploy to keep track of completed past actions, nor the present perfect – the what has been of who I now am – of the literary memoirist. It is more properly understood as the future anterior tense. The future anterior links a past event with a possible future upon which the past event depends for its significance. The split temporality intrinsic to the future anterior describes an already existing state of affairs at the same time that it stages the temporal practice through which that state of affairs 'will have been' produced.

The future anterior tense provided James with a mode of conjectural reading with which to challenge McCarran's usage. As we have seen, the McCarran bill purported to have represented a public will that it produced retroactively. The action James has employed the future anterior to produce 'will have repealed' McCarran legislation, retroactively. In *Mariners, Renegades and Castaways*, James correlates a past event – the collective revolt that did not take place in the past – as dependent on a future event – the repeal of the McCarran bill – by which the crew's revolt will have accomplished it. When he links the revolt that had not taken place on the *Pequod* with the possible future repeal of the McCarran legislation, the future repeal returns to the past to transform this virtual revolt into what will have been its legal precedent.[24]

As James traversed the temporal border separating Melville's symbolic mariners from his fellow wards of the Cold War state, he represented the state's linkage of its emergency measures with the doctrine of US exceptionalism as part of the 'knowledge' borne by Ellis Island's castaways. James's subsequent efforts to supplant the emergency state's monopoly over the representation of contemporary historical events led him to connect the unstoried cultural anteriority of the mariners, renegades and castaways with a future that could not have eventuated during the Cold War. James suggested that this other future also be understood as an alternative to the social and political conditions of the 1950s.

On 28 November 1952, to permit this fable now to catch up with James's allegorisation, the Trinidadian critic and writer C.L.R. James completed his book on Herman Melville, which he had begun while detained and awaiting deportation on Ellis Island. In the following passage James attests to the site from which he wrote as a significant aspect of its exposition:

Here was I just about to write suddenly projected onto an island isolated from the rest of society where American administrators and officials and American security officers controlled the destinies of perhaps a thousand men, sailors, 'isolatoes', renegades and castaways from all parts of the world. It seems now as if destiny had taken a hand to give me a unique opportunity to test my ideas of this great American writer. (pp. 132–3)

Throughout this passage, James has traded on heterogeneous understandings sedimented within the word 'destiny'. The range of meanings 'destiny' conjures up would include: the state's imperial progress; the belief in 'manifest destiny' through which it was rationalised; the violence with which state officials uprooted and then projected him onto Ellis Island; James's vulnerable political future; the chance configuration of events organising the conditions of the book's composition, distribution and transmission; the imagination informing James's critique of state policy; Melville's discontinued narrative intention; the process through which James has assumed, continued, reperformed and transmitted Melville's interrupted intention. All of the different values associated with 'destiny' converged in James's decision to write his book. That event has condensed this entire chain of connotations into an opportunity that feels pre-destined.

Having been resettled on Ellis Island as a displaced person lacking national citizenship and awaiting deportation, James articulated his experience of these serial displacements into the trans-temporal relay structuring the affiliation between himself, Melville's mariners and his fellow Ellis Islanders. Imagining himself as if projected into a future by Melvillean figures that were likewise lacking placement, James has transformed the involuntary condition of forcible displacement into the precondition for the dynamic motion destining him here.

Upon recasting his confinement within Ellis Island as if continuous with the political space Melville had imagined in 1850, yet non-synchronous with its temporality, then, James understood his stay on Ellis Island as an additional episode within Melville's masterwork. He thereupon experienced an uncanny oscillation between Melville's imaginary *Pequod* and his own political exile. According to the uncanny temporality underwriting James's commentary on *Moby-Dick*, Melville did not represent the contemporary political conditions of the *Pequod*'s crew, but those which will have prevailed on Ellis Island in 1952. The *Pequod* represented what Ellis Island will have been and Ellis Island constituted a memory of the *Pequod* coming from James's political present.

At the time of James's detention, Ellis Island was itself a highly contradictory space. It was a site where political refugees, migrant populations, nomads, expellees and the dispossessed intersected with the international trade and immigration policies that the state constructed to regulate their movements. Traversed by movements of people and information that were delocalised and transnational, Ellis Island resembled a federation of diasporas. The Island's culture included contributions from national exiles, as well as from colonials and postcolonials. It juxtaposed folkloric with transnational and cosmopolitan forms of expression.

The INS had resettled James on the Island so as to segregate him, along with other political deviants, from the nation's civic and public spaces. But writing about *Moby-Dick* while incarcerated on the Island enabled James to conduct an imaginary exchange of his immobilised condition of forced settlement for travel on a migratory vessel. This change of its geography transformed the Island ghetto into a site of local resistance wherein he criticised the government's assimilationist policies and disclosed the impossibility of internalising others within a homogeneous national space.

In place of submitting to the Ellis Island authorities, James positioned himself as if occupying the space splitting the narrative Melville intended from the security apparatus designed to censor it. Elucidating the difference between Melville's message and the fact that it could not be recognised as American opened up the paradoxical space of the postnational through which James transmitted the future of American Studies. In James's writing about *Moby-Dick* after having been detained on Ellis Island, the alternative Americas James discovered at work within Melville's work split at the seam where they would otherwise have been joined to the state. The administrative border of Ellis Island revealed the contour dividing the official national narrative from his re-narration.

The disciplines within the field of American Studies intersected with the United States as a geopolitical area whose boundaries field specialists were assigned the task of at once naturalising and policing. Previous interpreters of *Moby-Dick* had accommodated its themes to the discourse of US exceptionalism, through which they had demarcated and policed the national border. Rather than corroborating the exceptionalist imperatives organising the field of American Studies, James questioned the dominant discourses and assumptions within the field. He cast US exceptionalism as a national fantasy, installed within the field of American Studies, as an impediment to the emergence of this irrecuperably transnational movement. He brought the discrepant places and temporalities assembled on Ellis Island into critical relation with a field whose spatial boundaries were reflective of the binarised relations that pertained between the US and its others.

The coalition gathered under the banner 'mariners, renegades and castaways' interrelated multiple international as well as transnational locales. Its members associated the movement's democratising force with their shared condition of postnational migrancy. In place of corroborating the field's imperial imperatives, James's interpretation of *Moby-Dick* from the mariners' perspective had minoritised the classic. Quite literally dialogic, his interpretation has produced knowledges about *Moby-Dick* that have turned it into a means of exchange and cultural transaction that could not be confined by a national telos.

Mariners, Renegades and Castaways transported James beyond the US borders. In it James explored configurations of race and nationality in a transnational frame, and he conceptualised the United States as a geo-social space on the move across and between nations. After James extracted these extraterritorial properties from *Moby-Dick*, he rendered it impossible to determine to whose national culture it now belonged. The practices of aesthetic self-enactment that he generated out of it produced a fluctuating identity that avoided the state's categorical obsessions and challenged its belief that cultural identity is based on a national patrimony. In linking his experiences there with the floating culture on board the *Pequod*, James transformed Ellis Island into a mobile landscape whose geographically indeterminate space transgressed the national boundaries.

James thereby accomplished a transference of spatial and temporal properties which empowered him to re-describe the field of American Studies as, like Ellis Island, a site where becoming American had become indistinguishable from becoming 'mariners, renegades and castaways'. In effect, James reorganised the field as a space that Michel Foucault has called a 'heterotopia'. Written in a place that, while internal to the US, was external to the norms regulating other cultural spaces, *Mariners, Renegades and Castaways* permitted of the analysis, contestation and reversal of those norms. Heterotopia is the name of a space inhabited and defined by those who are passing through. It comprises transnational flows of people and information.

James reimagined the field as a postnational space that engendered multiple collective identifications and organisational loyalties. It convoked networks of association and of intersections that produced juxtapositions that confused the same with the different, the near with the far, that created and reflected social spaces that mediated with distant and dissimilar ones.

In 1953, James activated Melville's future memory to continue this interruptive process. He subsequently articulated the figures he recalled from within Melville's narrative with the 'unamericans' who, like him, had passed through Ellis Island. Having replaced the need for national belonging with their openness to unassimilated otherness, James constructed an open-ended circuit of transnational and international relations. The emergence in James's work of acts of postnational narration with the demonstrated competence to effect transnational and international relations that were then excluded from the official national narrative turn this work from the historical past toward a postnational future that has emerged within our historical present. Its recollection constitutes one of the possible futures of transnational American Studies.

NOTES

Reprinted from *Arizona Quarterly* 56:3 (2000), pp. 93–123, by permission of the Regents of the University of Arizona.

1. According to the itinerary James provided in *Mariners, Renegades and Castaways*, his examination was concluded on 16 August 1950 under the Act of 1918. The Internal Security Act was passed on 23 September 1950, and the Attorney General's decision was handed down on 31 October 1950. 'But my appeal was rejected under the McCarran Act. I had therefore been denied due process of law; the McCarran Act had been applied ... in the decision but could not have figured in the hearings.' C.L.R. James, *Mariners, Renegades and Castaways: The Story of Herman Melville and the World We Live In* (New York, 1953), p. 196.
2. Cited in Lisa Lowe, *Immigration Acts: On Asian American Cultural Politics* (Durham: Duke University Press, 1996), p. 9. David Campbell has observed the several ways in which the Cold War foreign policy resulted in the production of the national identity through the containment of threats to it. Foreign policy was understood as the 'disciplining of ambiguity and the contingency of global politics by dividing it into an inside and an outside, self and other, via the inscription of the boundaries of the state' (p. 64). National identity was structured in the power to exert visual control over the political imaginaries of other cultures.

> Danger was being totalized in the external realm in conjunction with an increased individualization in the internal field, the results being

the performative reconstitution of the borders of the state's identity. In this sense the Cold War needs to be understood as a disciplinary strategy that was global in scope but national in design. (p. 53)

In 'Political Prosaics, Transversal Politics, and the Anarchical World', Michael Shapiro and Hayward R. Alker (eds), *Challenging Boundaries* (Minnesota: University of Minnesota Press 1996), pp. 7–32.

3. Normatives can be seen as prescriptives or commands put into inverted commas that give them authority. The prescriptive says that 'X should carry out Y.' Its normative reformulation adds 'it is a norm (or z decrees) that x should carry out y.' In a democratic polity political and legal legitimacy are allegedly linked with the fact that the addressor of the norm (the legislator) and the addressee of the command (the legal subject) are one and the same. The essence of freedom is that the subjects who make the law are the subjects subjected.

Costas Douzinas and Ronnie Warrington, '"A Well-Founded Fear of Justice": Law and Ethics in Postmodernity', in *Legal Studies as Cultural Studies: A Reader in (Post) Modern Critical Theory*, ed. Jerry Leonard (Albany: State University of New York Press, 1995), p. 210.

4. Jean-Francois Lyotard has observed that a just society is one that recognises and allows all participants to have a voice, to narrate from their own perspective. It is desirable 'to extend interlocution to any human individual whatsoever, regardless of national or natural idiom'. Jean-Francois Lyotard, 'The Other's Rights', in *On Human Rights: The Oxford Amnesty Lectures*, ed. Stephen Shute and Susan Hurley (New York: Basic Books, 1993), p. 139.

5. James described the limitations the state had imposed on his 'I' in his representation of the following exchange when he requested that the District Director of the INS of the Port of New York send him to a hospital for the treatment of an ulcer. 'Mr. Shaughnessy's reply was that if I did not like it there I was not going to be detained against my will. I could always leave and go to Trinidad where I was born and drink my papaya juice.' James, *Mariners*, p. 166.

6. Jean-Francois Lyotard, *The Differend: Phrases in Dispute* (Manchester: Manchester University Press, 1983), p. xi.

7. At a time in which the legal apparatus for surveillance had been put into place to purge universities of politically heterodox activities, Richard Chase's *Herman Melville* continued the state's policing measures by other means. In '*Moby-Dick* and the Cold War', I discussed the Cold War mentality underwriting Melville criticism in some detail. *Moby-Dick* had entered the national canon as a sacralisation of the nation's struggle with global totalitarianism. The canonical reading had discerned in Ishmael's survival the signs of a decisive victory in the imaginary war. This reading might be understood as a belated effort to discharge myself of an indebtedness I had not known that I had incurred in writing that essay. In '*Moby-Dick* and the Cold War', I situated Herman Melville's novel within the cultural politics of the Cold War. The editors of a volume entitled *C.L.R. James: His Intellectual Legacies* sent me a reviewer's copy of

the book along with a note recommending that I read Cedric Robinson's essay 'C.L.R. James and the World System'. In it Robinson analysed my interpretation of *Moby-Dick* within the context of James's 1952 reading while incarcerated on Ellis Island. After observing that my refusal to find in Ishmael's narration a will that was any less totalising than Ahab's constituted 'an addendum to James's indictment of Ishmael', Professor Robinson complained that I had not taken my argument far enough. Had I adopted James's interpretive stance, it would have taken me beyond the boundaries of US national culture and into the multicentred analysis of transnational cultural relations. *The American Renaissance Reconsidered*, ed. Walter Benn Michaels and Donald E. Pease (Baltimore: The Johns Hopkins University Press, 1985), pp. 113–54.

8. James will draw incomplete parallels between the McCarran Act and Nazi totalitarianism throughout *Mariners, Renegades and Castaways*. In the following passage, James at first explicitly correlates the emergency measures of the McCarran Committee with related forms of totalitarian rule, but at the paragraph's conclusion he restricts the latter attribution to his experiences in Nazi Germany:

> The McCarran Act is an attempt to change the laws to correspond to the administrative policy. It may. But if and when the complete success has BEEN achieved, there will also have been achieved the complete demoralization of the staff of the Department of Justice and large sections of the American people. It is a comparatively simple thing to mobilize majorities in Congress to pass laws, and for judges and administrators to set out to apply them. But you cannot reverse the whole historical past and the traditions of a people by packaged legislation and loud propaganda. Certain policies demand total destruction of a legal system, its replacement by a new one, totalitarian indoctrination of the population in the new doctrine, and storm-troopers or G.P.U. men to enforce them. Try to carry them out by grafting them onto a traditionally democratic system and the result is complete chaos. I saw precisely that happen step by step to a whole nation between 1934 and 1939 (pp. 173–4).

9. Stuart Hall, 'C.L.R. James: A Portrait', *C.L.R. James's Caribbean*, ed. Paget Henry and Paul Buhle (Durham: Duke University Press, 1996), p. 12.
10. Walter Benjamin, 'Theses on the Philosophy of History', Hannah Arendt, ed.; Harry Zohn, Tr. *Illuminations: Walter Benjamin: Essays and Reflections* (New York: Schocken Books, 1969), p. 257.
11. *Congressional Record* 4/25/46:4993.
12. See William Connolly, *The Ethos of Pluralization* (Minneapolis: University of Minnesota Press, 1996), p. 139. Connolly draws upon Paul Ricoeur's elegant formulation of this paradox:

> It is of the nature of political consent, which gives rise to the unity of the human community organized and oriented by the state, to be able to be recovered only in an act which has not taken place, in a contract which has not been contracted, in an implicit and tacit pact which appears as such only in political awareness, in retrospection and reflection.

William Connolly, 'The Political Paradox', in *Legitimacy and the State*, ed. William Connolly (New York: New York University Press, 1984), p. 254.
13. Connolly, *The Ethos of Pluralization*, p. 139.
14. Among important recent discussions of US Exceptionalism, see Michael Kammen, 'The Problem of American Exceptionalism: A Reconsideration', *American Quarterly* 45 (March, 1993), pp. 1–43; and Joyce Appleby, 'Recovering America's Historical Diversity: Beyond Exceptionalism', *Journal of American History* 79 (September 1992), pp. 419–31.
15. Janice Radway, 'What's in a Name?' *American Quarterly*, 51:1 (1999), p. 4.
16. Louis Hartz, *The Liberal Tradition in America* (New York: Harcourt Brace, 1955), p. 5.
17. Chase, *Herman Melville*, p. vii.
18. Giorgio Agamben, *Homo Sacer: Sovereign Power and Bare Life* (Stanford: Stanford University Press, 1998), p. 24. The exception the state produces to engender the limits to the rule of democratic governance might also be understood to embody the rule that has produced the exception. As the limit internal to the national order but external to its conditions of belonging, the exception can consent to this non-position, or the exception can do what the 'young Oriental' did and turn the limit into legal grounds for supplanting the entire order.
19. Sylvia Wynter, 'Beyond the Categories of the Master Conception: The Counter-Doctrine of the Jamesian Poesis', in Henry and Buhle *C.L.R. James's Caribbean*, p. 72.
20. Michel Foucault has discussed the intimate relationship between the law and the disciplines' naturalisation of it:

> from the nineteenth century to our own day, [modern society] has been characterized on the one hand, by a legislation, a discourse, an organization based on public right, whose principle of articulation is the social body and the delegative status of each citizen; and on the other hand by a closely lined grid of disciplinary coercions whose purpose is in fact to assure the coherence of this same social body. Hence these two limits, a right of sovereignty and a mechanism of discipline which define, I believe, the arena in which power is exercised. But these two limits are so heterogeneous that they cannot possibly be reduced to each other. The powers of modern society are exercised through, on the basis of, and by virtue of, this very heterogeneity between a public right of sovereignty and a polymorphous disciplinary mechanism. The disciplines may well be the carriers of a discourse that speaks of a rule, but this is not the juridical rule deriving from sovereignty, but a natural rule, a norm. The code they come to define is not that of law but that of normalisation.

Michel Foucault 'Two Lectures', in *Power/Knowledge: Selected Interviews and Other Writings 1972–1977*, ed. Colin Gordon (New York: Pantheon, 1990), p. 107.
21. James provided this postnational site with the following description: 'The whole of the world is represented on Ellis Island. Many sailors, but not only sailors; Germans, Italians, Latvians, Swedes, Filipinos, Malays,

Chinese, Hindus, Pakistanis, West Indians, Englishmen, Australians, Danes, Yugoslavs, Greeks, Canadians, representatives of every Latin American country' (*Mariners*, p. 183).
22. Apropos of Melville's ethnographic imaginary, Richard Chase quotes Melville's description of Queequeg as 'George Washington cannibalistically developed'. 'Queequeg would do well on enough in a side show, a hideous savage, the son of a cannibal king. Such a face! It was of a dark, purplish, blackish-looking squares. And he worshipped a curious little deformed image with a hunch on its back, and exactly the color of a three days old Congo baby.' 'The other harpooners are also creatures of folklore: of prodigious strength, they are imposing in their natural dignity and devoted to the spirit of the hunt' (Chase, *Herman Melville*, p. 82).
23. C.L.R. James, *Beyond a Boundary* (London: Hutchinson, 1963), p. 163.
24. Jacques Derrida explains the significance of this retroactive temporality within the context of the *Declaration of Independence*. 'We the people', as Derrida has explained their emplacement within the paradoxical logic of a representative democracy,

> do not exist as an entity; it does *not* exist, *before* this declaration, not as *such*. If it gives birth to itself, as free and independent subject as possible signer, this can only hold in the act of the signature. The signature invents the signer. The signer can only authorize him- or herself, to sign once he or she has come to the end ... if one can say this, of his or her signature, in a sort of fabulous retroactivity.

'Declarations of Independence', trans. Tom Keenan and Tom Pepper, *New Political Science* 15 (1976), p. 10.

4
Beyond Boundaries: Cricket, Herman Melville, and C.L.R. James's Cold War

Christopher Gair

Even at a moment when postnationalism appears to have become the new orthodoxy in American Studies, an essay linking a sport indelibly associated with British colonialism, an author at the very core of the American literary canon, and the Cold War may seem to be taking its title's (cricket-inspired) metaphorical invocation of transgression too far. What does a piece that focuses much of its attention on a cricket match played in Australia in early 1933 hold of interest for scholars of American cultural relations? The game can hardly be claimed to have made a major impact on the United States' sporting consciousness, and for many Americans serves as an exemplary reminder of the differences between British and American cultures: What can be the point of a sport in which one match can be declared drawn after several days' play, beyond illustrating the need for American games (basketball, football, baseball) that can be watched at a single sitting, and that guarantee a victor at the end of the afternoon or evening? And what possible relation can there be between a sporting contest featuring Australia and England, played out on the other side of the world nearly 70 years ago, and the future of American Studies as an academic discipline?

The answer lies in my title's reference to C.L.R. James, whose professional career stretched from the 1920s to the 1980s, and whose political and cultural interests refused to be tied down by disciplinary constraints. James is rapidly becoming a key figure in postnational studies, being seen by critics such as Donald E. Pease as a pioneering practitioner of a methodology that would only emerge as a critical norm several decades later. Nevertheless, postnational Americanists have tended to fail fully to utilise those critical practices developed by James, and, as a result, remain complicit in the very privileging of the United States that they purport to deconstruct. By focusing specifically on James's writings most overtly *about* America, for example, Pease's version of postnational American Studies sustains preexisting notions of national identity, insisting – just like the American sports listed above – on versions of American exceptionalism, while simultaneously celebrating their demise. As an alternative, situating James's American writings alongside his thoughts on (among other things) cricket, the Caribbean, and colonialism, provides the blueprint for a more genuinely postnational approach, illustrating not only what is specific to US culture at a key moment in its history, but also the limits and ambiguities of its exceptionalism.

At the time of his internment on Ellis Island, James produced a reading of Melville that is suggestive of an approach to American Studies radically different both from the model that pertained at the time and subsequent paradigms. James based much of his reading on the analogy between the 'mariners, renegades and castaways' who constituted the crew of the *Pequod* – a collection of men from around the globe, united in the common pursuit of whaling – and his fellow detainees. Both groups are participants in what Pease calls a 'postnational social movement', and do not 'belong to a national community'. They therefore cannot be 'integrated within a nationalizing telos', with the result that, as Pease puts it, for James, US exceptionalism is cast as a 'national fantasy installed within the field of American Studies as an impediment to the emergence of this irrecuperably postnational movement'.[1]

I think that Pease is right to see *Mariners, Renegades, and Castaways* as a foundational document of postnational American Studies. Nevertheless, I believe that, in one fundamental way, he misunderstands the book, and that this misunderstanding imposes constraints on his challenge to the national multiculturalist paradigm. Although there is clearly an indubitable link between James's reading of Melville and his time on Ellis Island – a point that James goes to great lengths to stress in the final chapter of *Mariners* – I want to suggest that the model for his reading actually stemmed from two decades earlier, in the months following his arrival in England from Trinidad. Rather than emerging in the 1950s, first in *Mariners*, and then in *Beyond a Boundary* (his famous fusion of autobiography, history of cricket, and cultural analysis, published in 1963), James's methodology and logic appear in his understanding of the 'bodyline' crisis that threatened much more than the mere fabric of cricket in 1932–33.

This is not just a matter of over-simplification on Pease's part, or even merely an illustration of the need for scholars of the postnational to know something about how cultures beyond the United States understand themselves and function within models of postnational exchange. Rather, as a result of a combination of oversights, half-truths, and a focus on those of James's writings most obviously about America, Pease's approach remains locked within the national boundaries he claims to challenge. Despite its turn to the postnational communities of the *Pequod* and Ellis Island, his reading of James finally rearticulates the models of American 'national fantasy' that he purports to oppose. In order to reimagine *Mariners* in a truly postnational way (and thus to release its potential as a truly postnational text suggesting more radically postnational American Studies), it is necessary to locate it within a more complex network of transcultural relations, and, in the first instance, to look away from the United States.

In an essay called 'C.L.R. James at 80', E.P. Thompson remarked that 'I'm afraid that American theorists will not understand this, but the clue to everything lies in [James's] proper appreciation of the game of cricket.'[2] The comment could well be applied to Pease, whose recent essays provide only a passing account of James's early life and subsequent arrival in England, and of his interest in the game. For example, on the opening page of his introduction to *Mariners, Renegades and Castaways*, Pease calls James's secondary (high) school, Queen's Royal College, a 'British colonial university', and suggests that he travelled to England 'with the Trinidad cricket star Learie Constantine', and that it was his 'knowledge of cricket that provided him with the visa and the funds he required to make the trip'.[3] In fact, Constantine had been living as a professional cricketer in Nelson, a small industrial town in Lancashire, since 1929, and James joined him both to help Constantine with his autobiography and to complete his own study of the Trinidadian political activist, Captain Cipriani. In addition, James brought with him the manuscript of his only novel, *Minty Alley*, written in the late 1920s, but not published until 1936. In Pease's defence, of course, cricket does seem like a strange place to look for the origins of postnational American Studies. And yet, the fact that he does not seem at all interested in doing so is indicative of the extent to which much US-based postnational American Studies is unable to unmoor itself totally from its own national context, and continues to imagine the United States at the privileged centre of the postnational paradigm. Thus, although in

1952 James was seeking US citizenship (and had been a resident since 1938), his understanding of what that citizenship entailed involves a complexly interconnected sequence of migrations, from Trinidad to England and then America.

BODYLINE, 1932–33

The 'bodyline' series of five Test matches between Australia and England contested during the Australian summer of 1932–33 provided the perfect scenario for James to fashion his thinking on totalitarianism, occurring as it did in the months after his arrival in England, and immediately before the rise to power of Adolph Hitler. Essentially, bodyline was a new approach to bowling in which, rather than aiming at the wicket, the bowlers would bounce fast, short-pitched deliveries at the batsmen who, at that time, wore no protective headgear. As Neville Cardus, the senior cricket correspondent for the Manchester *Guardian*, explained it, the field was

> set mainly on the leg-side, in a semi-circle near the batsman's left hip, with two men placed deep. The ball was delivered at a terrific velocity, pitched short enough to rise, three or four times an over, in the region of the batsman's skull. If he merely shielded himself, and 'found contact', the crouching inner field caught the ball as it fell from his protective bat. If he desperately 'hooked' or 'pulled', he was most times caught from a great stroke on the leg-boundary.[4]

Although there had been small-scale experiments with bodyline beforehand, the ploy was fully developed by Douglas Jardine, the captain of the England team that visited Australia in 1932–33, to counter the phenomenal talent of the Australian batsman, Donald Bradman, whose unprecedented run-scoring abilities had resulted in a crushing defeat for the home team when Australia visited England in 1930. In order to grasp the significance of bodyline, both for James's emergent postnational paradigm and as a practice that seemed to undermine the core values of cricket – and that put diplomatic relations between Britain and Australia under severe strain – it is necessary to examine the events and protagonists involved in some detail. To make this explanation as straightforward as possible – since I suspect that many readers will not be well versed in the subtler intricacies of cricket – I will focus on just one game, the third Test match (or international) of the series, played over six days, from

13–19 January 1933, described by *Wisden* (the 'cricketer's bible') as 'probably the most unpleasant [Test match] ever played', and as a 'disgrace to cricket'.[5]

When the MCC team sailed for Australia in the autumn of 1932, Jardine set out with a specific purpose in mind.[6] He knew that the only hope of victory lay in finding a way to stop Bradman scoring. To put his feats in context, it should be noted that, over his international career, Bradman averaged 99.94 runs per innings, around 40 higher than anyone else has ever achieved. Whereas many batsmen regularly scored 100 runs or more in a single innings, Bradman had a habit of batting until he had made a double, triple, or (in domestic cricket) even quadruple century. In preparation for the tour, Jardine conducted extensive research into Bradman's technique, studying all aspects of his batting in a manner that would only become widely adopted in sports decades later. As a result, he believed that he had detected a weakness. Watching film of Bradman play on a rain-affected wicket, Jardine was convinced that Bradman was 'yellow', afraid of the short-pitched delivery that rose into his body.[7]

In order to deploy this strategy effectively, Jardine required bowlers who could bowl both quickly and accurately. In this, he was exceedingly fortunate, in that he could call upon Harold Larwood and Bill Voce, two former Nottinghamshire coal miners who had used their cricketing skills to escape the pit. Larwood, in particular, was a phenomenally strong and skilful bowler, mythologised in his days as a miner for his ability to work all night before bowling out the opposing team while clad in sand shoes, since he couldn't afford proper cricket boots. By the time of the 1932–33 tour he was at the peak of his career, and was recognised as the fastest bowler in world cricket – perhaps the fastest of all time. Voce was almost as quick and, because he bowled left-handed, offered a variant on the line of Larwood's attack.

In the 1930s, cricketing relations within the England team were still regulated by class. The eleven were split between 'gentleman', who had other sources of income and took no money for playing, and 'players', working class professionals who, although they earned not only prestige but also more money than they would in mines or factories, were paid poorly for their services. The team captain was, necessarily and unsurprisingly, a gentleman. But the composition of the side was not split merely along class lines: in addition, there were racial factors that further complicated relations. Jardine himself was a Scot, born in India, but sent to Scotland for schooling, before going to England to attend Winchester school and Oxford University. He rapidly gained a reputation as a strategist and as a fearless player, and was known (behind his back) as the 'Iron Duke'. Unfortunately, in the light of subsequent events, he had acquired a generalised hatred of Australians during his first tour there, in 1928–29, when his multicoloured Harlequins cap and white silk choker elicited much mirth and taunting from the crowd. From that moment, he is reputed to have referred to Australians collectively as 'bastards', and to have thought obsessively about how to defeat them at cricket. The other gentlemen in the team came from a range of different backgrounds: for example, the third fast bowler in the side, Gubby Allen, was actually born and raised in Australia, although he later became the epitome of the English establishment, devoting his life to cricket politics and even living in a house that backed on to Lord's cricket ground. Unlike the professionals, Larwood and Voce, who had little or no choice in the matter, he refused to bowl bodyline, and repeatedly defied Jardine's instructions to do so, although he always backed his captain in public. It appears that Allen calculated that he was integral to the team and that Jardine would not drop him.

In contrast, the Indian aristocrat and hugely talented batsman, the Nawab of Pataudi, paid the price for open defiance of his skipper and, by all accounts, close friend. Having scored a century in the first Test, which was also his international debut, he confronted Jardine about bodyline, which Pataudi saw as overstepping the ethics of the game. As a result, he was not selected in the team picked for the third Test and returned to England, having been told by Jardine that he would never play for his adopted country again. In a scene that echoes James's 1932 reading of Captain Cipriani as 'engaged in a series of struggles against the bad manners, the injustice, the tyranny, and the treachery of Crown Colony Government',[8] and which also anticipates his own later position on Ellis Island, Pataudi seems to have been 'outlawed' (to quote Hazel V. Carby's reading of *Captain Cipriani*) 'by the very ideologies instilled into him as a colonial subject', in other words, 'humanitarianism and "fair-play".'[9]

The final significant member of the tour party (at least, for my present purposes) was Pelham ('Plum') Warner, the manager of the side, and thus, nominally, holding authority over Jardine. Warner had been a highly distinguished cricketer himself before World War I, captaining England on tours to Australia and South Africa, and was a legacy of the 'Golden Age' – that period in cricket before the War characterised nostalgically for many, including James, by the daring and panache of the batsmen, who were more concerned with entertaining the crowd than with winning at all costs.[10] Like James, Warner originated from Trinidad (although he was white), and like James he had been raised to believe implicitly in the importance of behaving in the correct manner on the cricket field at all times. This was to lead to major disagreements between Warner and Jardine during the course of the match.

Bradman had been unwell and missed the first game of the series, which England won comfortably without deploying bodyline. In the second Test, the weather and pitch conditions rendered it relatively ineffective, although its use did fuel considerable resentment in the Australian team, crowd, and press, as well as unease in Gubby Allen and the England vice-captain, Bob Wyatt. Nevertheless, Australia won the match and squared the series. But events in Adelaide made everything that had preceded them seem trivial in comparison. Having scored a reasonable total of 341, the England eleven were preparing to take the field when Warner visited the dressing room and sought to persuade Jardine not to use bodyline. Apparently, Jardine was incensed and replied, 'We must each follow the dictates of our conscience.'[11] When the match restarted, Australia quickly lost a wicket, bringing Bradman to the crease – a moment that would transform not only the mood of the game, but also the place of cricket as a focus of colonial relations. Bradman scored a run from the first ball he received from Larwood, then watched as Larwood bowled a delivery that hit the Australian captain, Bill Woodfull, over the heart. After a lengthy delay, Woodfull decided that he could continue his innings but, before he had the chance to take strike, Jardine clapped his hands, the signal to adopt bodyline positions.[12] As a tactic, the move can be said to have succeeded: Bradman was quickly out, soon followed by Woodfull, who went to have treatment on his injury. At this point, Warner entered the Australian dressing room to apologise for the England team's tactics, and Woodfull replied, 'There are two teams out there, one of them is trying to play cricket.' The fact that an unnamed source (believed to be Bradman himself, although he always denied this) leaked the conversation to the Australian press further inflamed the situation.

When the game resumed on the Monday morning, Jardine ignored the barracking from the crowd and immediately set his bodyline field. After a few minor scares, the most serious injury of the match occurred, when Larwood hit the Australian wicketkeeper, Bert Oldfield on the temple, fracturing his skull, and, unsurprisingly, ending his participation in the match.[13] As Oldfield was carried from the field, the crowd started to burn Union flags, and Woodfull – a master, it would seem, of the soundbite – told Warner, 'This isn't cricket, it's war.'

England won the Test comfortably, but its outcome had consequences that reached far beyond the game of cricket. The Australian Board of Control sent a telegram to Lord's suggesting that unless bodyline was stopped 'at once', it would 'upset the friendly relations between Australia and England'. An unimpressed MCC sought guidance from Buckingham Palace, and the head of the British Mission in Australia consulted with the Australian prime minister. All agreed that bodyline should be abandoned before it dealt a serious blow to trade and industry between the two countries. Jardine, however, refused point-blank to accede to demands from Lord's and Warner to stop, and his team warned that they would not accept his dismissal. Therefore, the tour (and the tactic) continued, with England winning the series 4–1, and reducing Bradman's average to the mid-50s – exceptional for any other player, but well below his normal scores.

Before turning to the significance of this for James's critical methodology, a postscript should be added. Although there had been muted official support from England for Bodyline, and the English press had been largely supportive of *anything* that would lead to the defeat of the Australians, that support rapidly evaporated when the team returned to England. Reporting for the Port of Spain *Gazette*, in June 1933, James noted:

> The English had no mercy on the Australians. Now that the tour is over and the Ashes won, nearly every English writer and cricketer with the most bare-faced effrontery condemns body-line bowling, but when the Australians protested they shrieked to high heaven that there was nothing to it and the Australians were merely squealing.[14]

Jardine continued, briefly, to lead the side, but was condemned for using bodyline against India, an emergent team with no Bradman in their ranks, and became something of a cricketing pariah. As James put it in *Beyond a Boundary*, 'Jardine soon went, never to return'.[15] He did, however, display his courage in standing up to James's friend Learie Constantine when the West Indies adopted bodyline against England in 1933, playing his greatest innings during that series and, unlike almost everyone else, never complaining about the tactic. Larwood refused to apologise for what he had done, and never played for England again. Ironically, he emigrated to Australia in 1950 and lived there until his death in 1995, stating that the Australians better understood his situation and were more willing to forgive than the English establishment, which finally awarded him an MBE (presented by cricket-loving prime minister John Major) in 1993. Voce, too, initially refused to apologise, though he did return to the England side in 1936, having settled his differences with the cricket authorities. In contrast, Gubby Allen rose swiftly, to captain the MCC and England on their next tour of Australia in 1936–37.

FROM CRICKET TO MELVILLE

Although James was not employed as a cricket correspondent by the Manchester *Guardian* until April 1933, and did not cover Bodyline directly, it had a major and long-lasting impact on his thoughts not only about the game, but also about wider cultural and political developments. In *Mariners, Renegades and Castaways*, he notes just how significant this period was to his future thinking about the Western world, commenting that, after less than two years in England, by 1934 he felt that 'European civilization as it then existed was doomed', an opinion that he had not revised by 1953.[16] In order to understand this as a shift inspired by more than overtly political changes, it is essential to remember how important cricket had been to shaping his moral code, and how he used analysis of it to register social change. In a 1932 essay on the legendary former England bowler, S.F. Barnes, that provided James with the break into British sports journalism, he seems to intimate a reason why bodyline should have happened just three months later. Writing about Barnes, now aging and playing club cricket in Lancashire, James observed:

> To begin with, Barnes not only is fifty-nine, but looks it. Some cricketers at fifty-nine look and move like men in their thirties. Not so Barnes. You can almost hear the old bones creaking ... He is tall and thin, well over six feet, with strong features ...
>
> He fixed his field ... When every man was placed to the nearest centimetre Barnes walked back and set the old machinery in motion. As he forced himself to the crease you could see every year of the fifty-nine; but the arm swung over gallantly, high and straight. The wicket was slow, but a ball whipped hot from the pitch in the first over, and second slip took a neat catch.[17]

This passage has been read by Hazel V. Carby as an example of James's interest in the 'black male hero', and the male body as a 'work of art' displaying 'lines of beauty and power in action'.[18] Although the first part of this assertion is particularly strange, since Barnes was white – a point that calls much of her argument on the racialised body into question – Carby's comments on art and beauty demand special scrutiny here. Far from representing these things, Barnes – who started his career in the 1890s – appears to be a harbinger of the new and modern cricketers who would replace the graceful players of the Golden Age. James focuses on the Taylorised manner in which Barnes goes about his game: not only is his body represented as a piece of 'machinery', he is also absolutely precise in his setting of the field, applying the disciplinary principles of scientific management to his game, and 'husband[ing] his strength'.[19]

With his writings on bodyline, James refined these observations in a manner that linked cricket to wider social forces more explicitly. In *Beyond a Boundary*, James recalls how, in 1956, he was unable to agree with the Labour Party politician, Aneurin Bevan, in Bevan's mockery of 'such concepts as "playing with the team", "keeping a stiff upper lip", "playing with a straight bat" and the rest of them'. James recounts that he was 'engaged in a more respectful re-examination'. Tracing his differences back to his childhood games of cricket in Trinidad, and to his immersion at that time in books about the Golden Age, he comments that

> I never cheated, I never appealed for a decision unless I thought that the batsman was out, I never argued with the umpire, I never jeered at a defeated opponent, I never gave to a friend a vote or a place which by any stretch of imagination could be seen as belonging to an enemy or a stranger ... From the eight years of school life this code became the moral framework of my existence. It has never left me.[20]

Although there is nothing in his account of Barnes to suggest that James disapproves of what the master bowler is doing, when we combine it with the principles laid out above, it should not be hard to see what James made of Bradman (despite lifelong admiration for his skill and stamina) and of bodyline, and, subsequently, how his thinking would resurface in his book on Melville.

Writing about Bradman in 1934, James was full of praise for the master batsman's 'multifarious and unique' skills. Nevertheless, he was also concerned that such dominance was hazardous to the spirit of the sport, commenting,

> after the first excitement, this sort of thing becomes slightly monotonous ... The essence of any game is conflict, and there was no conflict here; the superiority of one side was too overwhelming... He will bat until he feels inclined to go.[21]

Looking back in *Beyond a Boundary*, James reflected on the reasons for such domination, and the response to it:

> I have gathered that even in Australia the attitude to him is ambivalent. They admire him, they are grateful to him, they love him, but they know that the disregard of the compulsions of everyday life, the chivalry that was always a part of the game, began to fade at the time he came into it. Sir Donald is not to blame. He was unfortunate in his place and time. The fact remains that in his own way he was as tough as Jardine.[22]

For James, both Bradman himself and Jardine's response to him are manifestations of the

> violence and ferocity of our age expressing itself in cricket. The time was the early thirties, the period in which the contemporary rejection of tradition, the contemporary disregard of means, the contemporary callousness were taking shape. The totalitarian dictators cultivated brutality of set purpose.

Although, as we have seen, James detected anticipatory traces of this change before bodyline, this, for him, was 'the blow from which "it isn't cricket" has never recovered'.[23] What is most significant is that, for James, both Bradman and the English response to him are products of this specific historical moment, in which challenges to the values and traditions of the game emerge from within:

> If Bradman continued his portentous career, a way of life, a system of morals, faced the possibility of disgrace and defeat just at the particular time when more than ever it needed the stimulus of victory and prestige. The men who had made it their special preserve were threatened not only in cricket. They were threatened everywhere. As is usual in such cases, they fought back blindly and were driven into extravagance and immorality.[24]

In *Beyond a Boundary*, James suggests that his feelings about bodyline were shaped by his thoughts about the wider forces of totalitarianism. Nevertheless, when his situation at the time is considered – a new arrival in England, living in (and caught up in the local intrigues of) a small northern industrial town, and working to complete his manuscripts and help Constantine with his autobiography – another narrative is suggested. In this, bodyline itself serves as the blueprint for his thinking in the early 1950s on Melville, American totalitarianism and more, at a moment when (as he put it in *Beyond a Boundary*) 'everything is at stake'.[25]

Although I am not claiming an absolute allegorical link between bodyline and *Mariners, Renegades and Castaways*, it is possible to map many of James's ideas about Melville onto it, in a way that illustrates an American Studies paradigm considerably more postnational and less Ameri-centric than the model proposed by Pease. Jardine, most clearly, is a type of James's Ahab in the manner in which, as James said of Ahab, he 'trampled upon' the 'sacred principles [of his civilisation], derided them, and set up instead his own feelings as a human being'. Like Ahab, Jardine is driven on his obsessive quest to turn his expert knowledge of his profession in a new and disastrous direction. Both men – remembering Jardine's 'We must each follow the dictates of our conscience' – are driven by motives that James identifies as the logical extremes of individualism prevalent in the West. In his own desire for revenge against Australians in general after their treatment of him in 1928–29, and his concentration of this urge into an unstoppable pursuit of Bradman, Jardine also anticipates Ahab's 'profound scorn for other pillars' of his national culture (pp. 5–6). Where Ahab turns the *Pequod* away from its original purpose of killing many whales and maximising profits in his pursuit of the white whale, Jardine abandons the morals and history of cricket in his own pursuit of Bradman. Although, of course, there *is* a difference, in that Jardine is still aiming to beat Australia, the game and its codes are forgotten in his single-minded obsession. In his ability to combine 'science, the management of things', and 'politics, the management of men', he once more anticipates James's Ahab as the 'embodiment of the totalitarian type' (p. 15), Taylorising his knowledge of the game to suit his own needs, and imposing those needs on a potentially hostile workforce.

In this, he prefigures James's understanding of Ahab's relation with his crew, since the combination of races and classes in Jardine's team in many ways parallels the function of the ship's officers and its band of 'mariners, renegades and castaways' in James's *Moby-Dick*. Although James never takes the step of telling the narrative from the other players' point of view, it is clear that, like the men on board the *Pequod*, they have different ambitions, but do not rebel because of their captain's strength of personality and the inability of the 'officer class' to counter him. Another passage from *Mariners* perfectly describes their situation:

> The men pursue whales ... sharing skill, danger, sweat and jokes. Ahab pursues his whale with foam-glued lips and inflamed distracted fury. Sometimes the men quarrel and fight, but the essence of their relation with each other at work or play is congeniality ... The men respond spontaneously to the immediate ... Ahab lives perpetually planning and scheming. (p. 29)

Where Larwood would run down the wicket to apologise when he hit batsmen, in apparently sincere concern for their well-being, Jardine pursued his quest without such short-term distractions, clapping his hands to signal bodyline, irrespective of the safety of the batsman, the state of a crowd ready to riot, or the consequences within and beyond the game of cricket. In this, he epitomises the 'weight of consciousness and of knowledge, absence of naturalness, lack of human association' also embodied in Ahab. For James's Melville, it is this combination in modern educated man that places society 'on the road to disaster'. In contrast, Larwood's combination of skill and humanity matches that of the *Pequod*'s harpooners, 'the most skilful seamen and most magnificent and generous human beings on board' (p. 30).

Although a mutiny on the part of Larwood, Voce and the other professionals in the team would be inconceivable given the workings of English cricket at the time, the other gentlemen could have deserted Jardine, and taken the professionals with them. But, despite the reservations of Allen and Wyatt, this did not happen. Again, James's *Pequod* seems analogous: as we have already seen in Jardine's furious response to the Nawab of Pataudi's objections to bodyline, the captain shares Ahab's totalitarian ambition to 'finish away altogether with men who think'. For each, it is 'his own ideas, his own feelings, his own needs [that] become the standard by which reality is tested and whatever does not fit into that must be excluded'. Where Hitler called this his 'intuition' and Jardine his 'conscience', James sees this absolute self-reliance as the mark of the 'degeneration' of the totalitarian into monomania (p. 50). In opposition, the representatives of the traditional virtues and values of cricket, the manager Warner and 'gentleman' Allen, are (despite the obvious major political and cultural differences) like the 'democrats' who (for James) capitulate to totalitarianism, too weak to stage any sort of meaningful resistance. Like Starbuck on board the *Pequod*, they know that their captain's actions are unethical and insane, and protest repeatedly, before capitulating to the passionate devotion embodied in their leader. Like Starbuck, Warner is unable to persuade Jardine to abandon his quest either when alone or in front of the men, and like Ahab, Jardine dismisses the protests with 'contempt'. And like Starbuck, Allen appears to lack respect for the professional players in the team, and never tries to enlist their support or align himself with them. For both, given that Jardine cannot be dismissed and will not resign from his post, there is 'no lawful way' (as Melville puts it) to stop him. James's cynical response to such inaction on board the *Pequod* is, 'That is it. There is no legal force by which to stop Ahab. So? Let him sink the ship with all on board' (p. 51). Much the same reading can be applied to bodyline.

Of course, there are limits to this analogy. In particular, there is no Ishmael in the bodyline narrative – a result of the near impossibility of the kind of movement from 'distinguished ... family' to worker in the team sports of a more rigidly class-determined English society. It took James's move from England to the United States in 1938 to identify this final type in his *Mariners, Renegades and Castaways*, and he admits in *Mariners* that, on arrival, he knew 'more about France and Russia and Ancient Greece and Rome' than about the United States, since 'little attention' was paid to them in the British and European educational systems (p. 159). But this is incidental to the narrative I have been constructing here: James's concern is with his discovery of a form of totalitarianism in America to match those in Europe, and he sees Ishmael as its intellectual representative. It is his own postnational identity, and the association between the conflict at an Australian cricket ground and his own place on the margins of American society enabled by such postnationalism, that make such a reading possible. The fact that for James, in contrast to the narrators of histories of American exceptionalism who shaped the emergent discipline of American Studies in the 1940s and 1950s, so little is different in America – with his treatment on Ellis Island, 'in miniature, a very sharp and direct expression of what was taking place in the world at large' (p. 127) – is fully illustrated by the extent to which such a mapping *is* possible.

CRICKET AND *AMERICAN CIVILIZATION*

Should we read this much into James's comments on cricket? After all, even a series as violent as bodyline cannot be said to have had the same consequences for world civilisation as the rise to power of Hitler or Stalin, or the treatment of political dissidents and aliens in the United States during the Cold War. It remained, just about, 'only a game'. The answer should be a resounding affirmative, not only remembering E.P. Thompson's comments, nor even James's own, on the importance of cricket. In addition, as he makes clear in *American Civilization*, James believed that, in the twentieth century, it was necessary to turn to popular culture in order to understand the 'violence, sadism, cruelty' that (for James) dominated the American scene during the Depression. In his description of the gangster films of the 1930s, James could almost be referring back to Jardine:

> Gangsters get what they want, trying it for a while, then are killed. In the end 'crime does not pay' but for an hour and a half highly skilled actors ... have given to many millions a sense of active living, and in the bloodshed, the violence, the freedom from restraint to allow pent-up feelings free play, they have released the bitterness, hate, fear and sadism which simmer just below the surface.[26]

Although, of course, Jardine and Larwood were not actually 'killed', their ostracism from the game bears a remarkable similarity to the fates of the movie gangsters punished for their desire to push individualism to its limits. And, in a striking synchronicity, James identifies the model for subsequent films as W.H. Burnett's *Little Caesar*, released in 1932, the year of bodyline.

JAMES'S COLD WAR

In the final chapter of *Mariners, Renegades and Castaways*, James makes explicit not only how personal his reading of Melville really is, but also how he deploys it to comment on Cold War American society. In it, he links his study to an account of his months on Ellis Island, and extrapolates to offer an analysis of the injustices of an American bureaucracy itself driven to totalitarian means in its opposition to the Soviet Union, and in its fear of communism. Although James's defence rests partly on points of law, he repeatedly stresses his ignorance of legal intricacies. Instead, his principal argument depends on appealing to historical precedent and the shared popular understanding of the meaning of the Constitution. In this, he appears to be drawing once more on the essential differences between law and practice in cricket, since (like the Department of Justice's refusal to grant him citizenship, in large part because of what he reads)[27] the magnitude of bodyline's seriousness resided in its breach of the spirit, rather than the mere letter, of the laws of the game. Jardine can therefore be seen as prefiguring not only James's Ahab, but also the state itself, in its deployment of emergency powers implemented in the name of national security. Thus, in response to the obstacles constantly placed between James and his desire for citizenship, he notes:

> The Department of Justice violated the most elementary principles of justice ... I ask the average American citizen to consider. The law provides that an alien should have a hearing; then the decision, if unfavorable, can be appealed to the Attorney-General. Then if the appeal is rejected, the matter can be taken to the District Court, then if need be to the Court of Appeals, and finally to the Supreme Court. What theory of law is it which cannot see that such a procedure could have originated only in a country where the traditional role of the immigrant and the tradition of civil liberties, are such as to have created for the alien every possible opportunity to make as good a case for himself as possible? Isn't it obvious that the only interpretation of such a procedure is that it was intended to break down barriers and not to set them up, to declare to the alien, and to the American citizens, and to the whole world that the United States took upon itself the responsibility of seeing that as far as possible he was treated as a potential citizen?
> ... By making it as difficult for me as possible even to exist, my spirit might be broken and I might throw up the whole case.

James appeals to the American people themselves to see that his treatment runs counter to the whole history of relations between state and alien. He goes on to say that the introduction of the McCarran-Walter Act in 1950, which enabled the state to exclude immigrants on political grounds (and which was used to expel him although it was passed well after he had completed the examinations necessary for citizenship), in no way reverses 'the whole historical past and traditions of a people' in its 'loud propaganda' (pp. 141–2, 144).

In response to a new law that he sees as un-American, James turns to the Constitution, which 'forbids the limitation of free speech and free expression of opinion of any person in the United States. It specifically does not say citizen: it says person, meaning anybody'

(p. 163). His argument, again, depends upon the sense of fair play that he had learned on the cricket fields of Trinidad as a young colonial subject, and upon recognition of the same values in people's understanding of the Constitution. Like that subject, as represented by figures such as Captain Cipriani and the Nawab of Pataudi, James adopts hegemonic discourse to expose the hypocrisies of those in power; and like Cipriani and Pataudi, his internalisation of that ideology cannot protect him from institutional assault. He is thus able to conclude that, although he is 'a person fit and proper to be a citizen and a citizen who would be of some value to his fellow citizens', he is denied this opportunity because

> only two types of persons are today suitable for citizenship: millionaires and others who come on their knees thanking God and all in sight that they have been fortunate enough to have been admitted to a place where bombs may not fall and meat is not rationed (p. 166).

Looking back from the perspective of 1960, James wrote to the Australian journalist, Jack Fingleton, who had played in the infamous Adelaide Test match,

> What I did [in *Beyond a Boundary*] was to show that body-line was a symptom of a degeneration in "it isn't cricket" which continues to this day, and that degeneration I relate to the declining standards of morals and values *in the world at large*[28] (my emphasis).

This comment both explains James's stance in the final chapter of *Mariners, Renegades and Castaways* and makes explicit the links between his writing on cricket and his prefiguration of postnational American Studies. James, of course, was far too experienced in the intrigues of politics to be genuinely surprised at the unfair treatment he received at the hands of the American Justice Department. What he recognised, however, were two things: first, the analogy between the ideals promoted in the unwritten codes he had learned as a boy playing cricket in Trinidad, and those enshrined in the US Constitution; second, the parallel between Jardine's totalitarian response to Donald Bradman's own obsessive run-scoring, Ahab's fanatical pursuit of the white whale, and the totalitarianism James identified in hegemonic American attitudes to what would-be American citizens should study. In combining these points, James was able to deploy his postnational representations in the construction of himself as an idealised American citizen, in an argument that combines points of law with appeals to the historical understanding of how that law should be applied. He thus developed a model for understanding the United States utilising a truly postnational framework, and incorporating, but never reducible to, elements drawn from a range of national identities. Unlike the postnational models that have emerged in recent years, James's paradigm does not privilege America. Instead, when read as one text within his ongoing investigation into globalised historical relations, *Mariners, Renegade, and Castaways* shows us that American Studies must often temporarily turn its back on 'American' themes if it is ever to understand the nation postnationally.

NOTES

1. Donald E. Pease, 'C.L.R. James, *Moby-Dick*, and the Emergence of Postnational American Studies', in this volume.
2. Quoted in Hazel V. Carby, *Race Men* (Cambridge, MA and London: Harvard University Press, 1998), p. 119.
3. Donald E. Pease, 'C.L.R. James's *Mariners, Renegades and Castaways* and the World We Live In', the introduction to Pease's edition of C.L.R. James, *Mariners, Renegades and Castaways: the Story of Herman Melville and the World We Live In* (Hanover, NH: University Press of New England, 2001), p. vii.
4. Neville Cardus, *English Cricket* (London: Collins, 1945), pp. 46–7. Cardus was one of the few establishment figures to continue to support bodyline's challenge to the 'mechanical domination of the batsman' once the players had returned to England, calling the English fast bowling in Australia, 'wonderful, thrilling and beautiful to behold' (p. 47).
5. Quoted in E.W. Swanton, *A History of Cricket*, Volume II (London: George Allen and Unwin, 1962), p. 44.
6. The MCC (Marylebone Cricket Club), based at Lord's cricket ground in London, continued to control overseas tours by the national team until the 1970s. The team would only play as 'England' in Test matches.
7. I am drawing on Swanton, *A History of Cricket*, pp. 40–7, Derek Birley, *A Social History of English Cricket* (London: Aurum Press, 1999), pp. 235–52, and the website http://www.334notout.com/Bodyline for much of the detail in this account.
8. C.L.R. James, *The Life of Captain Cipriani: An Account of British Government in the West Indies* (Nelson: Coulton, 1932), p. 1.
9. Carby, *Race Men*, p. 115. See Jack Williams, *Cricket and England: A Cultural and Social History of the Inter-War Years* (London and Portland, OR: Frank Cass, 1999), pp. 74–91, for an account of the importance of 'sportsmanship' in cricket at this time, and of the extent to which the game's codes were applied to other areas of English cultural life.
10. There is no doubt that, like many others, James, the colonial subject who had grown up reading innumerable accounts of the Golden Age,

had an overly nostalgic vision of this period in cricket history. Although batsmen like Ranjitsinhji, Trumper, and Fry were legendary for their desire to entertain, and for their ability to improvise, the nature of cricket was already being transformed by the phenomenal run-scoring feats of W.G. Grace, whose on- and off-field behaviour often failed to live up to the ideals of the game.

11. Again, see http://www.334notout.com/Bodyline for details of this confrontation. Jardine did not like the term 'bodyline', and always insisted that his tactics were both legitimate and within the spirit of the game.
12. Swanton records that

    Up to that moment there were sportsmen in Australia who had been unsuspicious of the physical intention behind Jardine's tactics – or who, at any rate, awaited further evidence before they condemned. Here to them, in this sinister gesture, was the proof... It is true to say that hereafter Jardine had scarcely a friend in Australia.
    A History of Cricket, p. 45.

13. Remarkably, Oldfield managed to return for the final game of the series.
14. C.L.R. James, *Cricket*, Anna Grimshaw (ed.) (London: Allison & Busby, 1986) p. 34.
15. C.L.R. James, *Beyond a Boundary*, (London: Serpent's Tail, 2000), p. 188.
16. *Mariners, Renegades and Castaways*, p. 154. Subsequent page references in the chapter are to this text.
17. C.L.R. James, 'The Greatest of All Bowlers: An Impressionistic Sketch of S.F. Barnes', Manchester *Guardian*, 1 September 1932. Reprinted in *Cricket*, p. 7.
18. Carby, *Race Men*, pp. 116–17.
19. *Cricket*, p. 8.
20. C.L.R. James, *Beyond a Boundary*, pp. 25–6.
21. *Cricket*, pp. 45–6.
22. *Beyond a Boundary*, p. 191.
23. Ibid., pp. 187, 188.
24. Ibid., p. 191.
25. Ibid., p. 192.
26. C.L.R. James, *American Civilization*, edited and introduced by Anna Grimshaw and Keith Hart (Cambridge, MA: Blackwell, 1993) pp. 122, 127.
27. See *Mariners, Renegades and Castaways*, pp. 125–67.
28. *Cricket*, p. 105.

5
The Odd Couple: C.L.R. James, Hannah Arendt and the Return of Politics in the Cold War

Richard King

A fascinating intellectual convergence of the Cold War period, specifically the 1950s, involved two quite different thinkers, C. L. R. James (1901–89) and Hannah Arendt (1906–75). This phenomenon is so interesting, in part, because they had such dissimilar backgrounds. Arendt came from a reasonably prosperous, secular Jewish family in Köenigsberg in East Prussia, while James hailed from a lower-middle-class black family in Trinidad. Arendt received the best education in theology and philosophy that early twentieth-century Germany had to offer – and that was very good indeed; but James never attended university at all, though he did well at the Queen's Royal College in Trinidad.

Still, there were crucial parallels between them as well. For instance, they shared a diasporic status, both having left – one involuntarily and the other voluntarily – the country of their origin. In that sense, they were also quintessential modern intellectuals, alienated from their political and cultural roots, though neither claimed superior virtue because of that. Although each was a member of one of the West's two great diasporic peoples, both came late to an awareness of the importance of ethnic/racial identity. Arendt later 'credited' the Nazis with having made her fully aware that she was a Jew. And it was only in London in the early 1930s that James became aware 'that an African, a black man, had a face of his own'. This was due partly to his friendship with Paul Robeson who, James recalled, 'taught me a lot about black people'.[1] Both Arendt and James were forced constantly to renegotiate the tension between universalism and particularism in their own lives and thought.[2]

Neither Arendt nor James was easy to place ideologically. Arendt, for instance, denied that she was a typical German leftist; rather she came, she said, from 'the tradition of German philosophy'.[3] Yet her relationship with the revolutionary left was more complex than this would suggest. She was a respectful but firm non-believer in Marxism; towards Stalinism and Marxism-Leninism, she was unashamedly hostile. Nor did she have much use for her contemporaries, the Frankfurt School theorists; and personal experience gave added bite to her theoretical disagreements with them. Still, from her second husband, Heinrich Blucher, himself a member of the German Communist Party until the mid 1920s, she learned much about the Jacobin–Bolshevik tradition and, indeed, helped radicals, some of them Communists, escape from Germany after the Nazis came to power. Finally, three of the most powerful and moving essays she wrote dealt with Marxists, albeit maverick ones: Walter Benjamin, Bertolt Brecht and Rosa Luxemburg.[4] Not accidentally, Arendt evoked Luxemburg's idea of 'spontaneous revolution' at the beginning of her analysis of the Hungarian Revolution, included in the second edition of *The Origins of Totalitarianism* (1958).[5]

James too had a problematic relationship with the Marxian left. Though he always described himself as a Marxist, he was never a member of any orthodox Communist party, but rather moved in and out of the Trotskyist movement until the mid 1950s. He spoke highly of figures such as Paul Robeson and W.E.B. Du Bois, despite their pro-Soviet stances after 1945. Contrary to Trotsky's pronouncements, James never accepted the idea that the Soviet Union was a 'degenerate' workers' state, which deserved 'critical support'. It was, he contended, the 'greatest tyranny known to human history'.[6] Like Arendt but unlike many others on the left, then and now, James had no trouble applying the term 'totalitarian' to the Soviet Union as well as to Nazi Germany. More importantly, in the late 1940s and into the 1950s, he rejected the Leninist idea of the vanguard party and the notion that 'real' Communism involved state control of politics through 'the Party' and of the economy by 'the Plan'.[7] Jamesian socialism saw the self-activity of the workers as the key element in revolutionising society, economy and polity. Finally, by the mid 1950s, he had ceased believing that revolution in the Third World would, or should, wait for proletarian uprisings in advanced capitalist societies to point the way.

In what follows, I want to pursue the similarities in the thought of Arendt and James in reference to three interwoven matters. First, both located the origins of politics as an activity and as a value in the Greek polis, particularly in fifth-century Athens. Second, both saw totalitarianism as central to the crisis of modernity, capitalist and socialist, and sought to address it in their work – James in his study of Herman Melville, *Mariners, Renegades and Castaways* (1953) and to a lesser extent *American Civilization* (1950), and Arendt in her *The Origins of Totalitarianism* and related writing of the early postwar period. Finally, both saw the Hungarian Revolution of October–November 1956 as one of the uniquely important events of their time. Only after Hungary did opposition to totalitarianism from within seem possible, and thus the overthrow for a few short days of the Soviet puppet regime helped dissipate the pessimism about democracy that blanketed Eastern Europe. In the wake of the Hungarian Revolution (for James the civil rights movement in the US South and the struggle for independence in the Gold Coast were equally important), each sought to re-imagine a conception of politics organised around the 'council system' and 'self-activity'. This led Arendt to formulate an alternative to the canonical grand narrative of Jacobin–Bolshevik revolutionary tradition. Their central theme, then, was the return of political activity and, by extension, political freedom to the tradition of democratic politics, once Western but now global in reach.

Moreover, by analysing this crucial period in each thinker's thought, the narrow terms within which James and Arendt are usually discussed will, I hope, be expanded. This will perhaps help give James's work greater prominence in mainstream Western political thought, while also suggesting ways that Arendt's writings can illuminate the politics of totalitarian domination *and* participatory freedom outside the narrow confines of the European tradition.

TOTALITARIANISM AND THE COLD WAR

How do James's ideas about totalitarianism as they emerge in his reading of *Moby-Dick* comport with Arendt's in *Origins*?[8] The point is not to engage in a one-to-one match-up or a connect-the-dots comparison, since the texts in question 'do' different things. In James's *Mariners*, what is at issue is an allegorisation of Melville's capacious, mixed-discourse novel, *Moby-Dick*, while Arendt's *Origins*, something of a behemoth of a book itself, combines economic, social, political and intellectual history, political thought, sociology and philosophical anthropology to try to take the measure of political modernity.

To engage with such a comparison, a few words about the term 'totalitarianism' itself are necessary. As already suggested, its use was by no means considered politically neutral, not at least to most participants in post-war ideological debates. Generally, 'totalitarian' was, and remains, what Hannah Pitkin refers to as a 'blob' term[9] – the sort of concept that encompasses everything the speaker or writer objects to about modern political and social reality. Prior to World War II, the left applied the term, which originated in the 1920s as a positive concept in Mussolini's fascist vocabulary, to Hitler's Nazi Germany, and often to the other fascist regimes in Europe, while conservatives applied it to Stalin's Soviet Union and usually to Nazi Germany as well.[10] In the post-war period, James, along with Arendt and some of the New York intellectuals, applied 'totalitarianism' to both the former Nazi regime and Stalin's Soviet Union. This, of course, was highly contentious, particularly with those on the left more inclined to give the Soviet Union the benefit of the doubt – that is, 'critical support' – and those who suspected that applying the term to the Soviet Union was a supposedly value-neutral way of red-baiting.

In fact, James justified his application of the term to both regimes, but was uneasy enough to want to explain himself. Thus, he wrote in *American Civilization*:

> In this volume there is made an identification of the regimes of Hitlerism and Stalinism under the common name of *totalitarian*. It must be understood that this implies no identity of regimes ... Politically speaking the differences between Stalinism and Fascism, particularly on a world scale, are of immense, in fact of decisive importance.[11]

Similarly, Arendt knew very well that Russia and Germany had vastly different political histories, and that National Socialism and Marxism-Leninism were ideologically far from identical. But, for her, similar outcomes did not imply identical origins or development. As she wrote in the early 1950s,

> Nazi Germany and Soviet Russia started from historical, economic, ideological, and cultural circumstances in many respects almost diametrically opposed, yet still arrived at certain results which are structurally identical.

In other words, it told her nothing she didn't already know to insist that Nazism and Stalinism were different in many respects.[12]

Moreover, by using 'totalitarian' to refer to both regimes, James and Arendt signalled their belief that, whatever role capitalism had played in the emergence of Hitler's regime in Germany, it was by no means the only explanation for this modern form of political (mis)rule. Those unfamiliar with *Origins* may be surprised to learn that Arendt identified late-nineteenth-century overseas capitalist expansion as a crucial factor in the historical emergence of totalitarianism in Europe. Specifically, she suggested that colonial rule by bureaucracy and secret police, along with ideologies of racial superiority, filtered back into Europe and helped prepare the ground for the racialisation of European politics.[13]

For his part, James explicitly distanced himself in *American Civilization* from any overly simple economic interpretation of totalitarianism:

> Many writers ignore totalitarianism in the United States or simply equate it with monopoly capitalism, finance-capital, etc. In my opinion all this is unpardonably superficial ... I aim at showing that the apparently irrational and stupefying behavior of people in totalitarian states is a product of modern civilization, not merely in terms of preserving property and privilege but as the result of deep social and psychological needs of man in modern life.[14]

Though James is not claiming here that the United States is a totalitarian state, his point is that more than just economic factors explain totalitarianism's appeal, and that evidence of those 'social and psychological needs' can be found in the United States. Arendt was more circumspect in using the term in reference to the United States, but she was scathing about McCarthyism and the climate of fear it had created.

Well into his reading of Melville's *Moby-Dick* as a prophetic delineation of the twentieth-century totalitarian leader, James formulates the main concern of *Mariners* as 'how the society of free individualism would give birth to totalitarianism and be unable to defend itself against it ... Melville's theme is totalitarianism, its rise and fall, its power and its weakness.'[15] James's thesis builds on the venerable trope of the ship as a society in microcosm. The *Pequod* itself represents the 'voyage of modern civilization seeking its destiny' (*MRC*, p. 19), even though there are neither women, nor children, nor families in *Moby-Dick*. In fact, the only representations of either parent–child or of heterosexual affections in the novel are associated with the society of whales rather than of human beings.

The instrument of the ship's destruction, the figure that embodies what James sees as Melville's prophetic vision of the fateful contradictions of modern industrial society is, of course, Captain Ahab. Ahab's unbridled individualism is reflected in more than the normal 'isolation of being in command' (*MRC*, p. 7). Still, through a combination of inspirational rhetoric, bribery and the threat of violence, Ahab is able to weld the crew into a single unit. As they commence the final hunt, Melville describes it thusly: 'They were one man, not thirty',[16] something which James explains as arising from the 'excitement of achieving a common goal' (*MRC*, p. 65). Later, Starbuck, one of the three ship's officers whom Melville collectively blames for the failure of the crew to revolt,[17] articulates the conventional expectations of the crew – and of course the ship's owners – when he says to Ahab: 'I am game for his crooked jaw, and for the jaws of Death too, Captain Ahab, if it fairly comes in the way of the business we follow, but I came here to hunt whales, not my commander's vengeance'.[18] This position is later reinforced by what the narrator claims is the motivation of the *Pequod*'s owners:

> the calculating people of that prudent isle were inclined to harbor the conceit, that for those reasons he [Ahab] was all the better qualified ... They were bent on profitable cruises, the profit to be counted in dollars from the mint. He was intent on an audacious, immitigable, and supernatural revenge.[19]

But they didn't know their man well enough.

However, Ahab's rage and desire for vengeance, claims James, can scarcely be attributed to 'some private individual suffering from megalomania, sexual crisis, or some such personalized difficulty, symbolical, but symbolical of human nature in general'. Rather, he must be 'seen as a specific type of person, at a specific point of historical time, produced by specific historical circumstances ...' (*MRC*, p. 56). Thus, what Ahab himself explains as a private hurt and outrage – that is, the intimate injury inflicted by the white whale – is read by James as integral to Melville's remarkable anticipation of the destructive tensions at work in modern industrial society.

The twin objects of James's interpretive animus are, first, those post-World War II intellectuals whom he scorned as caught up in their private 'neurosis' and 'incestuous desires, father-complex, mother fixation as the foundation of human personality and human behavior' (*MRC*, p. 102) and, specifically, Ishmael, who is the novel's narrator and himself a 'disoriented intellectual' (*MRC*, p. 42). Indeed, Ishmael foreshadows from within the text many of the post-1945 literary-critical readings of *Moby-Dick*. As though to anticipate the proliferation of symbolic and/or psychoanalytic readings of Melville's text, Ishmael's own hermeneutical probes fix on Ahab's deep unease and psychological projection:

> He at last came to identify with him, not only his bodily woes, but all his intellectual and spiritual exasperations. The White Whale swam before him as the monomaniac incarnation of all those malicious agencies which some deep men feel eating in them ...[20]

As mentioned, James also chastises Starbuck and the two other officers for failing to stand up to, much less lead a revolt against, their demented Captain.

Finally, there is the crew, the 'mongrel renegades, and castaways, and cannibals morally enfeebled'[21] by the inadequate leadership of the three officers. The crew James wants us to apotheosise is not the group that blindly follows Ahab to their death, but the crew at work together: 'Their heroism consists in their everyday doing of their work. The only tragic graces with which Melville endows them are the graces of men associated for common labor.' (*MRC*, p. 28) Thus, in the 'Try-Works' chapter, their 'common labor' in the diabolical conditions on-board the ship describes the fate of the industrial working class. It is their 'common labor' that indicates the promise of cooperative effort, but it is a promise that is destroyed by their exploitation by those who hold power on the ship and on land.

What, then, of Hannah Arendt's treatment of such matters? Above all, James and Arendt agree that the crucial motivation of totalitarian leaders was not utilitarian or rational in any conventional sense. Ahab scorns the profit motive, though he uses the love of gain to lure the men into committing to the chase after the white whale. Indeed, Melville captures the deep contradictions in Ahab's make-up when he has Ahab think: '... all my means are sane, my motive and my object mad',[22] a self-characterisation that anticipates the typology of modern rationality suggested by Max Weber and the Frankfurt School. Indeed, the most original aspect of Arendt's work had to do with the idea that totalitarian systems transcended all conventional political or economic calculation, while most of the Frankfurt School still implicitly held that the Nazis were acting within the broad parameters of political rationality – that is, comprehensible economic ends pursued by appropriate means, however horrible they were.

From another point of view, the Nazis, like Ahab, did operate according to a higher or different purpose – the desire for revenge against creation and against human nature. As Arendt insisted, the goal of the totalitarian regime was a population of superfluous beings who had lost all capacity for choice or spontaneity. The result would be an eradication of human plurality and difference by systematically destroying the individual's legal and moral personality, and then his or her sense of individuality itself.[23] Thus Melville's 'They were one man, not thirty' evokes in chilling terms the barely human, well-nigh anonymous inmates of the camps or the participants in the Nuremberg Rallies. For Arendt the central institution of the totalitarian order was the camp system, segregated by sex and overwhelmingly male, where terror was applied systematically for the purpose of reconstructing human 'being'. Arendt's central trope here echoes Melville's description of the unity of the crew: 'It substitutes for the boundaries and channels of communication between individual men a band of iron which holds them so tightly together that it is as though their plurality had disappeared into One Man of gigantic dimensions ...'[24] To Hobbes's Leviathan, Melville's Moby-Dick and Franz Neumann's Behemoth, we can add Arendt's 'One Man of gigantic dimensions' as a trope of gargantuan and grotesque power.

Another, more recognisable, goal of the totalitarian regime was the attempt to implement the central principle of the ideology. According to Arendt, this was 'race' in the case of National Socialism and 'class' in the case of the Soviet Union. Once the logic of race or class superiority was embraced, she feared that extermination was all but unavoidable. It is strange that, though James follows Arendt in focusing on the centrality of 'race' to National Socialism (and what he calls 'the Plan' to Soviet Communism), he hardly dwells on the importance of race, except to suggest that all nation-states privilege their own people in racial terms. The difference was that the Nazis 'decided to carry it to its logical conclusion ... The national race was the master race' (*MRC*, p. 13). But James's emphasis on the nation misses a crucial point of Arendt's analysis: Nazi ideology was actually hostile to the nation-state and subordinated German nationalism to the triumph of the master-race. Because James never went this far, his account of totalitarianism lacks the intellectual audacity of Arendt's work.

There is something to be said for James's jibes at post-war intellectuals as having retreated into the private realm and disengaged from political radicalism, but I find them out of proportion to the actual political importance of intellectuals. In addition, there is more than a hint here of a Lukácsian, anti-modernist strain in James's animadversions against 'neurotic' modernist intellectuals.[25] *Origins* includes an important discussion of the attraction that totalitarian movements had for intellectuals, who sought to combat the nihilism of modern life through real or vicarious action, especially violence and terrorism, which Arendt refers to as a 'kind of political expressionism'.[26] She too was deeply suspicious of the political judgment of intellectuals and academics, wherever they stood on the political spectrum; no wonder, after her own personal experience with Martin Heidegger and the example of her friend, Bert Brecht. Indeed, she once observed that it wasn't one's enemies but one's friends that one had to fear during the *Nazizeit*.

But one area of real disagreement between Arendt and James is over the importance of the totalitarian leader. A strong criticism of Arendt's *Origins* is that it seriously neglects the importance of the leader in the emergence, consolidation and augmentation of totalitarian rule. For Arendt, the totalitarian leader was different from the tyrant in not aiming for 'the tranquility of his own rule'. He was rather compelled by the restless 'imitation ... of the laws of Nature and History'. Above all, he was not really free, but 'the executioner of laws higher than himself'.[27] From this Arendt (strangely) drew the conclusion that no *specific* leader was essential to the functioning of a totalitarian system. This was a serious failure of historical judgment. That said, her actual analysis of Hitler's appeal was quite shrewd. She emphasised not his 'charisma' but his 'extraordinary self-confidence', which meant that he was always ready to act on his opinions – something that appealed to those paralysed by 'the modern inability to judge'. James himself sounded a good bit like Arendt (and Erich Fromm) when he claimed that intellectuals seek refuge with leaders such as Ahab 'to give them the protection from having to make choices ...' (*MRC*, 105). Beyond that, Arendt identified Hitler's 'greatest gift' as the will to implement the 'pure logic' of his ideology.[28] Still, there is in Arendt's thought little or no discussion of the ability of a Hitler or Stalin to galvanise isolated individuals into mass movements, or of any of the other ways these particular men held sway over their followers. Somehow, totalitarian movements and regimes would persist despite the fate of this or that leader.

But James rightly saw that *Moby-Dick* was a perfect specimen text for an exploration of totalitarian leadership. In fact, James does not present a structural or institutional description of the totalitarian regime separately from his presentation, drawn from Melville, of the hierarchies of power on a whaler. The constraints of the novel as a genre and the historical underdevelopment of modes of incarceration kept James from exploring the role of mass terror or anything like the camp system as crucial to totalitarian rule. Rather, his focus was primarily on the charismatic leadership of Ahab. For Melville and James, evil as it appears in the world is hyper-intelligent and mesmerising. Thus, representing radical evil fictionally runs the risk of making the figure of evil attractive rather than repulsive. Indeed, Ahab attracts sympathy as well as antipathy throughout the text. He is a wounded titan and thus also a suffering human being. Paradoxically, this is where Arendt's de-emphasis of the totalitarian leader and her later suggestion of the phrase 'banality of evil' to describe Adolph Eichmann capture a truth about the commonplace nature of most evildoers that glamorising a compelling figure such as Ahab misses. In that sense, Arendt's *Eichmann in Jerusalem* (1963) offers a perspective from which her own notion of radical evil in *Origins*, and Melville/James's fascination with Ahab, can be called into question, or at least put into perspective.

Mariners reminds us of James's lifelong interest in the nature of revolutionary leadership, a point at which he is more Hegelian than Marxist. One thinks here of the tragedy of Toussaint, who, like Ahab but without the demonic dimension, came to grief because of his isolation from his followers. 'Melville', writes James the literary critic and biographer, 'as every truly great writer, sees history in terms of men' (*MRC*, p. 30) rather than forces or structures. James expands on this fictional-biographical aesthetic when he begins Chapter 4 by identifying the way ideas are conveyed in fiction: '... the social and political ideas in a great work of imagination are embodied in human personalities, in the way they are presented, in the clash of passions, the struggle for happiness, the avoidance of misery.' (*MRC*, p. 115) Here, James might have added 'biography' to 'a great work of imagination'. The point is that, despite James's commitment to Marxism, he was always aesthetically and politically engaged by the problem of how to represent the powerful political leader.

Finally, I am not sure what to think of James's emphasis upon 'individualism' as part of the root cause of totalitarianism. One might see this as a conventional gesture towards a critique of capitalist culture as selfish and destructive of communal bonds, in which 'all that is solid melts into air'. But I suspect that a fuller diagnosis would focus on individualism, not as a cause, but as a symptom of the loss of meaning and bonds of connectedness under the conditions of modernity. Ahab's heedlessness of others, his willingness to transcend and transgress the established order of the whaler (and of normal society), and above all the voracious desire for vengeance that drives his quest, smack more of Nietzschean over-reaching than of the exaggerated liberal individualism of a John Stuart Mill. Ironically for a Marxist, James fails to explore the historical, as opposed to the personal, sources of Ahab's Promethean ambitions. In rejecting the profit motive that is central to the world he inhabits, Ahab might be said to transcend, rather than embody, the dominant economic forces of his time. In other words, Ahab finally emerges as a totally self-willed individual, one who bursts the bounds of community and history, but for idiosyncratic rather than representative reasons.

INTERVAL: 'AT ONCE NOT QUITE A CITIZEN BUT ALSO NOT YET NOT ONE'[29]

Arendt's *Origins* spoke powerfully to James's own condition as a stateless person, or at least as an alien in the United States. One lesson Arendt drew from the totalitarian era was that appeals to an abstract notion of human or natural rights, overseen by international organisations and dependent upon the good will of the global community for their enforcement, were useless in protecting those masses of stateless persons, national minorities and refugees who were so vulnerable to the Nazis in particular. They made up the reserve army of the superfluous, as it were, and we know the rest of the story. Based on that historical failure, Arendt insisted that in the future it was necessary to assert one basic right, itself grounded in human solidarity (admittedly not a significantly more compelling way of guaranteeing rights than an appeal to nature):

> For man, in the sense of the nature of man, is no longer the measure, despite what the new humanists would have us believe ... we shall have to create – not merely discover – a new foundation for human community as such.[30]

From this she went on to assert that

> The right to have rights ... should be guaranteed by humanity ... the fundamental deprivation of human rights is manifested first and above all in the deprivation of a place in the world which makes opinions significant and actions effective ... only the loss of a polity itself expels him from humanity.[31]

This was another way of saying that unless one belonged to a rights-recognising political entity, then so-called inalienable rights were without purchase or force. In belonging nowhere, one was politically and juridically nothing.

With this in mind, how then should we categorise the 'society' of the *Pequod*? Is it a kind of utopia of men drawn from all points of the compass and all races working together? Or is it a no-place, a space not of solidarity, but of naked vulnerability and incarceration? What James seems to have learned from his experience with the US government in the McCarthy era was that the *Pequod* was more like Ellis Island, as he suggests in the Introduction to *Mariners* (*MRC*, p. 3), than like the Athenian polis or a socialist community. Though American citizens were certainly vulnerable to the threat of loyalty oaths and Congressional committees, they allegedly could not be deported, and thus had the 'right to have rights'. Indeed, Donald Pease tells us that James had already taken the citizenship tests and met the requirements for citizenship when he was overtaken by the machinery of the McCarran Act that was passed two years *after* he began the process of obtaining citizenship.[32] Despite his strenuous appeals, James was deported in 1953.

Yet the argument against Arendt's position is also a strong one. It is that the nation-state is the problem rather than the solution. Creating nation-states with borders generates the very statelessness to which they are meant to provide the answer. As she all but predicted, the fate of the state of Israel demonstrates the tragic contradictions involved in founding a nation: Israel gave Jews a place in the world, from which they could not be expelled. At the same time, however, its founding created a mass of stateless Palestinians without any political place in which they had 'the right to have rights'. (And as James noted, each nation-state tends to see its citizens as a master-race or group.) Finally, James asserted his 'right to have rights' to the Immigration and Naturalization Service and to members of the US Congress, to whom he sent copies of *Mariners*. It didn't work, but his Melville book was itself a kind of Arendtian gesture, a (desperate) form of political action, of speaking to (almost) fellow citizens.

ANNUS MIRABILIS: 1956

'Why didn't the men revolt?' James wonders about the *Pequod*'s crew (*MRC*, p. 50). The happy answer is that they did, at least symbolically, in Montgomery, in the Gold Coast, and in Hungary, all at once, in the mid 1950s. For once, history improved on fiction. Writing in 1957 to his comrades in America, the London-based James reported on a conversation with Martin and Coretta King about Montgomery: 'It was one of the most astonishing events of endurance by a whole population I have ever heard of.' He then proceeded to link Montgomery with the 'Gold Coast Revolution' and with the 'Hungarian Revolution' as turning points in modern political history. These three events confirmed James's faith in the 'spontaneous creativity of the working class (and all other progressive classes) ...'[33]

James's small book, *Facing Reality* (1958), co-authored with Grace Lee and Pierre Chaulieu (aka Cornelius Castoriadis), focused on the working class in the Hungarian uprising of the autumn of 1956. Though a short-lived victory over the totalitarian regime propped up by the Soviet Union, the Revolution sent the message that the working classes everywhere were to take heart. An early paragraph contains the essential message:

> By the total uprising of a people, the Hungarian Revolution has disclosed the political form which not only destroys the bureaucratic state power, but substitutes in its place a socialist democracy, based not on the control of the people but the mastery of things. This political form is the Workers Councils ...[34]

And just a paragraph later: 'Workers' management of production, government from below, and government by consent, have thus been shown to be the same things'.[35]

Moreover, James made clear that socialism was the natural extension of collective group activity into every sphere of life. The councils embodied already existing socialism, not in the bogus form represented by Soviet-imposed governments, but in the sense that socialism 'exists. It is organized. It has to get rid of what is stifling it' and 'preventing it from tackling not only the immediate problem of production, but also the more general problems of society'.[36] James's crucial political concerns all came together in the Hungarian uprising – rejection of the bureaucratic state, organisation of people from the bottom up, the location of power in the workplace, and the effacement of the distinction between the economic, social and the political. The psychology of the working class, thought James, was profoundly shaped by the discipline of the industrial process learned on the ship-floor. What was acquired was 'mastery over production and social processes'.[37]

For Hannah Arendt, the Hungarian Revolution came as a great surprise. Never known for her willingness to admit a mistake, she nevertheless granted in her 'Epilogue: Reflections on the Hungarian Revolution' that:

> The Hungarian revolution interrupted these types of automatic occurrences and conscious or unconscious repetitions just when the student of totalitarianism had grown accustomed to them and public opinion [had grown] apathetic. This event was not prepared at all by events in Poland. It was totally unexpected and took everybody by surprise ... what happened here was something in which nobody any longer believed, if he ever had believed in it.[38]

Indeed, Hungary might be said to have revealed to Arendt that she was a kind of republican with democratic tendencies. The council system made manifest 'the voice of the people ... unaltered by the shouts of the mob and unstifled by the bureaucraticization of parties ...'[39] The experience there also reminded her of another, less obvious revolutionary tradition, as manifested in the American and French Revolutions, the Paris Commune of 1871, the emergence of Soviets in Russia in 1905 and 1917, and the soldiers' Raete (Councils) in Germany after World War I. Both Arendt and James ultimately identified this tradition of worker self-organisation and the council system of participatory democracy as the heart of the true revolutionary tradition of the modern West.[40] Like James, Arendt would surely have welcomed Solidarity in 1981 and the collapse of Communist rule in 1989 as direct legacies of Hungary and the forgotten tradition of modern republicanism.

Arendt and James agreed on much about the significance of the Hungarian Revolution. Both stressed its spontaneous nature, and its rejection not just of the Communist Party but also of all conventional political parties. Politics was present in the organisation and functioning of self-governing units throughout the society – in the workplace (and against the established unions), the military, among students, and in neighborhoods. This was politics 'from the bottom up'. Both agreed that an important goal of self-organisation was the diminution of centralised state power, something that Arendt, especially, saw as a way to strengthen rather than diminish political consensus. Arendt also emphasised more than James that the council system would help combat the corrosive effects of mass society. It was, as she later stressed, not only a site of action but also a source of order.

Still, James and Arendt parted ways on the relative emphasis to be placed upon the workers' versus the revolutionary councils. In contrast with James, who saw the workplace as the privileged site of self-government, and who emphasised the overlapping nature of the economic, social and political spheres, Arendt drew a distinction between the political and the economic spheres, which she would develop more fully in *The Human Condition* (1958):[41] 'The question whether economic, as distinguished from political, functions can be handled by councils, whether, in other words, it is possible to run factories under the management and ownership of the workers, we shall have to leave open.'[42] Arendt noted that the puppet regime of Janos Kadar seemed most threatened by the political councils, and shut them down first, while retaining some of the economic reforms suggested for the workplace. But generally the gap between 'citizen' and 'worker' in Arendt's thought was too wide to bridge, while it is difficult to see how James could privilege the workplace as the site of the emergence of self-governing activity when it was so clearly not the only place where such activity flourished in Hungary – and certainly not in Montgomery or the Gold Coast.[43]

Finally, subsequent writings of both thinkers would reveal, as mentioned earlier, a common source for their political ideas – the Athenian polis. For James, Athens was the great example of the self-governing polity in which the citizen body directly participated in the governing of the political order. Office-holding was determined by lot and for a limited time, thus keeping in check what Arendt would later call the 'rule of nobody' – that is, government by experts and bureaucrats. Conversely, Plato came under fire from James as being, to put it mildly, undemocratic: '*The Republic* was a perfect example of a totalitarian state governed by an elite.'[44] James was also intrigued by the way in which, at the annual festivals, the citizens were entrusted with the duty of judging the plays that were presented. For James, then, Athens had not only been a polity of self-government by free citizens, but a place where power and imagination, politics and culture, were unified rather than alienated from one another.

It would require more space than is available here to analyse the role that the Greek polis played in Arendt's thought, though it is also possible to over-emphasise its importance. Its classic statement can be found in *The Human Condition*, which was *not* available to

James when he was writing *Facing Reality*, since both books were published in the same year, 1958. What I would emphasise here is that Arendt's contention that action, speech and freedom were closely intertwined was based on her understanding of the politics of the polis *and* her discovery of the modern tradition of republican self-government in the period between 1955 and 1960. Thus, rather than emphasising their radically different nature and vast separation in time, it makes more sense to understand Arendt's classical and modern ideas of politics (and freedom) as closely related, though not without differences.

After all this, it was only in *Modern Politics* (1960), the transcript of a set of lectures he gave in August 1960 in Port-of-Spain, Trinidad, that James mentioned Arendt in his work. In a concluding note, 'A Few Words with Hannah Arendt', James listed *Origins* as indispensable 'for knowledge and insight into the totalitarian monsters', although James added that Arendt 'does not understand the economic basis of society'.[45] (This was neither the first nor the last time Arendt's work would receive this particular criticism.) But James was really interested in countering Arendt's claim that what had happened in Hungary was totally unexpected: '[T]hat everybody had given up hope is quite untrue ... we did not have to wait for Hungary. For us, as Marxists, totalitarianism is doomed.'[46] To make the case for the existence of a democratic political tradition *within* Marxism, James cited his own work and that of his colleagues at *Correspondence* and *Socialisme ou Barbarie* (such as Castoriadis). Arendt, I suspect, would have been more than skeptical, since for her Marx's concept of politics and the political was deeply compromised by his emphasis on the centrality of necessity in human affairs. But we have nothing to indicate, nor any reason to think, that she ever responded to James. For James, it was a long way from Ahab and the *Pequod*, but not so far at all from what he had hoped for from the mariners, renegades and castaways that made up its crew.

LESSONS

While Arendt is now recognised as a canonical figure in twentieth-century political thought, James and the tradition of anti-colonial political thought have been sorely neglected within mainstream political theory.[47] James lacked Arendt's sheer brilliance and originality as a political thinker, but his work is important for what it revealed about what was 'thinkable' as a dissident Marxist in the Cold War context, and as a Marxist generally. James also exemplified the way in which a black diasporic thinker drew upon European thought and history, not to reaffirm its superiority but to use – and modify – some of its central ideas in a non-European context. This was particularly the case with his *The Black Jacobins* (1938). In many ways quite Eurocentric, Arendt's work nevertheless was deeply concerned, particularly in *Origins*, with historical and political realities outside Europe. My overall sense is that the intellectual stature of both figures is enhanced rather than diminished by taking them out of their usual 'neighborhoods' (intellectual influences) and setting them down in new ones, as well as by playing them off against each other.

The work of Arendt and James also raises crucial methodological issues for political thought. Both took the *historical impact* of events, forces and actions, rather than static models, as the starting point for political thinking. Their primary interest fell neither on the economic nor institutional forces that block revolutionary action that are the preoccupation of orthodox Marxist historians and domination theorists, nor on the 'end-state' concepts – rights, justice, equality and freedom – that have been the staple of modern non-Marxist thought. Rather, they thought in, through, and against history. Their focus as political thinkers lay in their vision of politics as most centrally about participatory freedom and self-government in the broadest sense of those terms. 'Process' concepts, such as action, speech and self-determination were most significant for them. Freedom was not so much a status or a possession as an ongoing creation and experience.

For these reasons, their work is also most relevant for those 'in-between' situations when regimes collapse under pressure from external forces or from within. With that, power returns to the people, and the possibility appears of beginning again or expanding the realm of freedom. For neither was the state the only, or even the main, site of politics. Ultimately, their politics are less about classical revolution than 'rejuvenation' or 'revitalisation' or 'reconstruction' of the public realm where politics can once again exist. To be sure, their work did not exhaust the meaning of politics or freedom, but without their emphasis upon the crucial importance of the return of self-government, it is impossible to understand either how regimes retain legitimacy, or why they lose it.

NOTES

1. Hannah Arendt, '"What Remains? The Language Remains"', *Essays in Understanding* (New York: Harcourt Brace, 1994), pp.11–12; C.L.R. James, *At the Rendezvous of Victory* (London: Allison & Busby, 1984), p. 217.
2. See Richard H. King, *Race, Culture and the Intellectuals, 1940–1970* (Washington, DC and Baltimore, MD: The Wilson Center and Johns Hopkins University Press, 2004) for more detailed discussion of both figures in the terms laid out above.
3. Arendt, 'Response to Gershom Scholem', in *The Jew as Pariah*, ed. by Ron H. Feldman (New York: Grove Press, 1978), p. 246.
4. See Arendt, *Men in Dark Times* (New York: Harvest, 1968).
5. Arendt, 'Epilogue: Reflections on the Hungarian Revolution', in *The Origins of Totalitarianism*, second edition (Cleveland, OH: Meridian, 1958), p. 482.
6. James, *Spheres of Existence* (London: Allison & Busby, 1980), p. 121.
7. *At the Rendezvous of Victory*, p. 82.
8. Abbott Gleason, *Totalitarianism: The Inner History of the Cold War* (New York: Oxford University Press, 1995). Gleason's contention that totalitarianism was the central political concept of the Cold War period has a good deal to be said for it.
9. Hannah Fenichel Pitkin, *The Attack of the Blob: Hannah Arendt's Concept of the Social* (Chicago and London: University of Chicago Press, 1998). Pitkin notes that Arendt uses the term 'totalitarianism' in such a way that it often takes on a kind of will and agency of its own (see p. 95).
10. See Stephen J. Whitfield, *Into the Dark* (Philadelphia: Temple University Press, 1980) for a clear overview of the origins of the term 'totalitarianism'.
11. James, *American Civilization*, edited and introduced by Anna Grimshaw and Keith Hart with an Afterword by Robert H. Hill (Cambridge, MA and Oxford: Blackwell, 1993 [1949–50]), p. 39.
12. 'On the Nature of Totalitarianism', in *Essays in Understanding*, p. 347.
13. Aime Cesaire was also to make this point in his powerful polemic, *Discourse on Colonialism* (1955), as had W.E.B. Du Bois earlier.
14. *American Civilization*, p. 38.
15. C.L.R. James, *Mariners, Renegades and Castaways: The Story of Herman Melville and the World We Live In*, Introduction by Donald E. Pease (Hanover and London: University Press of New England/Dartmouth College, 2001 [1953]), p. 54. All page references will be included in the text hereinafter with the abbreviation *MRC*.
16. Herman Melville, *Moby-Dick Or, The Whale* (New York: Modern Library, 2000 [1851]), p. 797.
17. Melville, *Moby Dick*, p. 271.
18. Ibid., p. 235.
19. Ibid., p. 270.
20. Ibid., p. 267.
21. Ibid., p. 270.
22. Ibid., p. 269.
23. See Part 3 ('Totalitarianism') of *Origins* for Arendt's phenomenology of totalitarian domination.

24. *Origins*, pp. 465–6.
25. James's attitude echoes Edmund Wilson's objection to Franz Kafka's attitude towards authority as one of 'meaching compliance', as though that was all there was to say about Kafka.
26. *Origins*, pp. 326–40. She had in mind here 'action' intellectuals ranging from Bakunin and Nechayev to Rimbaud and T.E. Lawrence, Ernst Juenger and Bertolt Brecht. Among thinkers, she mentions Nietzsche and Pareto, but might also have listed Georg Lukács and, of course, Martin Heidegger.
27. Ibid., p. 347.
28. *Essays in Understanding*, pp. 291–5.
29. Pease, 'Introduction', *Mariners, Renegades and Castaways*, p. xxviii.
30. *Origins*, p. 434.
31. *Origins*, pp. 296–8.
32. Pease, 'Introduction', p. xxvi.
33. *The C.L.R. James Reader*, ed. Anna Grimshaw (Oxford and New York: Blackwell, 1992), p. 273; and *Spheres of Existence*, p. 117. Thanks to my colleague, Peter Boyle, whose paper, 'The Hungarian Revolution and the Suez Crisis', is a very lucid analysis of the momentous events of the autumn of 1956.
34. James et al., *Facing Reality* (Detroit, MI.: Correspondence Publishing Co., 1958), p. 6. For Castoriadis's account of his role in the composition of the book and his relationship to James, see 'C.L.R. James and the Fate of Marxism', in *C.L.R. James: His Intellectual Legacies*, ed. Selwyn R. Cudjoe and William E. Cain (Amherst, MA: University of Massachusetts Press, 1995), pp. 277–97.
35. James, *Facing Reality*, p. 7.
36. Ibid., p. 107.
37. Ibid., p. 7.
38. *Origins*, p. 482. Riots had broken out in Poznan, Poland in June 1956, and in late October the Soviet Union had accepted the new Gomulka government in Poland.
39. Ibid., p. 501.
40. See also Arendt, *On Revolution* (New York: Viking Press, 1965), Chapter 6, for a fuller account of this alternative revolutionary tradition.
41. Arendt had already delivered the lectures that later made up the core of *The Human Condition*, in the spring of 1956 in Chicago.
42. *Origins*, p. 498.
43. Hungarian philosopher Agnes Heller has suggested that Arendt 'romanticised' the situation a good bit, and mistakenly claimed that the people involved in the council system were opposed to having elected representatives: 'My difference with Arendt is that I was never against representation in politics. The members of the workers councils ... wanted dual political power representation and participation.' See Simon Tormey, 'Interview with Professor Agnes Heller (I)', *Revista de Filosofia* 17, (Julio–Diciembre 1998), p. 23.
44. James, *The Future in the Present* (London: Allison & Busby, 1980), p. 171.

45. James, *Modern Politics* (Detroit, MI: Bewick/ed, 1973), pp. 156–7. See also Kent Worcester, 'The Question of the Canon: C.L.R. James and Modern Politics', in *C.L.R. James's Caribbean* ed. Paget Henry and Paul Buhle (London: The Macmillan Press, Ltd, 1992), pp. 210–24.
46. Ibid., pp. 158–9.
47. Siep Stuurman, 'The Canon of the History of Political Thought: Its Critique and Proposed Alternative', *History and Theory* 39 (May 2000), 147–66. Stuurman suggests that there are two kinds of questions to ask about the canon of Western political thought: First, who is included or excluded, what voices have been attended to and which ones not? And, second, what are the proper 'objects' – that is, concepts, institutions and traditions – of political thought?

6

C.L.R. James's *American Civilization*

Bill Schwarz

Beyond a Boundary (1963) is a very strange book. Even for the time it was published, there was a distinctly old-fashioned tone to it, echoing the schoolboy memoirs of earlier generations. Many chapters evoke the exploits of long-forgotten cricketers. Yet the form of the book is deceptive, for its lyrical memories of a lost colonial order carry within them a devastating critique of England and its civilisation. This unnerving displacement between form and content has for long shaped the reputation of *Beyond a Boundary*. To its admirers it remains a classic, unmatched by anything around. Yet for every admirer there are many more who can't abide the thought of reading from beginning to end a book about cricket or, if they dutifully make a start, get nowhere with it. This must also have something to do with the devoutly English feel of the prose. After all, what could represent more profoundly the civilisation of the English than cricket? It is entirely characteristic that the great English historian E.P. Thompson – maybe tongue in cheek, or maybe not – said of James that 'everything' about him lay 'in his proper appreciation of the game of cricket', fearing that 'American theorists will not understand this'.[1]

There is, I think, some truth in what Thompson says. Those whom he chooses to designate 'American theorists' do indeed appear to find it easier to accommodate James's writings on American culture, while for English readers the American James can still seem rather distant, as if his American years represented only an inconsequential episode or interregnum. As all who know James's work will attest, this does him a disservice, for it was precisely his varying Atlantic locations that entered his imagination and made his life and work so powerful. More than that, James was a paradigmatic intellectual of the twentieth-century black Atlantic. For most of his life the principal axis of his activities lay between the Caribbean and Britain. After the birth of independent Ghana in 1957, and with the prospect that a pan-African future really was in the making, he became intimately involved with the Nkrumah regime. In the middle of the century, when he was in his thirties and forties, he was resident – albeit as an 'illegal' for most of his stay – in the United States. This too needs to be understood through the optic of the black Atlantic. Towards the end of his life, James looked back to his time in the United States as marking 'the most important years of my life', 'the high water mark' of what all agree is an extraordinary lifetime.[2] Seeing him in these Atlantic terms allows the putative division between an 'English' James and an 'American' James to be overcome. One of the great paradoxes, however, is that James's most 'English' work, *Beyond a Boundary*, could not have been imagined into existence without the work of great theoretical labour sustained in the United States. Although it is impossible to see this on the page, the conceptual structure of *Beyond a Boundary* derives directly from the political and intellectual insights developed in the United States.

To invoke the idea of the black Atlantic is necessarily to invoke the important and influential work of Paul Gilroy. His *The Black Atlantic* (1992) centred theoretically the issue of modernity and the making of the modern world. This theme, we shall see, preoccupied James as much as it did the figures that Gilroy discusses. Maybe James's work too can be understood as contributing to that 'counter-modernity' which Gilroy champions. But as I hope to show, James's conception of modernity was profoundly ambivalent – and from a contemporary perspective, in many ways disconcerting. I think this ambivalence derived partly from James's origins in the British West Indies, born into a Caribbean culture that preceded the great social rupture of the labour rebellions of the 1930s. This makes James (another paradox) a strangely old-fashioned tyro of the modern. Yet, at the same time, to come to James from this perspective provides a necessary Caribbean dimension to the complex figuring of the black Atlantic.

FROM ENGLAND TO THE UNITED STATES

When the English cricket season drew to its close in the late summer of 1938, James embarked for the United States; intending to return to Britain in time for the opening of the following season, he left behind all his books and files. He had political work to do for his section of the Fourth International, to which he was then dedicated. He journeyed as a professional agitator – Trotsky himself, it seems, wanting James in America in order for him to take on a leading role in the Negro struggle.[3] Maybe he made the trip to recover from a love affair that had run aground; maybe his British comrades had sent him in order to straighten him out, to rid him of deviations that, from this vantage in history, can no longer easily be detected; or maybe both were factors.[4] Before he left he returned to the Lancashire town of Nelson, where he had lived shortly after first arriving in England. His purpose was to visit his old friends from Trinidad, the Constantines, and he arrived, as he recalled many years later, 'dressed in my literary-political grey flannels and sports jacket'. Learie Constantine believed this no way for a West Indian to travel to America. He took him to the Co-op to buy him a new set of clothes, and presented him with his own, expensive, camera 'in a Newmarket case and straps'.[5] James, properly attired and with the accoutrements necessary for the modern traveller, was all set.

In the event James stayed in the United States for 15 years, from 1938 to 1953. In the first weeks he delivered two prepared lectures, one on 'Socialism and the Negro', the second on 'The Twilight of the British Empire', alternating between the two. While there, there is no evidence that the themes of *Beyond a Boundary* especially preoccupied him, apart from his checking the Test and county cricket results, which the *New York Times* then used to carry and, as he put it, his 'devouring' *Wisden*, the cricketing almanac beloved of devotees of the game.[6] Given this, it might appear as if James's long American interlude has no part in locating *Beyond a Boundary*.

But neither James nor those close to him in later life saw it like that. In *Beyond a Boundary* he described how he slowly broke with his own Trotskyist formation.

> In 1940 came a crisis in my political life. I rejected the Trotskyist version of Marxism and set about to re-examine my view of the world, which was (and remains) essentially a political one. It took me more than ten years, but by 1952 I once more felt my feet on solid ground, and in consequence I planned a series of books. The first was published in 1953, a critical study of the writings of Herman Melville as a mirror of our age, and the second is this book on cricket.[7]

Melville and cricket? What connection could they have? As a means to break with Trotskyism? As essentially political? This is far from any orthodoxy, aside from that which retrospectively has become known as 'Jamesian'. James himself indulged in many masquerades. It is not always clear when he relied on irony. But on this occasion there is no reason to suspect that irony is in play. In this instance, we need to read him in his own terms.

The book on Melville that James referred to was *Mariners, Renegades and Castaways*. This in turn was a spin-off extracted and refashioned from a huge, unpublished manuscript he wrote at breakneck speed in a few months at the end of 1949 and the start of 1950, which took for its title *Notes on American Civilization*. On completion, the first full draft of *Notes on American Civilization* was immediately sent out to his collaborators for comment, with a warning from James that '[t]his document is absolutely confidential', indicating the degree to which he himself perceived his study to possess the status of a political statement.[8] He explained to his chosen circle of critics that, when he had collated their various responses, he would recast the manuscript and produce something shorter and more focused, to 'be read on a Sunday or on two evenings'.[9] This never happened, and the original, unmodified text appeared in print only some 40 years later, under the title of *American Civilization*, the object of some dispute about its provenance in the James corpus.[10] It is clear, though, that *Mariners* was a component of the same investigation that James had launched in *American Civilization*, and there is evidence that even though *Mariners* wasn't published until 1953, for a time he was alternating between the two manuscripts.[11]

The connection between *American Civilization*, via the study of Melville, and *Beyond a Boundary*, is important to establish, first because, on the face of it, they have nothing in common; and second because James himself made the link between Melville and cricket, and accorded it great significance. In both we can witness James explicitly interrogating the precepts of a civilisation. And in both we can see a historical method peculiarly his own coming into effect. In this respect, *American Civilization* served James as a preparatory, experimental exercise – his *Grundrisse*, to draw an analogy from Marx scholarship – which made *Beyond a Boundary* possible. This needs to be emphasised, as it is still common to find *Beyond a Boundary* discussed as if it were a singular text, without precedent in James's intellectual life.[12] The achievements of James's ten-year labour of striving to think beyond Trotskyism lie in both *American Civilization* and *Beyond a Boundary*, where the reader can follow his discovery that there were 'large areas of human existence that my history and my politics did not seem to cover'.[13]

FREE ASSOCIATION

James was excited by the possibilities presented in America for the development of individual freedoms, and for the expansion of the self. In interpreting American civilisation he attempted to imagine a communism that would derive, not from sacrifice and the incessant disciplining of the individual, but from the expansion of the subjective possibilities of all: 'from the development and creation of the self'.[14] Within the Marxist orthodoxies of the time this was decidedly libertarian, if not heretical, in its utopianism. Much as *Beyond a Boundary* was written in an identifiably English intellectual idiom, so James's centring of the category of individualism in his reading of America was American in its fundamental sympathies. In each instance, the tenets of his own critique were drawn from the organising principles of the civilisation he was endeavouring to explain. If faith in the possibilities of individual freedom lay at the centre of the experience of the United States, as the most powerful symbol of what the civilisation was to mean, then that was where James would choose to centre his critique.

But it isn't as if this was merely a methodological tactic on James's part. He was certain that there was much to be learned from the American preoccupation with the social role of the individual. In approaching the question of emancipation in this way, he addressed what he called 'all the elements of life and liberty', which he believed to have greater potential for realisation in the US than anywhere else (p. 27). These he understood to be essentially civic liberties, which he described as 'a freedom of social intercourse' and, following Alexis de Tocqueville, 'an altogether exceptional capacity for free association', such that in America 'individuality and universality achieve a fusion unknown elsewhere' (pp. 28, 48). This was a conception of liberty that encompassed an early understanding of the politics of everyday life. It opened up for him specifically feminist issues, arising from the organisation of domestic relations, and led him to anticipate 'a revolution' which would bring about the emancipation of women (p. 203). It prompted him, too, to consider mass culture, not only as a commodified institution, in the manner of Theodor Adorno and Max Horkheimer, but also as a symbolic system which – to some degree – inevitably explored the deep-seated desires and fears of the American people. Over half a century ago, this expansive sense of the locations of politics – in the home, at the movies, within one's own innermost reveries – was radically daring to an extent that, today, may be difficult to appreciate.

This Jamesian story of American free association, in its rewriting of Tocqueville, had its darker side. Through this period James himself, we should recall, operated as a political militant in minuscule, firebrand

Marxist sects, forever splitting one from the other, in which the struggle was all. He had, he indicated, 'enveloped' himself in Marxism during these years.[15] In 1941 he spent a number of months organising sharecroppers in Missouri.[16] He lived for a while in Harlem – the ghetto Harlem of Chester Himes and James Baldwin. For long periods the FBI and the Immigration and Naturalization Service kept him under close surveillance. Not only was he living on the frontline of an upbeat, urban modernity, but so too was he placed in the vortex of the evolving imperatives of the Cold War. As I suggested, he regarded his *Notes on American Civilization* to be an internal political statement, circulated in confidence to the groupuscule. The drama of his thought at this time lies in his determination to bring within a single orbit the everyday culture of the American people with his insurgent conception of Marxism. Despite the conventional cast of his reading of the development of modern society, he knew well enough that even those aspects of contemporary life that he most admired were the creation of fierce social antagonism. He abhorred 'the pre-1914 belief in perpetual progress' and in the 'increasing rationalism of the human mind', thinking that it signalled nothing more than a 'rotten pile of falsehoods' (p. 200). The emphases that underwrite *American Civilization* – production *and* consumption; the public *and* the private; the social *and* the subjective; Russia *and* America – were for James the necessary revisions required for the renovation of Marxist politics. Or, as he perceived it, they enabled him to think his way out of the variety of Marxism bequeathed by Trotsky.

MELVILLE AND WORLD HISTORY

James was alive to the contradictory, double nature of modern life in America. He gave this, though, a characteristically forceful temporal theorisation, which can be followed most clearly in his discussion of Melville. In a letter to Constance Webb, James informed her: 'I read Moby Dick on Wednesday. It was an experience.'[17] Indeed. Melville he believed to be of the artistic stature of Aeschylus and Shakespeare; his grasp of the relationship between artist and society to have equalled that of Aristotle and Hegel; and *Moby-Dick* to be *the* American novel, Melville's being 'the finest mind that has ever functioned in the New World'.[18] When James reckoned he had discovered a thinker of truly universal reach he was not one for understatement. Like many more conventional readings of *Moby-Dick*, his is most concerned with the relationship between the crew of the whaler, the *Pequod*, and its monomaniacal master, Ahab. For James the crew depicted the people of America, composed of many different types, with distinctly different origins, brought into association, one with the other, by the work they do. This was an America, for both Melville and James, which so deeply prefigured the future that its narrowly national properties were superseded by an identification with a greater universalism. James quoted from Melville's *Redburn*:

> There is something in the contemplation of the mode in which America has been settled that, in a noble breast, should forever extinguish the prejudices of national dislikes. Settled by the peoples of all nations, all nations may claim her for their own. You cannot spill a drop of American blood without spilling the blood of the whole world ... Our ancestry is lost in the universal pageantry; and Caesar and Alfred, St Paul and Luther, and Homer and Shakespeare are as much ours as Washington, who is as much the world's as our own. We are the heirs of all time, and with all nations we divide our inheritance. On this Western Hemisphere all tribes and peoples are forming into one federated whole; and there is a future which shall see the estranged children of Adam restored as to the old hearthstone in Eden.[19]

If the crew represented the possibilities of a democratic future for humankind, Ahab represented for James its contrary, but a contrary equally universalistic in scope, anticipating a world of unprecedented subservience. Caught between the two, in this reading, stands Ishmael: the prototype of the modern intellectual, paralysed by the barbarism that confronts him, yet cut adrift from all that makes history move.

James chose to give this a contemporary ring, by seeing in Ahab the embodiment of reason transmuting into its antithesis, into madness and unreason. He is the figure through whom the totalitarianism of the twentieth century can be understood. The *Pequod*, in this frame, is the nucleus of modern industry – much as, for James, the plantation functioned in the Caribbean during the epoch of slavery. Commenting on the *Pequod* as a productive force in its own right, James notes:

> The last word, so far as the social significance of the book is concerned, must be with Ishmael [on what is] perhaps the most remarkable page. The *Pequod* has been converted into a factory at sea – the try-works. The factory is aglow, the oil is boiling. It is night, and Ishmael, the intellectual, suddenly feels that the whole spectacle is not within the bounds of reason.[20]

Melville dramatised the transmutation of reason into unreason nowhere more persuasively than in Ahab's renunciation even of the logic of capital accumulation. The dominating rationale of the *Pequod* was to bring together hands to work the ship; to master nature, in crossing oceans and in capturing the whales; to set in motion, when this had been done, the production, on an industrial scale, of many barrels of oil boiled down from whale blubber; and when this last objective had been achieved, to return to port to sell the oil on the market. With the new capital earned, the vessel would be refitted once more in order that the entire cycle of production and exchange could be repeated, in the shortest possible time. However, in his determination to wreak vengeance on Moby-Dick, Ahab's commitment to these objectives, and to the production of capital, collapses. He comes to be possessed, not by mastery to some purpose, but by mastery itself. In this lies Ahab's monomania: all around him, man and nature, must be subordinated to the dictates of a goal from which reason and humanity have been stripped.

This, in summary form, was James's interpretation. There is some ambiguity in his account about the role of the crew-members. It is not clear whether he wishes us to understand them to represent free, autonomous beings, exerting their own mastery over the productive complex with which they are charged, or whether they have come to be integrated into a system irrevocably organised by Ahab's drive for mastery, their reasoning faculties consequently 'reified', to use Adorno's term. At different moments he seems to suggest each is true. Although the reading of *Moby-Dick* that James presents is subtler than I have been able to indicate here, there are nonetheless legitimate doubts that register. His faith in the power of the crew to represent a new world, free from the insanity of Ahab, may be greater than Melville's text warrants. His reliance on allegory to establish the connections to the present – to 'The World We Live In', as the subtitle of *Mariners* has it – serves to flatten out distinct histories.[21] And his habit of pulling the text into the present, so that *Moby-Dick* comes to be a novel about Hitler or Stalin, can be just too crudely insistent. But in a larger sense, James's analysis of Ahab as figuring a new and momentous historical situation does present a dramatic truth. The dynamism of Melville's portrayal of the emergence of an all-encompassing, abstracted mastery is extraordinary. There is sufficient textual evidence, moreover, to suppose that there does exist a connection between Ahab's unreason and the social system of the *Pequod*, as a productive force over which he presides – the latter described by Melville as 'the material counterpart of her monomaniac commander's soul'.[22]

James accounted for Melville's imaginative genius historically, by placing him within a particular moment of world history. Much as Marx explained his admiration for the novels of Balzac by the fact that they expressed the profound social tensions of a period of historical transition – notwithstanding the manifest conservatism of the novels themselves – and much as Georg Lukács thought in similar terms about Walter Scott, so James understood Melville.[23] Melville, according to James, saw 'the characteristic social types of his day and because he lived at a turning point, *he saw also a characteristic social type of the age which was to follow*' (emphasis in original). He went on:

> The very greatest seem to be those who come at the climax of one age, but this is because the new age has grown up inside the old and they are watching both. This was the case with Melville. The old heroic individualist America he knew; but he could see as artists see that the old individualism was breeding a new individualism, an individualism which would destroy society.
>
> ... the greatness of a writer is revealed by the fact that peering and probing until he finds what he considers the fundamental types of his own period, he portrays what we in later years can see as the ancestors of what exist in our own world. (p. 76)

Explanations such as these presuppose the great writers of imaginative fiction to be inhabiting a kind of double consciousness. They live, or come to understand that they live, not strictly in two mental locations, but simultaneously in two historical times – the single vision catching in the same moment the old and the new.

Moby-Dick was first published in 1851. James saw it as an imaginative artefact constituted in the social and political crisis that preceded the Civil War (p. 82). This was a period to which he himself was drawn, having earlier planned and begun drafting a play about Harriet Tubman, in the style of his earlier drama on Toussaint.[24] As the historiography attests, this was not merely a conjunctural crisis, of short-term consequence. But nor was it, in James's view, only a crisis in the medium-term, out of which, after the spilling of much blood, there occurred a fundamental renegotiation of the founding principles of the nation. Rather he understood the 1850s and 1860s in America to mark a historical transition of epochal significance, not merely affecting the US nation-state, but launching a new phase in the organisation of the world-system.

TOTALITARIAN MASTERY

From this pivotal historical moment, James perceived the emergence of a nascent corporatism in which the human and natural world increasingly came to be mastered by an irrational drive for ever-greater productivity.[25] At the core of this system was the subjugation of men and women in the labour process itself, subsumed for every minute and every second by the dominance of exchange-value. James, borrowing from a European commentator, called this, in its complete form, 'Fordism' (p. 171). The organisation and management of labour required, he believed, the whole of the society to work as an integrated system, so that inherited divisions – between public and private, economics and politics, labour and leisure – fell away, and huge bureaucracies ordered the workings of everyday life. Every aspect of social life was caught up in a crazed, incessant Promethean transformation from which there could be no respite. Surveying his own America of the mid twentieth century, James concluded that at every point free association was under threat, confronted by 'so huge an apparatus of economic, social and political institutions that the freedom of the individual except in the most abstract terms does not exist' (p. 106).

This conception of modernity was based on a relatively simple temporal schema. James opened *American Civilization* by declaring:

> The American civilization is identified in the consciousness of the world with two phases of the development of world history.
> The first is the Declaration of Independence.
> The second is mass production. (p. 27)

Fundamentally in this scenario, the democratic moment of 1776 comes to be displaced by the arrival of mass production – a transformation prefigured imaginatively by Melville in his literary creation of Ahab. Thus, in *Mariners*, James is quick to point out that Ahab, the embodiment of the new phase of American life, signifies the destruction of the democratic promise of the new nation. Ahab was a man of Quaker upbringing.

His ancestors are among those who founded the United States. He was born about 1790 in New England. He therefore grew up in the period of expanding freedom after the War of Independence. America was the freest country in the world, and above all, in freedom of opportunity.[26]

Or again, looking back from his own moment of the middle of the twentieth century to the founding of the nation, he claimed it could offer no greater contrast to 'the heroic frontiersman, trader, sailor and artisan striving to be a capitalist of the early days' (p. 106). Thus *Moby-Dick* was to be situated, for James, deep inside the decisive transformation in the making of modern America, when the emergent social regime of mass labour first began to shatter the old, and when the present began to turn inside-out the democratic values of the past. *Moby-Dick* was both made possible by this particular conjuncture of historical forces, and – due to the greatness of Melville's own vision – it also announced to the world that it was occurring.

This world-historical reading of Melville is pure James. It is wonderful for its own largeness of vision, inviting us to consider how barely perceptible, deep historical forces entered, and were given form by, an individual human imagination. It is, at the same time, vulnerable on a number of more strictly historiographical grounds. In conventional historical terms, the chronologies James establishes must be open to doubt. He never makes it clear why 1851, or even the 1850s, should carry the burden of this epochal transformation. There is a convenience about this chronology, in validating the circumstances of *Moby-Dick*, which is overbearing. He was easily drawn to reading history through the figures of the epic literary imagination: Prometheus, Lear … and Toussaint. His determination to privilege Ahab analytically works to the same effect. In *American Civilization* it is apparent throughout that his conception of the evolution of the fully administered regime of the new American modernity was pitched at a relatively high level of abstraction; details of timing were never at issue.

Eighteen-fifty-one functioned as the symbolic moment of transition. The period from 1876 to 1919 demarcated the years when the new 'statism' was consolidated in American life (pp. 104, 105). And 1929 opened a new phase in the organisation of these general social tendencies, when their full barbarism was let loose. Thus James's estimation of another universal figure, in this instance Charlie Chaplin, was neatly bifurcated by the social collapse of 1929: before, his movies contained 'elements of the future' and defied the mechanised socialisation of everyday life; after 1929, they exhibited an increasing sentimentality. The earlier films, for James, represented 'the happy, carefree attitude of the United States up to 1929 (with its undercurrent of frustration and tragedy but not strong enough to dominate the emotions)' (pp. 132–5, 136–7).

These are curious formulations, in which the bad new days are counterposed, with precious little sense of complexity (and that in parentheses), to the good old days – 'heroic' and 'carefree'. James's attempts to reimagine the forces that had shaped American history were part and parcel of his own emancipation, as he believed it, from the intellectual constraints of Trotsky's Marxism. Yet we can also detect a vestige, or more, of the customary Trotskyist sensibility, in which the founding moment of freedom – the democratic breakthrough of the 1770s – is betrayed, and greater subservience follows.

These reservations are important, but they don't detract from the insights that follow. James understood American modernity to be a social system orchestrated by unreason, in which every facet of life was stamped by the irrationalities inherent in the productive process. Due to the complexity and intensified exploitation of the new mass labourer, its management required the integration of the whole of social life: the state, education, the family, private time, and so on. The integration of state and society was what made private and civic relations political as never before. 'This inter-relation of everything is a fundamental characteristic of our society', he wrote to Webb; 'And politics, art, life, love, in the modern world, all become so closely integrated that to understand one is to understand all.'[27] Or in *American Civilization*: 'Politics today comprises *all* aspects of life ...' (p. 141). This is what he meant by totalitarian: as much as on the *Pequod*, nothing remained untouched by the thrall of unreasoned mastery. But the 'integration' of life also carried within it the seeds of its own transcendence, prefiguring a future in which civilisation would overcome barbarism. It would require a politics sufficiently expansive to extend its reach to 'all aspects of life'. More particularly, and more provocatively, James perceived the potential for salvation: in the institutions of mass culture.

James always believed that the height of civilisation had been attained in ancient Greece, for Athenian society exemplified the democratic integration of politics and aesthetics, inseparable from life itself. Evidence for this completeness of life could be found not only on the Greek stage, but also in the classical appreciation of sport as a properly social activity. The dispute with Trotsky at Coyoacan on the politics of sport was for James a deeply serious matter, which must have influenced his later departure from the ranks. As a young boy, as he himself conceded, he had harboured vivid fantasies that it had been by misfortune that he had been born in colonial Trinidad, and that Greece was, by rights, his true home. This admission directly follows his account of the discussion with Trotsky:

> I believed that if when I left school I had gone into the society of Ancient Greece I would have been more at home than ever I have been since. It was a fantasy, but for me it had meaning. The world we lived in and Ancient Greece.

Unravelling the source of this fantasy prompted him to set about reimagining what cricket had meant to him, the project realised in *Beyond a Boundary*. 'The first task', however, 'was to get Greece clear.'[28] Greece was for James exactly what America was not. And yet in America the advances in the mechanical means for cultural reproduction – the record industry, the radio, the movies – had, he was convinced, created the possibilities for unifying the aesthetic realm with the life of the people.

When he opened his chapter on 'Popular Arts and Modern Society' in *American Civilization*, James informed the reader that it stood as the 'climax' of his narrative (p. 118). It was in popular art, he maintained, that the 'deep social responses' of the nation were mirrored, not in the work of recognised literary artists. This denigration of writers and of formally accredited intellectuals runs through *American Civilization*. In this passage he specifically cited Eliot and Hemingway, but the charge is a constant one throughout his American writings, and few authors of stature escaped his indictment (p. 119). The value he accorded to popular forms was given a certain polemical force by this concomitant disregard for established literary figures. Yet his was neither a simple populism nor a philistinism. His reading of modern literature was comprehensive, across all genres, his engagements with aesthetic questions serious and informed; and there were many authors he personally admired very much, including Eliot and Hemingway. His argument was based on two distinct propositions. First, he believed that modern writers, as a social grouping, were divorced from the principal currents of popular life. This is why he understood Ishmael to be symptomatic of an entire sociology of intellectual history.[29] His latter-day descendants could see, but could not act. Even when professing progressive causes they were incapable, in James's terms, of integrating their art with the new world that existed, buried and unformed, within the old.[30] Many of the most resourceful, even, were condemned only to repeat what had gone before – as James indicated in his claim that Norman Mailer's character of Croft, in *The Naked and the Dead*, was nothing more than a weak repetition of Ahab (p. 266-7). Second he saw intellectuals more generally as mental workers, placed in a society in which the organisation of mental work was functional to the continued exploitation of manual labour, in factory or field. Administrators, bureaucrats and ideologues of all stripes were required to keep the productive complex, in all its social dimensions, on the move. In consequence, they had for James a special responsibility for the increasingly totalitarian direction of American society.

Intellectuals, in this Jamesian scenario, do not get a good press. However, his analysis is not far distant from Gramsci's better known distinction between traditional and organic intellectuals. James's modern-day Ishmaels matched exactly Gramsci's notion of the traditional intellectual – formed by institutions created in an earlier society, continuing into the present, but separated from all that is vital in their own times.[31] Those whom James condemned as functional to the business of managing the new, social collective labourer were akin to Gramsci's organic intellectuals – and indeed, both James and Gramsci identified those mental workers associated with Fordism, and with the corporate state characteristic of the Fordist era, as a peculiarly modern manifestation of this type of intellectual.[32] While Gramsci was explicit that, in addition, there existed a stratum of intellectuals organic to the forces seeking a democratic future, James tended to assume this by implication. On occasion, though, he too can be found identifying those intellectuals who 'express in scientific, artistic and political form the ideas which spring from new economic and social developments' (p. 226). But both knew that *this* intellectual would be different in form – in function as well as in outlook – from the traditional man of letters, whose only raison d'être was to cultivate his own sensibilities.

MASS CULTURE

Every so often James – in 'prophetic' or 'ecclesiastical' mood, in Derek Walcott's words – would issue confident proclamations that philosophy was at an end, or that the age of great literature had passed.[33] It's not that James was hostile to either, in themselves. But he did believe that, insofar as their structure of thought was based on abstraction and divorced from the realities imposed by history, they were in essence outmoded. Philosophically he followed Marx, in supposing that abstracted truth would, at the moment of social emancipation, become realised in history, embodied in the actions of the oppressed. But actually existing Americanised mass culture, he insisted, was neither abstracted nor divorced from the lived historical realities of the people. In 1932, on first arriving in Britain, James had subscribed to a typically British common-sense viewpoint about the vulgarity of the Americans. There is no evidence, however, of this recidivism being manifest at any moment during his years in the United States. From very early on, he became a keen wireless listener, expressing a pleasure for US radio with an enthusiasm he had never mustered for its British counterpart.[34] Soap operas and movies entered his soul. 'The movies, even the most absurd Hollywood movies are an expression of life', he wrote in a letter to Constance Webb,

> and being made for people who pay their money, they express what the people need – that is what the people miss in their own lives … Like all art, but more than most, the movies are not merely a reflection, but an extension of the actual, but an extension along the lines which people feel are lacking and *possible* in the actual.[35]

Movie-goers, he insisted, were not 'passive recipients', and he found it 'totally unhistorical' to assume that they were. 'The idea that movie-makers spend their time thinking about how to use movies in order to maintain capitalist society is nonsense' (pp. 122, 123). The predicament of American individualism was, in this period, played out most fully – in its symbolic dimensions – within the popular arts. The true heirs to Shakespeare and Melville he deemed to be Chaplin and D.W. Griffith.[36] This was not 'a matter of making futile comparisons between the relative aesthetic values of Shakespeare and Chaplin', but a question of how they were positioned, and positioned themselves, in world history.[37] The early fictionalised character of Charlie Chaplin, the private detective living in the shadows of the mean streets, the cowboy in the western – all represented an emergent universal expression of the true American individualism, which had been obliterated in the drive for irrational mastery.

> … in modern popular art, film, radio, television, comic strip, we are headed for some such artistic comprehensive integration of modern life, that the

spiritual, intellectual, ideological life of modern peoples will express itself in the closest and most rapid, most complex, absolutely free relation to the actual life of the citizens tomorrow. In fact it cannot be escaped. It is being done in the totalitarian states already. But whereas among the Greeks free expression was the basis of intellectual life, the integrated expression of the totalitarian states is the result of the suppression of free expression. In one case, therefore, we have perhaps the greatest intellectual civilization known to history; in the other case, we have barbarism ... We have now reached a state in modern society where this integration must take place or the complexity and antagonisms of society will destroy the personality. Society is already on the road to ruin through its inability to resolve the contradictions which are preventing this integration. (pp. 150–1)

What James described as the 'comprehensive integration of modern life' meant that, more than ever, politics operated in all domains of social activity: it was, essentially, displaced. In turn, the movements of world history, he seemed to be saying, had come to be located more deeply within the everyday experiences of the mass of the people. His aspiration for a new politico-cultural form, with the capacity to express the actual needs and longings of the American people – universally – gave no sign of diminishing. This is what, in James's mind, modernity made possible. It carried the potential that the comprehensive humanity once known in the ancient world might be realised in the new social conditions of modern life. The conceptual and political shift apparent in *American Civilization*, though, turned on the belief that this future could be imagined not only through the emblematic heroes of great tragic fiction, but within the everyday practices of modern life itself: in which people fell in love, went to the movies, ordered ravioli and meatballs. For in this everyday world the yearning for the new, free from the dominion of unreason, existed everywhere on the surface.[38]

RACE

Two questions remain. The first arises from the issue of race. James, like other West Indians in his pan-African circle, saw no pressing need to connect the subjective injuries he experienced as a result of racism with the political task of securing black emancipation. The obligations of the latter required the former to be brushed aside as of no political consequence. This understanding of the politics of race remained unchanged throughout his years in the United

States, despite his growing appreciation of the political significance of the individual self. He had been invited to America specifically to participate in the Negro struggle. His early commitments were militantly pan-African. But he was conscious of himself as a black man who had been formed within the British world. He perceived the US as no black native son or daughter could. He claimed, in retrospect, that he hadn't really understood 'the question of race or what real racial prejudice was until I had been to the United States'.[39] He recognised that 'America is the most fanatically race-conscious country in the world', while at the same time giving the impression that he was not personally implicated.[40] Faced with the prospect of travelling through the South, from New Orleans to New York on his return from Coyoacan, he confessed to feeling 'a slight nervousness' – adding, 'I shall get through of course, unless someone goes out of his way to annoy me ...'[41] He was aware that he didn't behave like an American negro, and we can sense that he took some pride in the confusion this created. Many years after the event he recounted this story of his time in a black neighbourhood in South Carolina:

> I used to go into town to buy this or that paper and I used to walk back past a man who owned a shop. I had been staying there for some weeks and after a while when I would go up to the town I would say to this man: 'Hello, how are you?' We would talk a bit and one day he said: 'You are no Negro, you know.' I answered: 'What are you talking about?' He said: 'You are a black man it is true, but you are not a Negro.' I questioned him. I said: 'What makes you think that?' He replied: 'From the way you walk along here. You are not one of these Negro fellows.' I had some general idea of what he was talking about.[42]

He worked politically with many black militants, and in so doing sustained some of his most important friendships in the United States. Various collaborative publishing plans were mooted with Richard Wright, Ralph Ellison and others. Wright, it appears, was always ready to talk about the personal costs of racism. James was more reticent. According to Constance Webb he expressed astonishment at the length at which she and Wright discussed the matter, with James present but not wishing to participate: '[I]t never preoccupied him'.[43] And yet we also know from her accounts – if not from his – that, as we might have assumed, James did indeed find himself immediately confronted by racial hostility:

Nello and I were married by a justice of the peace in New Jersey with two bigoted policemen as witnesses. They almost dared us to kiss after the ceremony and became red in the face with anger when we did so. Neither of us really wanted to exhibit our personal feelings, simply wanted to get away as quickly as possible. But neither could we allow such blatant and rampant bigotry to go unnoticed. In some fear and trembling we embraced, brushed our mouths together quickly, and hurried out of sight. Our fear was real, not imagined. As far away as Greenwich Village, a most bohemian liberal area, black and white couples were being attacked and beaten, often dragged from restaurants. And New Jersey was notorious for its hatred of blacks, particularly when they coupled with whites.[44]

James's attempts to integrate all aspects of his analysis of modern life could not overcome his own reticence about race. His ambivalence is striking. Many sympathetic to James are shocked how, alongside Charlie Chaplin, he could elevate D.W. Griffith as one of the great universal American artists when his most famous film, *The Birth of a Nation* (1915), worked explicitly to heroise the Ku Klux Klan.[45] One can read *American Civilization* and know nothing of the film's allegiance to the dictates of white supremacy, nor of the political mobilisation by black political groups to ban it from being screened. 'Griffith', claimed James, 'writes the epic of the ordinary man' (p. 248). James's reading is entirely formalist. But something of his ambivalence is caught in his wry observation that he would picket the movie in the morning, then sneak back to watch it at a later showing.

American Civilization directly addressed the Negro question, with James arguing for the necessary autonomy of black politics. 'The Negro struggle has a validity, a strength, a democratic, a "socialistic" value in itself.'[46] At the same time he envisaged that, because of their social position in the United States, blacks would play a leading role in the socialist struggle, just as they had throughout in the making of the West. The black churches he believed to be exemplary manifestations of the American spirit of free association. Indeed, his early pan-African emphasis diminished as he came to see the specifically American elements of the struggle for black emancipation.

No greater torture for an American could be devised than that which the American Negroes suffer, to see others no better than they have the elementary rights of which they are deprived. The twisted bitterness of the Negro people is an index of the suppressed angers which permeate the vast majority of the nation. In the passion of the church services and singing of the very poor, in the responses to the great Negro bands in dance-halls and sometimes in theaters in the Negro districts, can be felt a passion, a tremendous elemental social force, which many who note it, like to fancy is primitive, of the jungle. It is nothing of the kind. It is modern Americanism. (p. 209)

This determination to understand that blacks historically had been active in the making of modern America, that they were in his own times fully modern subjects, and that in the future they would take a leading role in bringing about freedom for all: this for James was axiomatic. It is of the first importance.

But if the argument is pushed too insistently the difference between black and white is effaced. All are American, all are modern, and the only thing that distinguishes the locations of black and white in modernity is a matter of degree. Something of this conflation is apparent in the temporal structure outlined in *American Civilization*. Within the text, the Civil War functions as the pivotal historical moment in which the fate of the new nation was determined. In making the case, James argued that this was due to the fact that, in the aftermath, capitalist accumulation took off in the North, allowing 'the popular masses' to be 'slowly disciplined by big capital'.[47] In this reading, neither slavery nor abolition appears as a decisive issue, which reflects a puzzling judgement from the author of *The Black Jacobins*.[48] His is a perspective centrally organised around the North: it turns on the development of the capitalist mode of production, in its Northern variant, and on the consequent imposition of a new phase of modernity. The 'popular masses' appear to be the workers of the North – the 'ordinary' white men of Griffith's preconceptions – rather than the slaves who had been disciplined by the plantation, or the freed men and women locked into the subservice of the share-cropping system: the 'one-eighth of the whole population' to whom Lincoln made tribute in his second inaugural, a speech much admired by James. It is difficult to imagine the blacks in the South finding themselves in a position to enjoy the fruits of the 'carefree' republic which James lauded, or looking back to the heroic, founding moments of the democratic nation. For whom had America been 'the freest country in the world'? The stress of his recounting of the Civil War falls on the winners who functioned as the agents of modernisation. Black America, in this scenario, has no sociological specificity: it is destined merely to follow in the wake of the dynamic modernisers of the North. It's not that James denied the self-activity of the blacks,[49] but his interpretation leaves little room for understanding anything other than the vision of modernity inspired by the victors in the North. Within this frame, one can see how James could imagine American Negroes *participating* in the fulfilment of the project that an irrational, unfinished modernity had bequeathed. But would they create an America in their own image? Where did their bid for universality find expression?[50] On these questions James was silent. This may turn out to be as much about 'Westernness' – or its close cognate, modernity – as it is about race per se, as James's friend Richard Wright was to discover. James was always alert to the agency of the black masses. But, characteristically, this was an agency he imagined to be exercised within a field of activity inscribed in his own preconceptions of what modern civilisation represented. This remained for him, essentially, the classical Western lineage. That this offered much there can be no doubt, for it is the source of much of the vitality of James's thought. That it also limited what was possible must also be true. In Wright's words,

To be a functioning and organic part of something is to be almost unconscious of it. I was a part, intimate but separate, of the Western world, but I seldom had to account for my Westernness, had rarely found myself in situations which challenged me to do so.[51]

In America James's intellect underwent many extraordinary transformations. Like Adorno and Horkheimer, he knew the dangers that modern life carried deep within itself. But the terms on which he felt called upon to account for *his own* investments in the civilisation that had nurtured him remain difficult to fathom. These difficulties mark the limit-point of James's political imagination. This, however, he knew well enough himself, for why else – in his later years – would he claim as his own the identity of 'black European'?[52]

JAMES'S MARXISM

The relations between race and modernity present one overarching issue that arises from James's reading of American civilisation. A second concerns the theoretical resources he drew upon to develop his study. In seeking to break from both Stalinism and Trotskyism, James returned to the idealist traditions, particularly to Hegel, from which Marx's own thought had emerged. Theoretically, this was a procedure typical of much of the aptly known Western Marxism of the mid twentieth century. This was a body of thought which – in reaction against the hard, positivist materialism of official Soviet Communism – endeavoured to reconnect Marxism to a more directly human conception of social life, in which human agency and the activity of the human imagination assumed a renewed centrality. Gramsci's prolonged encounter with the philosophical idealism of Benedetto Croce, for example, was symptomatic, re-enacting for Gramsci the theoretical journey that Marx himself had undergone in *his* critique of Hegel. To this extent, James was a paradigmatic Western Marxist.[53]

In 1948, a year before he started working on *American Civilization*, he published in mimeographed form his long analysis of Hegel, *Notes on the Dialectic*.[54] Many in the James camp regard this as a work of great standing. This is not my position. Although it may have served James well politically, I am not persuaded by its philosophical value, and this, after all, was the purpose of the book: to clear the rubble so that he could grasp the philosophical foundation of what Marx was about. There is no point in rehearsing these disagreements here. The perceived need to return to Hegel, and to read Marx through Hegel, was not at this time James's perception alone, but a common theoretical strategy impelled by a wish to see Marxism reinvigorated, freed from a politics subservient to Stalinism. Even if one is skeptical of the way that James conducted this as a philosophical venture, there can be no doubt that it did work politically, enabling him to put at the very centre of his theoretical world the reasoning self-activity of social actors. Henceforth, his emphasis fell on the capacities of the oppressed to overcome – to 'leap' over – the givens of historical necessity.[55] Nor any longer did he imagine a politics in which an organisational vanguard was necessary in order for the people to see and make for themselves their own future. His study of the dialectic signalled the intellectual *coup de grace* for his erstwhile Trotskyism.

Within this broad, complex tradition of Western Marxism he adopted distinctive, minority political positions. His eventual conclusion that Stalin and Trotsky shared the same theoretical universe was one. His conviction that the Soviet Union reproduced the essentials of capitalism was another. For James, the Soviet Union represented 'a last desperate attempt under the guise of "socialism" and "planned economy" to reorganize the means of production without releasing the proletariat from wage-slavery'.[56] What many intellectuals of the time found to be singularly positive about the Soviet Union – the attempt to exert rational controls over economic life – James considered to be most destructive:

> Their primary aim is not world revolution. They wish to build factories and power stations larger than all others which have been built. They aim to connect rivers, to remove mountains, to plant from the air, and to achieve these they will waste human and material resources on an unprecedented scale. Their primary aim is not war. It is not dictatorship. It is the Plan. In pursuit of what they call planning the economy, they have depopulated Russia of tens of millions of workers, peasants, and officials so that it seems as if some pestilence sweeps periodically across the country. In pursuit of their plan, they have placed and intend to keep millions in concentration camps. Their purpose is to plan.[57]

Productivism like this was anathema to James. It was indeed Ahab in another guise, given to mastery for no other purpose but mastery itself. So far as he was concerned it was here, not in the institutions of mass culture, where the categorical collapse of reason into unreason occurred.

The precondition for countering productivism, in the US and in the USSR, James concluded, was to understand that the economy was based upon the sensuous activity of the labourer. Labour needed to be conceived in itself as a human activity, directed towards the human end of self-realisation. It was about the socially creative process, not about its instrumental ends. Any division of labour that compromised this led, he maintained, not simply to misery in the workplace but to the burgeoning system that he described as totalitarian. The contradiction between barbarism and civilisation was rooted in the act of labour, for it was in the labour process itself that exploitation prevailed, and that the humanity of the workers was stripped from them.

> That is the whole secret of present society. It took me years to learn. The productive capacity is solved. The problem is not a higher standard of living or no unemployment. The problem ... the strictly scientific, *economic* problem, the solution of the capitalist crisis, lies in precisely the recognition of man as MAN. That is Marxism, that is Marx's philosophic theory, that is his economic theory, that is his political theory.[58]

James wrote this in 1944. He took it, as he made clear, to be the core of Marxism: not just as a politically inspired interpretation, but as its very truth.

This Marxist humanism cohered in James's mind in the middle years of the 1940s, and it remained with him, without serious revision, for the rest of his intellectual life. Those familiar with Marx will recognise the proximity between the positions James arrived at in the 1940s and those adumbrated by the young Marx 100 years beforehand, in the 1840s. This is not by chance.[59]

Those most immediately connected to James in his political grouping, the Johnson–Forest Tendency, were the intellectuals in New York. At some distance, but an organic part of the collective political life of the group, were the car workers in Detroit. The workers on the line received, and were expected collectively to discuss, the political theses – and the more general philosophical ruminations – produced by the New York branch. They would come off their shift, open the packages of the instalments of James's mimeographed thoughts on the Hegelian dialectic, which ran to many pages, and read them through the night. As Martin Glaberman recalled:

> I can still remember when I saw the first draft of *Notes on Dialectics*. I was drilling holes in crankshafts at the Buick Division of General Motors in Flint, Michigan ... The impact was unbelievable. Rereading it over thirty years later, it still makes a powerful impression. On the days that a section of the document came in the mail we would sit up late into the night reading and discussing it. Each day we would wait for the mail to see if another section had come. That was pretty remarkable for a book that was difficult then and is difficult now (although it is not as difficult as taking Hegel neat).[60]

This required not just stamina, but a kind of intellect that we, in a later age, might properly marvel at. In turn, the Detroit workers would write about their own experiences on the frontline of Fordism, and send their writings to the New York intellectuals, who would incorporate the findings into their philosophical explorations. If these exchanges still reproduced the divisions between mental and manual labour, they also signified an attempt to reflect on what these disparities in power meant, and to elaborate a politics that worked towards their transcendence. In the course of this philosophical work, James and his collaborators, Raya Dunayevskaya and Grace Lee, got to hear of the existence of Marx's *Economic and Philosophic Manuscripts of 1844*. They did so first from reading, and then by corresponding with,

Herbert Marcuse – who, we should remember, was also one of the exiles from Frankfurt, close intellectually at this time to Adorno and Horkheimer.[61] These early *Manuscripts* of Marx were not then widely known, and certainly not in the English-speaking world: no full translation appeared until the early 1960s. Dunayevskaya prepared an early, though partial, translation in May 1943, which underwent a number of revisions at the hands of Lee, and which was then eventually published by the Johnson–Forest group in the summer of 1947. This was a text of Marx's which caused much excitement among radical scholars in the 1960s, when it appeared in full: James had published portions of it some 20 years earlier, and absorbed its arguments long before most English speakers had even known of its existence.

Marx's central thesis in 1844 had been on the estrangement, or alienation, of the labourer in the moment of labour itself. He argued that the commodity produced by the workers exercised a power over them, divesting them of their humanity: they themselves became reified, estranged from what was essentially human within their own selves. This estrangement, according to Marx, was a social as much as a subjective, psychological process; and it led not only to estrangement within the self, but also to the alienation of worker from worker. The political project, in consequence, needed to restore the humanity of the workers, collectively and individually. This required the evolution of a non-alienated form of collective 'association' – 'free association', in James's Marxisant rendering of Tocqueville – and the maximal encouragement of human creativity, both within the labour process, and in the wider sense of men and women producing, or realising, themselves as social beings in the body politic as a whole.[62] In 1947, in his published commentary on the *Manuscripts*, James employed these categories to give conceptual shape to his characteristic reading of American civilisation, insisting that Marx's humanism lay at the core of his economic theory.[63]

James took these early theorisations of Marx's as his own, providing his gloss on them in order that they could illuminate contemporary realities a century after Marx. It is in America that we can see him engaged in the theoretical work that would carry him through to *Beyond a Boundary*. The battle between civilisation and barbarism was rooted for James in the activity and organisation of labour. Modernity, in this perspective, with its strong Hegelian input, was the incomplete story of humanity's progressive self-realisation, in which men and women would ultimately become reconciled with their own humanity.

> We are the fruit of 2000 years – not to go back further. The classical world was very different from ours. The large mass of men were slaves. They were not considered as human. To-day every person is theoretically a human being, with human rights. They are often deprived of these rights. But at least, theoretically, they are ours. It took the ruin of the Graeco-Roman civilization to establish that.[64]

What had been conceded in thought needed to be made actual.

James's elaboration of a Marxist humanism was conducted without the sophisticated philosophical learning that many of its more famous practitioners possessed, and he knew full well that he was 'no philosopher'.[65] He was, as we have seen, skeptical about the virtues of formal philosophy, favouring what he termed 'the habit of the concrete'.[66] It came into being in the United States – in New York, California and Nevada – rather than in continental Europe, and these American realities pressed in. Its purpose was political, consciously deployed as part of a day-to-day political struggle. And a black man from the British Empire, who was proud to declare his allegiance to the civilisation of Europe, authored it. If in form James was a paradigmatic Western Marxist, his blackness and his locations further complicated this already complex designation. As much as Frantz Fanon – West Indian too – his Marxist humanism took him to unexpected places.

NOTES

An earlier version of this essay appeared in *Atlantic Studies*, vol. 2:1 (2005), pp. 15–43. *Atlantic Studies* is published by Taylor and Francis, http://www.tandf.co.uk/journals.

1. E.P. Thompson, 'C.L.R. James at 80', in Paul Buhle (ed.), *C.L.R. James: His Life and Work* (London: Allison & Busby, 1986), p. 249.
2. James to Lyman and Freddie Paine, and to Grace Lee and James Boggs, 24 February 1976, cited in Scott McLemee, 'Introduction', James, *On The 'Negro Question'* (Jackson: University of Mississippi Press, 1996), p. xiv.
3. Kent Worcester, *C.L.R. James: A Political Biography* (New York: State University of New York Press, 1996), pp. 50–1.
4. Ibid.
5. C.L.R. James, *Beyond a Boundary* (London: Stanley Paul, 1968), p. 128.
6. James, 'Return of a Wanderer: Comparisons between 1938 and 1953', first published in the Manchester *Guardian*, 7 October 1953; reprinted in C.L.R. James, *Cricket* (London: Allison & Busby, 1989), p. 71.

7. James, *Beyond a Boundary*, pp. 29, 48.
8. Constance Webb gives a different impression, suggesting that the book was to be 'our own', rather than having the imprimatur of James's political groupuscule, the Johnson–Forest Tendency, and was to have been published commercially. See *Not Without Love: A Memoir* (Lebanon, NH: University Press of New England, 2003), p. 238.
9. C.L.R. James, *American Civilization* (Oxford: Blackwell, 1983), pp. 26, 38. Subsequent page references are provided in parentheses in the text.
10. See Anna Grimshaw and Keith Hart, 'American Civilization: An Introduction' and Robert Hill, 'Literary Executor's Afterword', both in James, *American Civilization*.
11. Webb, *Not Without Love*, p. 252.
12. Though for contrary views, with which I concur, see Hill, 'Afterword', pp. 293, 325; Grimshaw and Hart, 'Introduction', pp. 16–19; and Grant Farred, 'The Maple Man: How Cricket Made a Postcolonial Intellectual', in Farred (ed.), *Rethinking C.L.R. James* (Oxford: Blackwell, 1996), p. 205.
13. James, *Beyond a Boundary*, p. 149.
14. Letter from James to Webb, April 1944: C.L.R. James, *Special Delivery: The Letters of C.L.R. James to Constance Webb* (Oxford: Blackwell, 1996), p. 111.
15. Letter from James to Webb, 4 January 1940, in James, *Special Delivery*, p. 64.
16. See C.L.R. James, 'With the Sharecroppers' (1941), in Scott McLemee (ed.), *C.L.R. James On the 'Negro Question'* (Jackson: University of Mississippi Press, 1996). C.L.R. James, George Breitman, Edgar Keemer et al., *Fighting Racism in World War II* (New York: Monad Press, 1980) contains four early articles by James on the black struggle.
17. Letter from James to Webb, 28 July 1944, in James, *Special Delivery*, p. 167.
18. James, *Mariners, Renegades and Castaways: The Story of Herman Melville and the World We Live In* (Detroit: Bewick/ed, 1978), pp. 81, 99, 139.
19. Cited in James, *Mariners, Renegades and Castaways*, pp. 91–2. The passage can be found in Herman Melville, *Redburn: His First Voyage* (Evanston and Chicago: Northwestern University Press and The Newberry Library, 1969), p. 169.
20. James, *American Civilization*, p. 83. The passage James refers to comes from Herman Melville, *Moby-Dick* (London: Penguin, 1994), pp. 401–5.
21. These points are made by William E. Cain in 'The Triumph of the Will and the Failure of Resistance: C.L.R. James's Readings of *Moby-Dick* and *Othello*', in Selwyn Cudjoe and Cain (eds), *C.L.R. James: His Intellectual Legacies* (Amherst: University of Massachusetts Press, 1995).
22. Melville, *Moby-Dick*, p. 404.
23. S.S. Prawer, *Karl Marx and World Literature* (Oxford: Clarendon Press, 1976), pp. 94, 181; Georg Lukács, *The Historical Novel* (London: Merlin Press, 1962), pp. 32, 41. At one time Marx planned to write a study of Balzac's *Human Comedy*.
24. Letters from James to Webb, 15 December 1943, 4 February 1944, and March or April 1944, in James, *Special Delivery*, pp. 82–4, 95–100 and 100–1.

25. The most concise political expressions of these theorisations can be found in C.L.R. James, F. Forest (Raya Dunayevskaya), and Ria Stone (Grace Lee), *The Invading Socialist Society* (Detroit: Bewick/ed, 1972; first published 1947); and C.L.R. James, Raya Dunayevskaya and Grace Lee, *State Capitalism and World Revolution* (Chicago: Charles Kerr, 1986; first published 1950). I can't address here James's important critique of the official Communist movement that, fundamentally, equated the totalitarianism of the US system with that of Stalinism.
26. James, *Mariners, Renegades and Castaways*, p. 2.
27. Letter from James to Webb, 14 June 1944, in James, *Special Delivery*, p. 123.
28. James, *Beyond a Boundary*, pp. 43, 151–2.
29. For a clear indication of the overarching argument, see James's 'Neurosis and the Intellectuals', Chapter 5 of *Mariners, Renegades and Castaways*.
30. There are many instances, but for an encapsulation of the greatest economy, see C.L.R. James, 'To and From the Finland Station: A Review of *To the Finland Station* by Edmund Wilson', in Scott McLemee and Paul Le Blanc, *C.L.R. James and Revolutionary Marxism: Selected Writings of C.L.R. James, 1939–1949* (Atlantic Highlands, NJ: Humanities Press, 1994).
31. See especially James, *American Civilization*, p. 261.
32. Antonio Gramsci, 'Americanism and Fordism', in his *Selections From the Prison Notebooks* (London: Lawrence & Wishart, 1971).
33. Derek Walcott, 'A Tribute to C.L.R. James', in Cudjoe and Cain, *C.L.R. James*, p. 38; C.L.R. James, Grace Lee and Pierre Chaulieu, *Facing Reality* (Detroit: Bewick/ed, 1974; first published 1958), p. 65; and James, *American Civilization*, pp. 265–6.
34. Letter from James to Webb, undated [April 1939], in James, *Special Delivery*, pp. 45–7.
35. Letter from James to Webb, 1 September 1943, in James, *Special Delivery*, p. 73.
36. Thus he began his 1954 Paris lecture: 'I propose to show that artistic creation in the great tradition of Aeschylus and Shakespeare finds its continuation today in films by D.W. Griffith, Charlie Chaplin and Eisenstein.' C.L.R. James, 'Popular Arts and the Cultural Tradition', in Anna Grimshaw (ed.), *The C.L.R. James Reader* (Oxford: Blackwell, 1992), p. 249; and James, *American Civilization*, p. 35.
37. James, 'Popular Arts', p. 250.
38. See especially letter from James to Webb, undated 1944, in James, *Special Delivery*, p. 192.
39. C.L.R. James, 'Africans and Afro-Caribbeans: A Personal View', *Ten.8*, 16 (1984), p. 54.
40. Letter from James to Webb, 1944, in James, *Special Delivery*, p. 182.
41. Letter from James to Webb, undated [April 1939], in James, *Special Delivery*, p. 45.
42. James, 'Africans and Afro-Caribbeans', p. 54; and for a comparable recollection of him, Paul Buhle, *C.L.R. James: The Artist as Revolutionary* (London: Verso, 1993), p. 74.
43. Webb, *Not Without Love*, p. 133.

44. Cited in Selwyn Cudjoe, '"As Ever Darling, All My Love, Nello": The Love Letters of C.L.R. James', in Cudjoe and Cain, *James: His Intellectual Legacies*, p. 232. But see too James's letter to Webb, 2 August 1948, in James, *Special Delivery*, p. 313.
45. Conversation with George Lamming, Atlantis Hotel, Bathsheba, Barbados, 28 August 2001.
46. Letter from James to Webb, February 1945, in James, *Special Delivery*, p. 203.
47. Letter from James to Webb, July 1944, in James, *Special Delivery*, p. 165. The previous year he had argued that the Civil War needed to be understood as the US bourgeois revolution – C.L.R. James, *Education, Propaganda, Agitation* (Detroit: Facing Reality, 1968), p. 33.
48. Contrast this to W.E.B. DuBois's *Black Reconstruction in America* (London: Cass, 1966), first published in 1935. It can't be that James was unaware of this, though he makes no reference to it. By 1971 he was claiming that the argument that DuBois made for blacks in the Civil War was exactly comparable to the argument that James himself made about blacks in the making of Haiti: '*The Black Jacobins* and *Black Reconstruction*: A Comparative Analysis', the second of three 'Lectures on *The Black Jacobins*', *Small Axe* 8 (2000).
49. See for example C.L.R. James, 'Negroes in the Civil War: Their Role in the Second American Revolution' (1943), in James, *The 'Negro Question'*.
50. In the 1940s *the* issue to explore in this regard would have been black popular music. James commented a little on jazz (which he believed weakened after 1929), but rather more on the classical European traditions – *American Civilization*, p. 137. There is no anticipation of the kind of arguments that, a decade later, would discuss the transition from slavery to citizenship in terms of black vernacular music, most notably in LeRoi Jones, *Blues People* (New York: Morrow, 1963).
51. Richard Wright, *Pagan Spain* (London: Bodley Head, 1960), p. 164.
52. There are a number of instances – see for example John Bracey, 'Nello', in McLemee and Le Blanc, *James and Revolutionary Marxism*, p. 52.
53. For a discussion of this tradition, which unaccountably excludes James, see Perry Anderson, *Considerations on Western Marxism* (London: Verso, 1976).
54. C.L.R. James, *Notes on the Dialectic: Hegel, Marx, Lenin* (London: Allison & Busby, 1980).
55. James, *Dialectic*, p. 148.
56. James, Dunayevskaya and Lee, *State Capitalism*, p. 7.
57. James, *Marines, Renegades and Castaways*, p. 12.
58. Letter from James to Webb, undated [1944], in James, *Special Delivery*, p. 138.
59. In what follows I have been much influenced by the analysis of Robert Hill, 'Literary Executor's Afterword', pp. 312–19.
60. Martin Glaberman, 'Review of *Notes on Dialectics*', *Race and Class* 23:1 (1981), p. 97.
61. For the correspondence with Marcuse, see Aldon Lynn Nielsen, *C.L.R James: A Critical Introduction* (Jackson: University Press of Mississippi, 1997), p. 104. The decisive text here was Herbert Marcuse, *Reason and*

Revolution: Hegel and the Rise of Social Theory (New York: Oxford University Press, 1941).
62. For Marx's conceptualisations of association, see *Economic and Philosophic Manuscripts of 1844* (Moscow: Progress Publishers, 1974), p. 109.
63. C.L.R. James, 'On Marx's *Essays from the Economic-Philosophical Manuscripts*', in his *At the Rendezvous of Victory: Selected Writings* (London: Allison and Busby, 1984), p. 71.
64. Letter from James to Webb, undated [1944], in James, *Special Delivery*, p. 191.
65. Cited by Scott McLemee, 'Afterword: American Civilization and World Revolution. C.L.R. James in the United States, 1938–1953 and Beyond', in McLemee and Le Blanc, *James and Revolutionary Marxism*, p. 225.
66. Letter from James to Webb, 11 October 1947, in James, *Special Delivery*, p. 304.

7
C.L.R. James and the Politics of the Subject, Culture and Desire

Anthony Bogues

In my private mind ... I was increasingly aware of large areas of human existence that my history and my politics did not seem to cover.[1]

C.L.R. James, *Beyond a Boundary*

My objective, instead, has been to create a history of the different modes by which, in our culture, human beings are made subjects.[2]

Michel Foucault, *The Subject and Power*

Towards the end of his first American sojourn in the late 1940s, C.L.R. James became increasingly aware that, even though his theoretical and political work in what was then called the Johnson–Forest Tendency[3] had broken new ground in Marxist theory, something was amiss. In 1944 he observed in a letter to his second wife, Constance Webb, that he had become 'more and more interested in all aspects of life, as in our modern society all aspects of life become more closely inter-related'.[4] The late 1940s marked a turn in James's theoretical and political thinking.[5] This turn was shaped in part by James's efforts to grapple with a notion of politics in which there was an additional dimension to the moral economy of the proletarian revolution. This dimension revolved around the question, 'What did men live by? What did they want? What did history show that they wanted?'[6] Sylvia Wynter, in a remarkable essay on James, notes that his first question allows him to 'deabsolutize the material representation of man's identity when it asks the question central to the *cultural life* of man'.[7] It would be easy to say that James at this point was reaching for a politics of culture, for a politics and historical understanding of the human that was grounded in what Stuart Hall has suggested in his definition of culture as the 'actual grounded terrain of practices, representations, languages and customs of any specific society'. To that definition Hall adds this comment: 'I also mean the contradictionary forms of common sense which have taken root in and helped to shape popular life.'[8]

Such a position would be too facile, however, and would immediately locate James's later work as anticipatory of cultural studies. Besides, it would posit a history of ideas or intellectual genealogy in which phases smoothly flow from one into another. Moreover, this might make us miss the complex questions with which James was grappling in the late 1940s, 1950s and 1960s. These questions, I want to suggest, are framed by the post-World War II period, and revolve around the following issues: the nature of totalitarianism; the different ways in which workers' revolts (particularly the Hungarian Revolution of 1956) had raised new questions about the nature of human society and politics; and, finally, the historic meanings of the ending of colonial empires. In grappling with these questions, James executed a series of theoretical moves that allowed him to probe his own highly developed brand of independent Marxism, and then to pry open a different space that had been partly closed in the different renderings of Marxism. If, in the 1930s, Gramsci, pushed by the failures of the European proletarian revolution, asked about the nature of political consciousness and ideology, and posited the answer of hegemony, James went in another direction. Instead, he wondered about the conditions that would allow for 'self-realization, creativity based upon the incorporation into the individual personality of the whole previous development of humanity'. In this connection he would declare that 'Freedom is creative universality, *not* utility.'[9]

James's major writings and concerns between the late 1940s and the publication of *Beyond a Boundary* in 1963, therefore represented an extraordinarily fertile period in which he sought forms of political understanding of human society that were not premised upon a philosophical anthropology of material redemption, but rather upon the human as primarily a social figure, whose desire revolved around giving his or her creative powers full play. This capacity did not require the conditions of 'full' economic development, and therefore was a departure from conventional Marxist theory, since Marx, it will be remembered, envisioned the stage of communism as the decline of necessity creating the conditions for the full flowering of individual talents. James, on the other hand, signalling his shift from the laws of material redemption, dispenses with the laws of necessity and locates the human as a concrete being with possibilities in the present. The most explicit enunciation of this shift was James's increasing preoccupation with the questions of what men wanted, and the relationship of this desire to freedom.[10]

In *American Civilization* James had already signalled that freedom was the central thrust of what men lived by. He notes in a sarcastic comment in the chapter titled 'The Struggle for Happiness' that the perspective which argues that people only wanted things like better working conditions, more leisure, or security, was one that reduced '[m]ankind to the level of horses and cows with an instinct for exercise'.[11] There are two things that I think might be useful in making sense of both the shifts in James's theoretical gaze during this period (from the late 1940s to 1962) and what that gaze means for contemporary life today. We will first turn our attention to the questions of desire.

WHAT DO MEN WANT?

When James asks this question in *Beyond a Boundary*, it is immediately followed by another question: 'What do men live by?' This suggests that there is an organic connection between what men want – a form of desire – and what human beings live by. Following his usual method, James further complicates these questions by also suggesting that history had shown what it was that men wanted and lived by. But very quickly he recognises that what human beings desire and live by changes, since it is impacted upon by historical temporality. James's preoccupation with the question of what men live by is a concern about desire and its various meanings. His posing of the question is laden with assumptions of self-consciousness, and generally follows the line of Hegel's claim in the *Phenomenology of Spirit* that 'self-consciousness in general is Desire'.[12] This new gaze of James allows him to develop a theory of the human in which the core human desire establishes itself in a form of freedom that he calls the 'good life'. James observes in *Modern Politics*,

> this is some idea of what I mean by what is the good life – the individual in relationship to the society. It is *not*, it never has been, merely a question of what the vulgarians call 'raising the standard of living.' Men are not pigs to be fattened.[13] (emphasis in the original)

For James, therefore, desire was rooted in the social.

This was a different optic from that of Freud, in which desire is linked to fantasy and the productions of the unconscious. It is also different from the Lacanian position, whereby desire is the gap between need and demand, and is therefore seen as lack. Judith Butler observes that Lacan's conception of desire means 'the impossibility of a coherent subject'.[14] Gilles Deleuze and Felix Guattari, in *antioedipus*, offer a sustained critique of desire as lack or fantasy. They argue that if desire is about lack, then desire 'produces an imaginary object that functions as a double of reality'.[15] Arguing that the creation of lack is a function of the market economy and part of the 'art of a dominant class',[16] they suggest that desire 'always remains in close touch with the conditions of objective existence; it embraces them and follows them, shifts when they shift and does not outlive them'.[17] If we agree that desire is firmly within the realm of the social, then the issue that forces itself upon us is not so much the psychoanalytical one about self-formation, but rather the *political* one about subject-formation. From James's perspective, the issue becomes how the relationship between desire and freedom opens up new fields of human living, and therefore of community. I want to suggest that this is currently one of the most important political problems of the contemporary world.

The twentieth century was one in which conceptions of freedom were central to many social and political struggles. From the 1917 Russian Revolution, to the anti-colonial and anti-racist struggles, and the anti-fascist battles and feminist movements, the conceptions of freedom served both as clarion call and as a practice that would herald something new in human living. Ernesto Laclau, making a distinction between freedom and emancipation, has argued that emancipation is not an 'act of creation but instead of liberation of something which precedes the liberating act'.[18] He further makes the point that the discourses about emancipation have yoked together 'incompatible lines of thought ... the full representability of the social ... [and] the chasm which makes a social objectivity ... impossible'.[19] In the end he argues for a version of freedom that is beyond emancipation, and calls for the 'end of emancipation and [the] beginning of freedom'.[20]

James makes no such distinction, and in a 1947 essay titled 'Dialectical Materialism and the Fate of Humanity' he invokes both Marx and Hegel in asking the question, 'What is man?' His purpose in asking this was to suggest that there is an essential striving of human beings towards freedom. He writes, 'The history of man is his effort to make the abstract universal concrete. He constantly seeks to negate what impedes his movement towards freedom and happiness.'[21] For James, this freedom was to be found in two things:

firstly, the ways in which workers would control production through their self-organisation and, secondly, the closing of the perceived gap between the society and the individual. In the latter, the individual would become self-actualised. Here the question was not so much about wealth as about movement. Again taking his cue from Hegelian dialectics and Marx's notion of freedom as creating one's own nature, and therefore the actualisation of possibility in the overcoming of necessity, James observes in *Modern Politics* that '[t]he citizen is alive when he feels that he himself in his own national community is overcoming difficulties'.[22]

Self-realisation through movement, the overcoming of difficulties – these for James are the grounds of freedom. It is the drive for freedom constructed through movement that men live by. The freedom that is created by these processes is what they desire. In James's mind, this striving for freedom disconnected from the laws of necessity was missing from his earlier historical and political understandings. In spite of this recognition, James did not further explore the different ways in which freedom could be organised as a set of discourses and human practices that would rest on domination and power. In other words, he was not interested in how the possibility of the language of freedom could become a terrain for domination. It was not that desire would morph into an imaginary mirror, and therefore itself become an ideological trap, but rather that, in contemporary modernity, forms of politics could be constructed that would make efforts to shape desire itself, thereby creating modalities of power that could become regularised in everyday life. This point allows us to begin to explore questions absent from James's political thinking, concerning the nature of hegemony and its construction into various forms of rule and power.

HEGEMONY, POWER AND FREEDOM

In conventional radical thinking, the concept of hegemony is not often linked to that of language. Although hegemony is conceived as the cultural yeast of political rule, how that cultural yeast is constructed, and what layers of our social experiences it taps into, are often given secondary consideration. At other times, hegemony is conflated with ideology. Raymond Williams, however, observes that ideology is about the 'actual consciousness of both dominant and subordinated classes'.[23] Hegemony is about something more fluid and mobile – it is more about what Williams calls 'practical consciousness'. It is a 'body of practices and expectations, over the whole of living ... it is a lived system of meanings and values – constitutive and constituting'.[24] What Williams left out of this definition is the role of language and discourse in constructions of hegemony. Ludwig Wittgenstein makes the point that to imagine a language is 'to imagine a form of life'.[25] The speaking of language is therefore about forms of life, emphasising the point that Fanon makes so well in *Black Skin White Masks*, where he states that '[t]o speak means to be in a position to use a certain syntax ... but it means above all to assume a culture, to support the existing weight of a civilization'.[26] Central to language is its power to name and, as the Caribbean novelist and critic George Lamming noted, 'A name is an infinite source of control.'[27] But, given the capacities of language, what happens when freedom as a language and set of practices becomes hegemonic?

James's answer to this is to suggest, in *American Civilization*, that, '(1) freedom has been lost in modern industrial production (2) that the outstanding social fact of the United States is that the population has gone a long way on the road to recognizing that freedom has been lost'.[28] Of course, James here is unclear about the ways in which freedom has been constructed in American society. His reading of de Tocqueville's *Democracy in America* was in large measure uncritical. However, James is accurate when he observes that conceptions of freedom and liberty were foundational in the history and dominant narrative of American society. The question, however, was not about a nostalgia for lost freedoms, but rather how power shaped the content of that freedom; how freedom became a driving discourse of power in American society, and in doing so became, in Tocqueville's words, 'habits of the heart'. These habits become 'common-sense', in Gramsci's phrase. In James's words, 'The Europeans wrote and theorized about freedom in superb writings. Americans lived it.'[29] Tocqueville also wrote that the '[l]ove of Liberty defies analysis ... It is something one must feel, and logic has no part in it.'[30] It would seem to me that both Tocqueville and James, in their understandings of American freedom, were attempting to construct meanings of freedom that were attached to desire. In this sense, desire was not only Hegelian self-consciousness, but also an end in itself, once it expressed itself as freedom and a form of lived experience. But what about the meanings of freedom?

There are many historical, political and philosophical narratives about American freedom. These narratives have to be complicated, of course, by the discourses, political and social practices of those who were denied any vestiges of freedom or liberty in the American covenant – in particular the black slaves and the Native American population. The typical narrative is that, over time, the American covenant has enlarged itself, taking into its fold those who were left out at the inaugural moment. So the dominant story of American freedom is about ever-wider circles of inclusion.[31] However, there are at least two things that problematise this narrative. The first is obvious: given the nature of the exclusions and their historic length, what precisely was the nature of this lived experience of freedom? In other words, how did racial slavery shape American freedom? And the second is critical for our contemporary world: how did American freedom fold into conceptions of the providential destiny of America and its manifest destiny as the 'city on the hill?' These two things make it clear that freedom is not a neutral word that matches desire. Rather, as it becomes a hegemony framing the practices of power it must become contested. James misses this contestation or, when he acknowledges it, roots it only in mass production. For example, he observes in *American Civilization*:

> But careful investigation by trained observers … shows that political ideas of the workers are one thing, the deep responses to their work … [are] something else … Therefore, over and over again, the same workers who express as far as general politics are concerned, conservative and even reactionary sentiments will immediately turn around and express with regard to their daily work sentiments with the most revolutionary implications conceivable.[32]

James attributes this duality to the primacy of the productive process, an idea that was, of course, located in the Marxist notion that the conditions of economic life and production would force the worker to see the radical possibilities of a new society. James's formulation of the duality establishes a wall between the so-called general political and the conditions of mass production. In *American Civilization* this was to appear as a point of tension in his thought. This tension notwithstanding, James attempted to shift his gaze from political economy to the domain of popular culture. Indeed, it is the section in *American Civilization* on popular arts that has given the text its importance in what can be called 'James studies'.

In this section James establishes the argument that different art-forms (particularly film) represent, 'if only negatively … some of the deepest feelings of the masses, but represent them within common agreement – no serious political or social questions which would cause explosions'.[33] He also makes the point that 'the mass is not merely passive ... The film strip, radio drama are a form of art which must satisfy the mass, the individual seeking individuality in a mechanized, socialized society, where his life is ordered at every turn.'[34] Not only is James at this point taking a different position from that of Adorno and others of the Frankfurt School, who argued that popular culture was mass deception;[35] he is also suggesting that, in a society in which forms of hegemony close spaces for resistance, cultural production may give us clues about forms of resistance. This closing of space was for James marked by the emergence of totalitarian states in the post-World War II period. In these states, James argued, there was the integration of 'every aspect of life, production, politics, entertainment, aesthetics, sport into a single whole and [its imposition] with the utmost ruthlessness upon the mass of the population'.[36] What James was therefore reaching for in his discussion of popular culture were signs of how a different kind of integration could occur outside of the totalitarian state: 'It is the writer's belief that in the modern popular art, film, radio television, comic strip, we are headed for some artistic comprehensive integration of modern life.'[37]

At work here is James's notion of the 'good life' as integration of the individual and social personality. This would then become the ground for freedom and self-actualisation. Of course, we now know that James ignored the commodification process in cultural production, and how that process is linked to forms of hegemony – in other words, as Stuart Hall demonstrates, the manner in which popular culture is itself contested.[38]

At this point I want to return to a discussion of American freedom as a set of hegemonic discourses and practices, and to remark on James's silences about this dimension of American civilization. Finally, I will suggest how what Sylvia Wynter calls James's poiesis is one useful aspect of contemporary radical thought that should inform our present.

AMERICAN CIVILISATION AND FREEDOM

Michel Foucault's work on power focuses on how 'power applies itself to everyday life ... marks [the subject] by his own individuality ... imposes a law of truth on him ... It is a form of power that makes individuals subjects.'[39] But power is not a nebulous thing, and takes form through a series of discourses, customs and practices in a society.

There is a way in which the founding narrative of a society can become not just the dominant ideology, but hegemonic as it seeps into the practices, into the desires of the population constructing ideas about life and its meanings. This narrative becomes *the truth* of life, the universalism of human life. In the case of America, freedom has become this universal, structuring the field of actions and of belief. What this means is that American imperial power acts with a series of rationalities in which freedom becomes the central value. To this value is added the notion of chosenness.[40] In early American history, the Puritans, in reworking the Hebrew tradition, made themselves God's chosen people, and therefore imagined America as the New Israel, in which humankind would be finally reconciled with God. Jonathan Edwards, one of the most important figures of eighteenth century American history, made the point that America had been conceived as 'the most glorious renovation of the world'.[41] This sense of a new adventure, of a new civilisation, a world-historical community, was dedicated, in the words of David Humphreys, an officer in the revolutionary army, 'to embrace humanity's cause, a world of our empire, for a world of our laws'.[42] Very quickly this empire was to become, in Thomas Jefferson's words, paraphrasing Edmund Burke, 'an empire of liberty'. The 'empire of liberty' would mean that what was important to American power was to construct ways of life. Those ways of life covered all dimensions of the human, and rested on two conceptions. One was American economic power and the values of the market economy, and the other was the integration of republican democracy with the conception of freedom. The objective of American power was to create a 'civilisation'. In American history this practice of creating a certain form of 'civilisation' was deployed upon the Cherokees. Theda Perdue and Michael Green note how this programme

> struck at the most basic way in which societies organize themselves – according to gender ... The 'civilization' program had to teach Indians to appreciate the value of private property and the marketability of land ... 'civilization' eventually encompassed a broader cultural transformation including Christianity, formal education and republican government, but the changes in economic values remained at its core.[43]

Critical to this process of 'civilisation' was also the construction of white womanhood as a marker of the Anglo-Saxon ideal, since the Cherokee men were allowed to marry white women once they accepted the 'civilisation' programme. Those men who became Cherokee elites were also allowed to hold black slaves. American imperial power has historically organised itself around questions of culture, about creating a certain kind of human who would regulate him- or herself into a willing subject. Given racial oppression, the normative terms of this 'civilisation' were white male supremacy. The objective of American imperial power still remains the creation of a set of hegemonic practices in which its power could be nestled. In the present, the clearest indication of this is what has become known as the Bush doctrine.

In the November 2002 'National Security Strategy of the United States' we find the following sentences:

> The great struggles of the twentieth century between liberty and totalitarianism ended with a decisive victory for the forces of freedom – and a single sustainable model for national success: freedom, democracy and free enterprise ... These values are right and true for every person, in every society – and the duty of protecting these values against their enemies is the common calling of freedom-loving people across the globe and across the ages.[44]

This passage sums up a long history of American imperial power deploying itself as the cause of freedom. The issue here is not the hypocrisy of American imperial freedom, but rather that freedom has become a set of discourses and practices that now limit the possibilities of the human. We have in this version of history arrived at the end of history, the terminus of our possibilities. One should be careful here to not present a one-sided view of the deployment of American power. As the historians Fred Anderson and Andrew Cayton have illustrated, the American 'empire of liberty' has been organised through war. They make the point that the 'quest for liberty and the pursuit of power together have created an American historical dialectic catalyzed and made dynamic by war',[45] confirming Gramsci's observations that power has two sides to it.

James's work on *American Civilization* did not address any of these points. There is no hint in the text of any of the imperial adventures of America. We do not know for certain if he had seriously studied W.E.B. Du Bois's *Black Reconstruction* at that time – something he was to do seriously in the 1960s, giving semester-long history classes at Howard University and what was then Federal City College in Washington DC, on the text.[46] However, the silences in *American*

Civilization strangely follow those in Tocquville's *Democracy in America*. This is not surprising, since James himself notes that he 'propose to write an essay closer to the spirit and aims of de Tocqueville than any other of the writers who have followed him'.[47]

I want to suggest that the silences in the text were in part due to James's suspension of his colonial past. For example, James was writing long after the Spanish American War had taken place, and Jose Martí had already called to our attention the nature of American imperial power. By temporarily suspending his colonial past, James wove into the text a number of silences. The rebuttal to this view might be that James was trying something new; that he was responding to his own desire to understand American civilisation other than as a political economy; that he was part of an intellectual current preoccupied with totalitarianism in the mid twentieth century; and finally that he was responding to the series of texts that had appeared at the time about America. All of this would be true, but only partly so. James makes it known that he was writing this text 'as a stranger who has lived in the United States for twelve crucial years'.[48] But what kind of stranger was he? It would seem that if James had not suspended his own colonial past, then he might have thought of American civilisation in radically new ways. It is accurate to observe that he significantly departed from many elements of Marxist theory. However, these departures did not allow him to grapple with the complex meanings of freedom in America. In the end the value of *American Civilization* to our understanding of James's thought is that it seems to begin a period where he is searching for a new paradigm for his studies of history and politics. This paradigm of human study would focus on the desires of human beings as illuminated by history. The method was of course to be illustrated fully in *Beyond a Boundary*.

BEYOND CAESAR'S REGION

In reflecting on his theoretical turn, James notes that in the 1940s there was a crisis in his political life. When the crisis was resolved, James claims he planned a series of books, one on Herman Melville and the other on cricket.[49] This claim is noteworthy, since it reveals that James had now firmly turned his intellectual powers to issues of literary criticism and cultural history. James's work on Melville, *Mariners, Renegades and Castaways: The Story of Herman Melville and The World We Live In*, has been studied as a critical example of his importance to post-World War II American literary history. Donald

Pease makes the point that James's interpretation of *Moby-Dick* 'challenged the conventional understanding of Melville's work'.[50] In this text, James posits a theory of literary production in which the great writer is the 'unsurpassed interpreter of the age in which we live, its past, its present and its uncertain future'.[51] He elaborates on this when he earlier observes, in discussing Melville's writing talent: 'it is startling but before you read a page you get an idea of what a great imaginative writer can do, and what philosophers, economists, journalists, historians, however gifted, can never do'.[52]

It is clear that here James wants to suggest that, while the conventional methods and perhaps disciplines that attempt to study human society have some merit, it is only in great writing that we come close to any really profound understanding of ourselves. Not only is this a major departure from conventional Marxist political economy, but it also claims a different gaze for the study of the human. It is why I want to suggest that *Beyond a Boundary* takes the form it does. It is not a cultural history of cricket per se. But by writing the text in a semi-autobiographical mode, James was able to function as a writer grappling with the 'imaginative structures'[53] of human life. These structures and their interpretation became for James the most important elements in our attempts to understand ourselves. It is this fact that Wynter points to when she observes that there is a Jamesian poiesis: the 'imaginative structures' to which James calls our attention are the ways in which humans reconfigure their humanness, the ways in which representations become constitutive of culture and society. In this frame, sports, art, and other forms of so-called cultural representation become the sites from which human beings affirm their desire for forms of life. We might remind ourselves here of a Jamesian quote: 'Men are not pigs to be fattened'.[54]

In making this shift, James draws our attention to a certain quality of aesthetics. Following M.M. Bakhtin's distinctions, Wynter argues about how James's collapse of high and popular cultures in *Beyond a Boundary* created an aesthetic that was organically linked to politics.[55] She further makes the point that the aesthetic 'redefined the mode of existence in what was now not the polis of the whole body of the people'.[56] In this shift, politics was no longer only about class relations: at stake were a series of conceptions about the purpose of the human. The cultural history of cricket then became the site from which West Indian anticolonialism and nationalism would find their feet in the deepest impulses of the mass of the West Indian population. It is from this perspective that we should read the figure of Matthew Bondman.

Matthew Bondman is introduced on the first page of the text. He resides beside James in the small district of Tunapuna, and is the very first character to whom we are introduced. His living besides James is already a juxtaposition, for James resides in a house in which his family were typical of the 'Christian black' subjects that had been constructed in the post-emancipation period of Caribbean society.[57] And, as he himself notes about his grandfather, 'My grandfather went to church every Sunday morning at eleven o'clock wearing in the broiling sun a frock coat ... Respectability was not an ideal it was an armour.'[58] In opposition to this 'Christian black' subject was Bondman. James describes him as an 'awful character, dirty ... he would not work ... his eyes were fierce, his language violent, and his voice was loud'. He would also walk barefoot. There is nothing of the Christian black colonial subject here. Compare him to James's grandfather, for example. However, James's family all agreed that this character that James describes as a ne'er-do-well could bat. James notes, 'Matthew, so crude and vulgar in every aspect of his life, with bat in hand was all grace and style.'[59] What accounted for this? James does not venture any easy explanations. But the rest of the text is in great part about how cricket became constitutive of Caribbean nationalism and the West Indian personality. There was no excuse for Bondman's general comportment in the minds of the 'Christian black' colonial subject, but by his batting Matthew Bondman openly demonstrated the capacities of the Caribbean peoples then under the heel of British colonialism.

However, there is an added complication about Bondman. This figure was *the colonial* subject. Yet in his comportment he had thrown off the armour of respectability, which the colonial power had created as the marker for his humanity. Bondman did not wear shoes, perhaps in part because they may have been a luxury for him. But he may also not have worn shoes because, in early-twentieth-century Caribbean society, many people growing up in rural, or even semi-urban centres did not wear, or often 'judge'[60] shoes. Growing up bare-footed these persons only wore shoes on special occasions. It is not that he did not wear shoes on his feet, because if this were so while he was playing cricket James would have noted it, and he would not have been allowed on the practice pitch. But the notice about shoes was about a subject in rebellion, who in the semi-urban areas refused to conform to what was deemed right. In other words, Bondman represented the rebellious colonial subject who broke all the colonial rationalities of subject-formation. It is by coming to the figure of Bondman that James is able to detail the new areas of his politics and history. I do not mean here that James only recognises the self-activity of the working-class or oppressed groups through the figure of Bondman. Rather, I want to suggest that this recognition in *Beyond A Boundary* is different.

In James's work, the self-activity of the working class is rooted in production, in the formation of workers' councils, of soviets of rank-and-file organisations. In the figure of Bondman, James pays attention to a different sort of rebellion and self-activity. It is a self-activity that reconfigures *self*, that establishes a set of practices that completely break the mold of the subject.

James's turn to this form of politics again, as was typical of his method, takes him back to a study of Greek society. In discussing the centrality of games to Greek life, James cites Solon's response to a query that 'You would have to be there'. In other words, this is a human activity in which emotions, desire, the body and the intellect all fuse in moments of play. But it is serious play. It does not distract from the business of politics. It is itself a site of politics. James confirms this when he writes in the chapter on W.G. Grace,

> A famous liberal historian can write the social history of England in the nineteenth century, and two famous socialists can write what they have declared to be the history of the common people of England and between them never once mention who was the best-known Englishman of his time.[61]

James's criticism announces that he is now finished with the conventional historical method, which refuses to take into account all human activity. This is a new beginning for James, and an outline for how the study of human society should occur. It is not only a question of subaltern history, or history 'from below', but rather of *what* is it we should study in order to offer profound understandings of human society. For James, Matthew Bondman was similar in many respects to the crew of the *Peqoud* in Melville's *Moby-Dick*. He applauds Melville's writing in *Moby-Dick* where the author states: 'if then to meanest mariners, and renegades and castaways, I shall hereafter ascribe high qualities, though dark; weave round them tragic graces ...'[62] This then is James's gaze. How do those who are oppressed reconfigure their humanness in the midst of domination? To put this another way: What forms of life, if any, are created in opposition to the power and domination?

In the contemporary world, such a gaze has become extraordinarily difficult, since at first blush it seems that hegemony has closed down all avenues, incorporated different forms of life and bent them to suit the market and the imperial power of America. But the might of hegemony does not necessarily capture all things. It seeks to, but there is no law that says it must succeed. There is another history of freedom, another set of discourses about the human that were forged in what the Latin American thinker Enrique Dussel calls the 'underside of modernity'.[63] Perhaps it is to these discourses and practices that we must turn to realign radical political thought, and to give it the energy that is required to struggle against domination. In making that move, the work of James in the period from the late 1940s to the early 1960s may be a useful guide.

NOTES

Thanks to Geri Augusto for her usual fine critical reading, which made this a better chapter.

1. C.L.R. James, *Beyond a Boundary* (London: Serpent's Tail, 1996), p. 151.
2. Michel Foucault, 'The Subject and Power', in Michel Foucault, *Power: Essential Works of Foucault 1954–1984*, ed. James D. Faubion (New York: The New Press, 2000), p. 326.
3. For an examination of the theoretical and political work of this tendency, see Anthony Bogues, *Caliban's Freedom: The Early Political Thought of C.L.R. James* (London: Pluto, 1997), Chapters 4 and 6.
4. Cited in Bogues, *Caliban's Freedom*, p. 133.
5. This turn is illustrated by James's preoccupation with coming to terms with the meanings of the human. His book on American civilisation, his writings on Herman Melville, his lectures on William Shakespeare, and then almost a decade later his lectures in Trinidad on modern politics, all point to James searching for a missing element which he thought his early historical and political thought did not cover. Many commentators on James use the semi-autobiographical text, *Beyond a Boundary*, as the definitive marker of this turn. I would suggest that it can be seen both in his 1944 letters to Constance Webb and the draft of what became published as *American Civilization*. This was not a turn to cultural matters per se; rather James was beginning to walk the path that many other radical anticolonial thinkers did; that is, grappling with the question: What is the human?
6. *Beyond a Boundary*, p. 151.
7. Sylvia Wynter, 'In Quest of Matthew Bondsman: Some Cultural Notes on the Jamesian Journey', in *Urgent Tasks: Journal of the Revolutionary Left* 12, Summer 1981. Special Issue, 'C.L.R. James: His Life and Work', p. 54.

8. Stuart Hall, 'Gramsci's Relevance for the Study of Race and Ethnicity', in David Morley and Kuan-Hsing Chen (eds) *Stuart Hall: Critical Dialogues in Cultural Studies* (London: Routledge, 1996), p. 439.
9. C.L.R. James, *Modern Politics* (Detroit: Bewick Editions, 1973), p. 115 (emphasis in the original).
10. Given the limitations of space in this essay, I will focus on James's single authored writings during the period. This means I will not look at books like *Facing Reality*. The discussion of this and other co-authored texts during this period can be found in my forthcoming second volume on James's political thought.
11. C.L.R. James, *American Civilization* (Oxford: Blackwell, 1993), p. 166.
12. Cited in Judith Butler, *Subjects of Desire* (New York: Columbia University Press, 1999), p. 7.
13. *Modern Politics*, p. 105.
14. Butler, *Subjects of Desire*, p. 186.
15. Gilles Deleuze and Felix Guattari, *anti-oedipus: capitalism and schizophrenia* (Minneapolis: University of Minnesota Press, 1983), p. 25.
16. Ibid., p. 28.
17. Ibid., p. 27.
18. Ernesto Laclau, *Emancipation(s)* (London: Verso, 1996), p. 1.
19. Ibid., p. 5.
20. Ibid., p. 18.
21. C.L.R. James, *Spheres of Existence: Selected Writings* (London: Allison and Busby, 1980), p. 83
22. *Modern Politics*, p. 100.
23. Raymond Williams, *Marxism and Literature*, (Oxford: Oxford University Press, 1977), p. 109.
24. Ibid., p. 110.
25. Ludwig Wittgenstein, *Philosophical Investigations* (Oxford: Blackwell, 1997), p. 80.
26. Frantz Fanon, *Black Skin, White Masks*, (New York: Grove Press, 1967), pp. 17–18.
27. George Lamming, ' The Negro Writer and his World', in Richard Drayton and Andaiye (eds.), *Conversation: George Lamming: Essays, Addresses and Interviews 1953–1990* (London: Karia Press, 1992), p. 38.
28. *American Civilization*, p. 107.
29. Ibid., p. 31.
30. Cited in David Hackett Fisher, *Liberty and Freedom: A Visual History of America's Founding Ideas* (Oxford: Oxford University Press, 2005), p. 715.
31. The most recent example of this is the extraordinary work of the historian David Hackett Fischer in his massive volume, *Liberty and Freedom*.
32. *American Civilization*, p. 167.
33. Ibid., p. 123.
34. Ibid., pp. 123–7.
35. These arguments can be found in Theodore Adorno and Max Horkheimer, *The Dialectic of Enlightenment* (London: Verso, 1979).
36. *American Civilization*, p. 162.
37. Ibid., p. 150.

38. For an exemplary discussion of this point, see Hall's essay, 'What is Black in Black Popular Culture?', in Gina Gent (ed.), *Black Popular Culture* (Seattle: Bay Press, 1992), pp. 21–36.
39. Michel Foucault, 'The Subject and Power' in Foucault, *Power*, p. 331.
40. It should be noted that this is not unique. The Huguenots in South Africa did the same thing.
41. Cited in Anders Stephanson, *Manifest Destiny, American Expansion and the Empire of Right* (New York: Hill and Wang, 1996), p. 17. In this section I closely follow the arguments posited by Stephanson.
42. Cited in Stephanson, *Manifest Destiny*, p. 19.
43. Theda Perdue and Michael Green, *The Cherokee Removal: A Brief History with Documents* (Boston: Beford /St Martin Press, 1995), p. 25.
44. George W. Bush, 'America's Responsibility, America's Mission', in Andrew Bachevich (ed.), *The Imperial Tense: Prospects and Problems of American Empire* (Chicago: Ivan R. Dee, 2003), p. 5.
45. Fred Anderson and Andrew Cayton, *The Domination of War: Empire and Liberty in North America 1500–2000* (New York: Viking, 2005), p. xxiv.
46. Interview with Geri Augusto on James's activity in Washington DC during the late 1960s and early 1970s. Augusto was a member of the Center for Black Education at the time. The Center worked closely with James and its bookstore and press, Drum and Spear, was responsible for the reissuing of James's 1938 book, *History of Negro Revolt*. The book was reissued in 1969 with a new section that summed up worldwide black revolt between 1938 and 1969. This interview occurred in December 1997 in Boston.
47. *American Civilization*, p. 31.
48. Ibid., p. 30.
49. James discusses this in *Beyond A Boundary*, p. 19.
50. Donald E. Pease, 'C. L. R. James's *Mariners, Renegades and Castaways* and the World We Live In', in C. L. R. James, *Mariners, Renegades and Castaways: The Story of Herman Melville and the World We Live In* (Hanover: University Press of New England, 2001), p. xiii. The text, of course, has a strange history. Written by James when he was on Ellis Island awaiting the final judgment on his immigration and deportation order from America, its political purpose became James's attempt to convince the American authorities not to deport him. The book was sent out to numerous officials and figures in American society in an effort to persuade them to take up James's case. The attempt failed. However, one significant consequence of the attempt was a sharp exchange between James and George Padmore, in which the latter notes (in a letter to James) that the last section of the book disturbed him and others. The debate between James and Padmore about this is evident in the letter James wrote to Padmore on 22 June 1953. I thank the late Jim Murray for bringing this letter to my attention.
51. *Mariners, Renegades and Castaways*, p. 124.
52. Ibid., p. 41.
53. The phrase is taken from Michael Sprinkler, *Imaginary Relations: Aesthetics and Ideology in the Theory of Historical Materialism* (London: Verso, 1987), p. 33.
54. C.L.R. James, *Modern Politics* (Detroit: Bewick/ed, 1973.), p. 105.

55. Sylvia Wynter, 'In Quest of Matthew Bondman', in Paul Buhle, ed. *C. L. R. James: His Life and Work* (London: Allison and Busby, 1986), p. 133.
56. Ibid.
57. For descriptions of this see Horace Russell, 'The Emergence of the Christian Black: the Making of a Stereotype', in *Jamaica Journal* 16: 1, 1983, pp. 51–71. Another important work on this is the excellent comparative study by Catherine Hall, *Civilising Subjects: Metropole and Colony in the English Imagination 1830–1867* (Chicago: University of Chicago Press, 2002).
58. *Beyond a Boundary*, pp. 7–8.
59. Ibid., p. 4.
60. It is interesting to note the word used in Jamaica for the wearing of shoes. One 'judged' shoes, suggesting that there was an issue of when and why shoes were worn. It is also interesting that during the rise of the anticolonial movement in Trinidad, the central subaltern figure was often seen as the barefoot male figure.
61. *Beyond a Boundary*, p. 159.
62. *Mariners, Renegades and Castaways*, p. 17.
63. For a discussion of this concept see in particular Linda Alcoff and Eduardo Mendieta (eds), *Thinking From The Underside of History: Enrique Dussell's Philosophy of Liberation* (Boston: Rowman and Littlefield, 2000).

8
C.L.R. James, Critical Humanist
Brian W. Alleyne

In this essay I will discuss the hybrid approach to culture and politics found in the work of C.L.R. James – an amalgam of Marxism and anti-colonialism, informed by a cultural consciousness shaped strongly by European classics, and especially English literature. I argue that James's work was humanist because it centred on human needs and creative potential, and universalist because it sought to articulate a vision of history that encompassed all of humanity, while remaining aware of the contradictory and often exclusionary ways in which humanism and universalism have developed as designs for life. I label James a *critical* humanist because he held fast to a vision of a better society, while criticising the more unsavoury aspects of Eurocentric variants of humanism. Since the 1960s, in particular, many critics have cast doubt on humanism's claim to speak on behalf of all people, and sought to expose universalist rhetoric as a disguise for domination and exploitation. Without denying such trenchant criticisms of humanist ideas, I will argue that James's work suggests that there is much worth salvaging in the humanist project.

The critical conception of humanism that shapes James's work imagines people as makers of life projects, individually and collectively. It is a particular kind of social imaginary that works with the dual premises of agents and structures. The late sociologist C. Wright Mills said of the 'sociological imagination' that it should enable the understanding of how the social and historical interact with the personal. For Mills, the central problem to which social science should address itself is that of the relation between 'private troubles' and 'public issues'. In *The Sociological Imagination* (1959), Mills analysed the rise of bureaucratic and technical structures in modern society, showing that, though on the one hand they permitted great improvements in the material well-being of most people (in the developed world, at least), on the other they had the unfortunate effect of isolating the individual amid impersonal processes and organisations. This contradictory experience of modernity ought to be addressed, for Mills, by an imaginative standpoint that seeks to understand how the individual biography is related to social and historical forces.[1]

Though Mills was concerned with issues of social research, his ideas are applicable to broader intellectual and political projects of the kind that occupied James throughout his life. James worked across disciplines, largely as a revolutionary intellectual, and so his lifework cannot be reduced to conventional models of an academic, or even a generic intellectual career. Nonetheless I want to locate him, tentatively, within the fields of intellectual work that are concerned with interpretation – the social sciences – and with critique in the Kantian sense of making judgements – the arts. Moreover, I see James as emerging from an intellectual tradition of social-realist writing that comes out of the nineteenth century, when novelists as well as social investigators made the lives of ordinary people the subjects of their texts. Here again there are connections to Mills, who himself saw some fiction as displaying the qualities of sociological imagination.

In what follows I will explore James's critical humanism in four areas. First, I will discuss his early fiction, placing him in a context of social-realist writing that connects early-twentieth-century English Caribbean novelists to metropolitan Euro-American developments in realist fiction. Second, I will look at James's relationship to the 'Western canon' of literature, from which he drew inspiration; this is one of the more controversial aspects of James's reception as a radical thinker, especially among some in the field of Black Studies. Third, I will look at James's reading of political and social change in the colonial West Indies through the lens of cricket. Fourth, I will turn to James's reflections on US society around World War II; I compare him to Theodor Adorno, and suggest that while Adorno was too dismissive of popular culture, his distrust of US mass culture seems sound from a contemporary standpoint. While James was sometimes uncritical in his reading of US mass culture, his ideas are productive for critically engaging the present moment of US hegemony and the so-called clash of civilisations.

JAMES'S SOCIAL REALISM

Two people lived in me: one, the rebel against all family and school discipline and order; the other, a Puritan who would have cut off a finger sooner than do anything contrary to the ethics of the game.[2]

Beyond a Boundary (1963)

Cyril Lionel Robert James was born in 1901 in rural Trinidad, then a British colony. He died in London in 1989.[3] As a young man he found the colonial lower-middle-class milieu into which he was born and raised to be mainly dull and overly concerned with imitating the mores of the British middle class. He began to develop a method that sought below the surface appearances of individuals and events for underlying essences, which he believed caused people to act and events to occur in particular ways. This method had its genesis in his early engagement with the lives of working-class people, albeit as an educated member of the lower middle class who wished to become a writer. The first aspect of James's critical humanism that I will discuss involves his development of social realism in his early fiction.

Realism, as an artistic and critical sensibility and as a cultural movement, sought to come to terms with the transformation of social life brought into being by modernity.[4] Realism was the characteristic mode of the nineteenth-century novel, interacting in complex ways with the development of Western societies, both representing and being shaped by that development.[5] The realist novel represented people in society, especially the emergent bourgeois societies of Western Europe and North America. Further, it sought to portray people and society in the state of disenchantment that resulted from modernity. The character in a realist novel was one intended to be identified as someone who *could be* just like the reader: this reader was the new bourgeois individual who, from the eighteenth century onwards, began to express an aesthetic sensibility more concerned with individual life and sentiment than the classically oriented outlook of the European aristocracy. The 'ordinary man' going about his ordinary business, came into his own – 'ordinary' here meaning bourgeois. In making the ordinary person the subject of the text, realist fiction made a political statement that was in keeping with the gradual expansion of civil liberties and representative democracy in Western societies at the time.

The realist commitment to representing ordinary lives would shape the emergent fields of urban sociology and, especially, social anthropology, with the pioneering anthropologists drawing on the conventions and strategies of realist fiction in creating a new kind of textual world, which they named 'ethnography'[6] – literally, 'the writing of culture'. The concern of both the realist novel and realist ethnography was with representation, indeed faithful representation. The authority (in both senses of the word: validity and the quality of being written by someone) of the realist ethnographic text was established by the acceptance of the claim, 'I was there', by the persona of the objective observer at work, and ultimately by the acceptance by the reader of the possibility of representation.[7] Representation is the raison d'être of the realist ethnography, as of the realist novel.

These developments can offer insights into the development of indigenous writing in the English Caribbean. Though the pioneering early-twentieth-century English Caribbean authors were descended from the Western European tradition of nineteenth-century realist novel-writing, they differed in that they were concerned with individual character only insofar as it exists in a social context shaped more by European colonialism outside Europe than by bourgeois European society at its heart. For critic Ken Ramchand,

> Although West Indian novelists are aware of the main pattern of the nineteenth-century English novel – an analysis of the character in relation to the manners and morals operative in a given period – it follows from the formlessness of West Indian society, and the existential position of the individual in it, that such a pattern is not one that seems relevant or comes spontaneously to the writer from the West Indies.[8]

Selwyn Cudjoe's assertion that resistance to colonialism is the dynamic force behind Caribbean literature,[9] if taken on-board, gives us a clue as to why so many authors from this region chose the social-realist mode of writing: these authors have tended to address themselves to issues at the societal level, as opposed to the level of the deep psychology of the individual; for them, the struggle against colonialism had to operate on a level beyond that of the individual if it was to have any social effect. In *The Trinidad Awakening: West Indian Literature of the Nineteen Thirties* (1988), Reinhard Sander sees some early Caribbean realist writing as being critical in the sense of advocating a specific political project, in addition to being social-realist. James's early fiction was certainly social-realist. Moreover, we may trace the development of a critical perspective, as defined by Sander, in James's early non-fiction, especially in his *Case for West Indian Self-Government* (1933).[10]

What we may loosely term an ethnographic sensibility shaped early English Caribbean social-realist writing as it did 'mainstream' realist fiction. Extended periods of exposure to plebeian life (these were as proto-ethnographic, paternalistic and voyeuristic as the excursions of respectable authors into nineteenth-century working-class Manchester or Paris), were a feature of the careers of a number of these English Caribbean authors. Trinidadian Alfred Mendes, for example, spent several months living in a barrack yard[11] in Trinidad in order to prepare for the writing of his novel *Black Fauns* (1935): this period of what the anthropologist terms 'participant observation' was intended to lend verisimilitude to the novel, to capture the mannerisms and speech, the milieu, of the barrack yard characters.

James based his first novel, *Minty Alley* (1936), on his own exposure to barrack-yard life. In *Minty Alley*, the main character, Haynes, is a young man of the lower middle class, a bookstore clerk; he has got to move to a room in a barrack yard because of a family misfortune. Haynes's story illustrates the life of the lower class through the eyes of a middle-class protagonist who gradually grows to understand his new milieu by immersion – rather like the classic work in anthropology, where the anthropologist would immerse herself in the environment of interest, *Minty Alley* can be read as both testament and ethnography. There is more than a little of James in Haynes: in a 1973 lecture James stated,

> Now, the novel that I wrote I made the hero of the novel, not the hero but the chief character, myself at the age of about 18 – knowing nothing, ignorant, my head full of books, and I go to these people who are not so much proletarian but they are plebeians, they live the ordinary life.[12]

Haynes throws off the blinkers of a 'respectable' upbringing as he grows used to life in the yard; he learns about the vitality of plebeian life, of the necessity for constant struggle to affirm the self in the face of adversity. The concerns of the later Marxist humanist are foreshadowed here: in the novel James was fictionally inscribing some of his first insights into class conflict in Caribbean society. In its quasi-ethnographic realism, *Minty Alley* is a kindred text to Friedrich Engels's *The Condition of the Working Class in England* (1844) or W.E.B. Du Bois's *Philadelphia Negro* (1899). James/Haynes developed his knowledge of lower-class life in colonial Trinidad's capital city through observation and participation, just as Engels or Du Bois did in pursuit of their more conventional research projects in Manchester and Philadelphia. James's explorations into plebeian life in Trinidad were crucial to forming his early critical consciousness; in this sense we can read *Minty Alley* as a kind of fictional ethnography.

JAMES AND THE CANON OF WESTERN CIVILISATION

One of the most distinctive features of James's life and work is the great respect that he held for European culture in the form of its 'great men' and 'great works'. James was schooled at a time when non-European intellectuals were not nearly as hostile to the European canon of great works of literature as is the case nowadays. With Black Power, the modern women's movement and decolonisation as historical accomplishments, it is perhaps not now easy to place one of the founders of pan-Africanism, who was also a fervent fan of Ancient Greece and of Shakespeare. James was, though, no unreflective creature of European 'high' culture:

> It was only long years after [leaving school] that I understood the limitation on spirit, vision and self-respect which was imposed on us by the fact that our masters, our curriculum, our code of morals, *everything* began from the basis that Britain was the source of all light and leading, and our business was to admire, wonder, imitate, learn; our criterion of success was to have succeeded in approaching that distant ideal – to attain it was, of course, impossible.[13]

James held that the common fact of being human was of greater importance to social transformation than characteristics such as race or gender or nationality. He stressed *inclusion*: the inclusion of all human beings which humanism promised, but never quite delivered. Further, James held that Enlightenment, though conceived and initiated by privileged men in Europe (for historical and *not* socio-genetic reasons – James was a lifelong Marxist), is the common property of all humankind: it is the struggle of the others – European working-class men and women, and non-Europeans – against colonial domination that brought the ideal of Enlightenment closer to reality; the French, American and Haitian revolutions are emblematic of this struggle. Enlightenment is, on this understanding, a global, hence universal project.

James's respect for 'Western Civilisation' in its guise of the 'canon' of great books and great men has raised doubts on the part of some who are suspicious of non-European intellectuals who pay respect to European cultural models. In a 1984 interview the following was put to James: 'Some Caribbean intellectuals of your generation could be accused of excessive veneration for Western culture and implicitly downgrading the African and New World roots of their own languages and culture', to which James replied:

I do not know what are the African roots of the language and culture of Caribbean intellectuals. I am not aware of the African roots of my use of the language and culture ... The basis of our civilisation in the Caribbean is an adaptation of Western civilisation.[14]

James's early connection of European philosophical tradition with the struggle of black people in the Atlantic world, which occupied him in the 1930s, has interesting parallels with the political and intellectual development of Angela Davis in the United States in the 1960s. Like James before her, Davis was shaped by a traditional education in Western (that is, white canonical) literature and philosophy, which she adapted to her purposes as a Black radical writer and activist, as she recounts in her *Autobiography* (1974). Also like James, she had early developed a sophisticated consciousness of the historical and political complexity of racism, and she committed herself early on to struggle against racist oppression. But the most telling point of similarity is in her drawing on a Western philosophical tradition and building of a political project of struggle against racism as part of a wider struggle against capitalism: contests over race, class, and gender (in the consideration of which she went far beyond James) are constructed in her *Women, Race and Class* (1983), and *Women, Culture and Politics* (1990) as critical moments in the struggle against the inhumanity of capitalism and imperialism. A defining feature of both James's and Davis's work is the complete refusal of essential black identity as a basis for understanding and seeking to transform racially stratified society. In Davis's recent work on the prison-industrial complex in the United States – especially in an interview in *Race & Class*[15] and in *Are Prisons Obolete?* (2003) – she shows how brutalised Black labour is coerced into conditions of super-exploitation in the service of late capitalism. For Davis, US prisons are overflowing with black men not because these men are black, but because they are that fraction of the underclass who have lately proved most difficult to police, and therefore to exploit; so incarceration facilitates their control by US state power and the coerced extraction of their labour-power for the profit of US capital. In Davis's work on prisons we can read echoes of James's own pioneering analysis of Atlantic slave labour in *The Black Jacobins* (1938). This historical and structural reading of how a section of the working class comes to be racialised is a characteristic strand of what Cederic Robinson terms 'Black Marxism',[16] in which Black authors simultaneously bring an awareness of racialisation and racism to Marxist thought, while drawing on theories of class struggle to explain the development of racialisation and racism in the modern era.

James's *Black Jacobins* and Du Bois's *Black Reconstruction* (1935) are two foundational texts in the Black Marxist tradition. Both authors set out to understand the role that Atlantic slavery played in the development of European capitalist modernity. The relationship of blacks to Marxism has always been complex. Any number of Black radicals have turned for critical ammunition to the Marxist tradition, but, as Anthony Bogues has demonstrated, the experiences of blacks in left-wing parties and the reception of blacks as Marxist thinkers has been mixed.[17] George Padmore and Claude McKay both broke with the US Communist Party; Claudia Jones and Angela Davis worked to bring an awareness of race and gender to the praxis of that same party. James himself had sometimes strained relations with comrades in the British and American Trotskyist movements, disagreeing with them over a number of issues, including that of race.

The colonial, the cricket-loving black Marxist who was an enthusiast of English literature and classical studies, James was a complicated amalgam of influences, which is best explained, I suggest, in terms of a transcendent political perspective. In drawing on European intellectual traditions to the extent that he did, James may seem quaint to a younger generation of black critics. We must remind ourselves that he drew as much on the revolutionary as on the elite currents in European thought. As much as James was fascinated by classical Greece and by Shakespeare, it was the movement of the Paris masses during the French Revolution that he made his European touchstone for the Haitian Revolution. The movements of masses in revolutionary periods were at least as significant to James as the ideas of European philosophers; this dual interest is emblematic of, and arguably partly derived from, the hybrid character of Caribbean society and culture. In drawing upon classical Greece, while at the same time insisting on the indispensable role of colonised people in constituting modern Western civilisation, James was a *bricoleur*: he combined seemingly disparate elements to construct a conception of history and culture which would be adequate to life in the modern world. James had a hybrid world vision.[18]

CRICKET AT WORK AND PLAY

In his work on cricket, especially the renowned *Beyond a Boundary*, we see James combining insights from social science with sociocultural criticism and reflections on his own biography. James was the first to develop systematically the idea that West Indian cricket offered a promising standpoint from which to analyse the social context into which it was inserted, and in which it developed.

For most of the twentieth century, cricket in the West Indies was organised into clubs that recruited their members on ascriptive class and colour criteria; West Indian teams were captained by upper-class white men, even when they were of demonstrably inferior cricketing ability to their working-class counterparts.[19] James argues that the masses of people in the West Indies, without a voice in the government of the colonies, found some release for their passions on the playing-field and in the spectator stand.[20] He goes on to show, using the dilemma he faced in deciding which cricket club to join after leaving school, that the class and colour stratification of Trinidad in the early twentieth century manifested themselves on the cricket pitch. Indeed, for James cricket was a faithful mirror for West Indian society:

> From its beginning to this day cricket in the West Indies has expressed with astonishing fidelity the social relations of the islands. The early island teams consisted for the most part of Englishmen in the colonies associated with local whites, and black plebeians who were dignified by the title of professional bowlers. These bowlers were more ground attendants than professionals in the accepted modern sense. Some of them had come to the nets where their batters practised, picked up the ball and bowled, sometimes without shoes. The brown-skin or black middle class produced a few good players but there was a sharp social gap between Englishmen and white or light-skinned members of the upper classes and the black plebeians who bowled so well that they were sometimes given an opportunity to make a precarious living by their skill.[21]

James broke new ground in showing that cricket was one of several sites where colour-coded class struggle in the colonial Caribbean was played out: white for the ruling class, brown/mixed for the middle class, and black and Asian working class and peasantry. This struggle was one of the most important social dynamics in English Caribbean history.[22] With regard to cricket, much was at stake: acceptance by the right cricket club could open doors to all kinds of social and political privileges. The colonial ruling class wished to hold cricket as a bastion of their right to rule and to set social and moral examples to those they deemed their inferiors. The intermediate strata, the middle class, strove earnestly for the status and privileges of the elite, by virtue of their comparable economic and educational accomplishments. At the same time many members of the middle class wished to distance themselves from the masses, who were themselves engaged in bitter struggle for what most of us would nowadays take as basic human rights: the vote, literacy, equality before the law, a living wage, and basic public services.

James shows how cricket was a palliative for the unjust situation of the mass of people being denied elementary political and civil rights; for people without the vote, the game came to carry part of the weight of their desire for a public corporate presence. On the field, teams from the various clubs 'represented' the classes from which their members came. More than just pride would be at stake in a match between an upstart working-class club and a middle-class club: social identities were shaken or strengthened by the outcome of many a game.

The teams and their supporters brought the full weight of their social positions and expectations to the cricket ground. In a sense, the cricket ground met a need that was more than just recreational: the coming together of hundreds or thousands of supporters met one of Marx's criteria for the development of class consciousness – that is to say, a number of persons similarly positioned in the social system coming together on a regular basis to further a collective enterprise. The cricket ground served as a sort of public sphere for the disenfranchised masses of the West Indies – or rather, those who were not fully citizens in the wider society, who had no political representatives of their own choosing, became citizens in the quasi-polity of the cricket ground. The players on the team supported by these plebeians became their elected representatives – elected by popular acclaim – and were expected to 'give the opposition hell', especially when the opposition was a team from the ruling class.

James makes it clear that triumph on the cricket field for a working-class club was a pyrrhic victory in the larger social context, which remained intact, whatever the outcome of the game. In itself, cricket was not revolutionary: only when it articulated revolutionary currents in the wider society was it an agent of progressive change. Such articulation did not occur often. The strict rules of cricket, and its ideology of fair play, respect for opponents, and respect for duly constituted authority, served usually to blunt the progressive and even revolutionary possibilities of the collective enterprise of cricket for the masses. Though cricket was something of a public sphere for the working class, albeit a most limited one, the very nature of cricket itself militated against the benefits of that limited public sphere being realised beyond the time of a game and the space of the cricket ground. In the final analysis, cricket remained a game, and quite a polite one at that. No popular cultural form is inherently revolutionary, even if it can be shown, as in this case, that such a form displayed distinct elements of rebellion against the existing order. The popular is not necessarily the revolutionary; part of the slyness of hegemony is that self-confident ruling classes, in the exercise of hegemony over others, can adjust to upsurges of rebellious activity, while ultimately holding fast to their power.

In the first decade of the twentieth century, as the West Indian masses began to organise their own cricketing public spaces, their collective passion to define themselves against the hegemony of the local ruling class was partly redirected by that very ruling class onto an external 'enemy'; an enemy that was constructed in the game of cricket itself. In this period, touring teams from England became a part of the West Indian cricket scene. Some of the energy that might have gone into struggling through cricket against the local elite and its subordinate fellow travellers was channelled into beating the touring English at their own game. This 'international' sporting enterprise, with its resistance carefully limited to giving the touring Englishmen a good game, was one into which the West Indian elite sought to incorporate the masses, in a subaltern role. The organisational structure of the game remained under the control of the ruling class, who had the resources to construct a quasi-national cricket consciousness – one which papered over the social contradictions of colonial society and directed energies into so-called inter-colonial/international competition.

Nonetheless, there were times when cricket would articulate social tension with unusual effect. In 1960, a controversy over the captainship of the West Indian team would see the power balance swing from the ruling-class administrators to the masses. Despite the unquestioned ability of working-class players, up to 1960 the West Indian cricket team was captained by white men of the ruling class, exemplary of the continued survival of the view that only 'Gentlemen' should lead a team, whatever the composition of that team (and naturally, gentlemen in the colonial West Indies were quintessentially ruling class and white). The elite clubs in the region continued to practise apartheid in their policies of membership, and even in seating arrangements at the grounds. This was a situation that would not sit well with the growing nationalist consciousness. Matters came to a head in 1960: the social tensions that had been both sublimated and acted out in cricket flared up over the campaign to have Frank Worrell named as captain of the West Indies team. Worrell, a superb cricketer, was eminently suited for the job. The West Indian masses would hear of no excuses for the traditional selection of a ruling-class, white captain. After an intense popular campaign in which James was himself involved in a leading role, Worrell did become captain. This event was a symbolically important staging point in the maturation of West Indian cricket as a popular cultural expression. We should note too that in 1960 the issue of West Indian federation as a means to gain independence from Britain was very much alive.[23] In the final pages of *Beyond a Boundary* James wrote of the close of the West Indian tour of Australia in 1961, when under Worrell's captaincy they were to make their first major international impact:

> I caught a glimpse of what brought a quarter of a million inhabitants of Melbourne into the streets to tell the West Indian cricketers good-bye, a gesture spontaneous and in cricket without precedent, one people speaking to another. Clearing their way with bat and ball, West Indians at that moment had made a public entry into the comity of nations. Thomas Arnold, Thomas Hughes and the Old master himself would have recognised Frank Worrell as their boy.[24]

What we have in James's account of these events is a cultural and political study that seeks to integrate individual and collective concerns: the development of Worrell as a cricketer and personality is sketched against the backdrop of the heightened nationalist fervour of 1960. James saw personalities developing in, being shaped by, *and* influencing society; he offers many sketches of these processes at work in his portraits of cricketers in *Beyond a Boundary*.

The Worrell campaign, as it unfolded within the movement towards West Indian independence, was the expression of an aspiration held by an entire community. We get the sense, from James's account, as in E.P. Thompson's formulation (1968), of class as a process whereby some people come to see themselves as having interests in common as against some other people: in this case the working people of the West Indies were seeing conflict between their own interest in achieving political self-determination and the continued rule of the British colonial office, along with its local cohorts. Nationalism and class struggle combined in this campaign, as they have done elsewhere in the colonial world. The narrative of the Worrell campaign is unrolled on a necessarily large scale (James writes of the 'West Indian masses' and 'the Australians'); nonetheless, like Thompson, James is not working with an abstract category of class (or of nation or race): his accounts are built around human agents, around people who inhabit (constitute as well as being constituted by) class positions, as well as strongly conditioning national and racial identities.

Cricket in the colonial West Indies, like the fiercely competitive system of colonial education, was a 'strategy of containment'[25] – in the hands of the colonial rulers, it deflected questions about the social order by constructing a mythical space, the level playing-field on which was enacted a competition where players supposedly left their social personae behind in the dressing room. In the mythic space of cricket, no bloodstain of oppression, no blemish of racist exclusion or British supremacist practice could soil the white flannels of the players. The creation of such mythic spaces in sport is what, for James, is a particularly British contribution to modern civilisation: they made of team sports a space in which social tensions could be mediated. How the colonised turned the strategy of containment towards insurgent ends is James's special contribution.

A JAMESIAN TAKE ON US HEGEMONY AND THE CLASH OF CIVILISATIONS

The final element of James's thought that I want to assess concerns his reflections on US society and culture during and immediately after World War II. While this aspect of his work is in my view weaker than his writings on Atlantic slavery, colonialism, or cricket and society, I suggest that James may nonetheless help us to think critically about the new era of US hegemony and the 'clash of civilisations' that is supposed to have been heightened after 11 September 2001.

Both C.L.R. James and Theodor Adorno – especially in *Dialectic of Enlightenment* (co-written with Max Horkheimer, 1944) and in the essays collected in *The Culture Industry* (1991) – wrote on the emergence of the mass media in the US; their work is suggestive for analysing the spread of US hegemony through its cultural industries. Both men were sojourners for a time in the United States during and immediately after World War II. These common points in no way compensate for the obvious differences between the two. Adorno is remembered as a brilliant Hegelian Marxist critic, and more controversially as the enemy of mass and 'massified' culture; he is generally read as a stern-faced critic of the authoritarian tendencies of late capitalism and the related hegemony of the culture industries. He has drawn the ire of a number of critics because of his negative comments on jazz.[26] In contrast, James has, with the posthumous publication of a manuscript he wrote in the 1940s (*American Civilization*), been looked at anew as an insightful commentator on US popular culture of the 1940s, possessing a prescient vision in his favourable assessment of the democratising potential of mass-cultural forms like the cinema, the comic strip and mass-circulation magazines. By contrasting the critical perspectives of James with those of Adorno, who shared a concern that Marxism must treat culture as a relatively autonomous sphere, I will highlight further James's critical humanism.

C.L.R. James's understanding of enlightenment and modernity, like that of Adorno, was a dialectical one. And, like Adorno, James was not tempted to take the nihilistic route of total rejection of modernity. For James, there was much in modernity that was worth saving, and he would have had no time for its dismissal as a cultural formation that is reducible to the ideology of bourgeois European men. Still, he was ambivalent towards modernity, though his ambivalence had a different source from Adorno's. James, the Anglophone black colonial turned Marxist revolutionary, occupied the insider–outsider position that many commentators have seen as characteristic of black people in the modern Western world system. The black subject is a peculiarly positioned, even liminal figure in the grand narratives of modernity, as pointed out by Paul Gilroy.[27] James is almost the paradigm case of such a figure, and his ambiguous modern black subjectivity was the source of his ambivalence towards modernity.

In *Mariners, Renegades and Castaways* (1953) James builds a critical reading of modernity around Herman Melville's novel *Moby-Dick*. James sees the *Peqoud* as modern society in microcosm – organised rationally and dependent upon technology for its continued existence – and reads *Moby-Dick* as a dialectical tale of modernity. Like Adorno in the *Dialectic of Enlightenment*, James in *Mariners* is concerned that the social organisation of modern society, while potentially liberating for the individual, is tendentially oppressive. Though the interdependence necessary to survival could have led to a communalist micro-society aboard the ship, the social structure of the *Pequod* in fact reproduces the class, ethnic and knowledge–power inequality of mainstream modern society.

James's vision of what modernity might become was inspired by transcendent emancipatory political projects like the French and Haitian Revolutions, yet he was demonstrably aware that such ideas and projects were ideals whose realisation had constantly to be struggled for – they were always unfinished. This openness, rare in a Marxist who began his career in the 1930s, is manifested in James's early attempts to incorporate non-class aspects of social differentiation more seriously into his revolutionary praxis. Well before the coming to prominence of identity politics he debated Trotsky on the so-called 'Negro Question';[28] in the 1940s, anticipating some of the concerns of cultural studies, he was writing (in *American Civilization*) on the democratising possibilities of cinema and the comic strip. James was more comfortable with the American[29] mass and popular culture industries than Adorno, but went perhaps too far in the opposite direction: he made an insufficiently critical appraisal of these forms and of the structures and institutions that produced and disseminated them.

James's experiences as a radical labour activist during his American years (1938–53) were crucial both to his elaboration of a critique of communist vanguardism and to his development of a popular democratic reading of modern American society. Against the praxis of the vanguard party, James held that the key to revolutionary struggles lay in peoples' spontaneous self-organisation in all spheres of life. Autonomy was not only a political issue for James, but was also a cultural imperative. He saw the Americans, in their shedding of European class distinctions and conventions, as moving towards a democratisation of cultural form – if not production – exemplified by the cinema, the comic strip and the mass-circulation magazine. The popular arts were a space where what James saw as a uniquely American pursuit of happiness and individual self-fulfilment was played out.

James was aware that not all Americans were equal, and that class, race and gender impacted differentially on individual Americans. He pursued his thesis of American exceptionalism because of his belief that societies were characterised in different historical epochs by typical personalities – that is, Hegelian world-historical individuals. Hamlet was the archetypal European personality on the threshold of modernity; Toussaint L'Ouverture and Napoleon Bonaparte were the world-historical individuals in the age of revolution that started in the late eighteenth century; Melville's Ahab was the archetype of the alienated individual under industrial capitalist society. James applied this method to his reading of American popular arts, seeing in the comic strip character Dick Tracy, for example, the archetype of the rugged individualist pursuing a moral code that transcended the everyday compromises that are typical of life in capitalist society.

This development was not without its flaws. James's romanticism and his own disillusionment with European society led him into an extraordinarily uncritical celebration of the popular-democratic ideology of the American ruling class.[30] What could have so blinded the otherwise staunch anti-imperialist Marxist? When James drafted *American Civilization*, the break-up of the European empires had become a real possibility, and the horrors of World War II had brought into question again the (always questionable) notion of a culturally superior, in the sense of a more civilised, Europe. But the handover of imperial power from Britain and France to America was still in its earliest stages. American neo-imperialism was not yet fully up to speed, though Washington's Caribbean and Central American interventions, beginning with the annexation of Spanish territories in 1898, should have alerted James that there was going to be trouble with the *pax Americana*.

In the 1940s it was perhaps too early for James to have seen that the pursuit of happiness by the 'American people' was sometimes in reality a pursuit of happiness by America's ruling blocs, implemented at the expense of the freedoms and well-being of many who did not have the good fortune to be born (White, middle class and male) American. The tragedy of Native Americans should have sounded another warning note. James's young and bold America would change, from 1948 to 1968, into a major enemy of self-determination in the Third World. In the early twenty-first century, the United States is a bloated colossus astride an increasingly inequitable world disorder, over which the neoconservative US elite appears to be losing the control that the US has held since the end of World War II. In contrast to James's benign reading in *American Civilization*, Adorno would perhaps nod knowingly at what America and the rest of the world have become at the start of the twenty-first century.

Though James in *American Civilization* was at times blind to US imperialism, his work as a whole has much to offer for a critical engagement with the contemporary moment of US hegemony under capitalist globalisation. Despite signs of US weakness, a new mood of Western triumphalism has been growing since the demise of the Soviet Union. The 1990s would see the US and, to a lesser extent, Western European economies resurgent, while Japanese stagnation and the 1997 Asian economic crisis took the shine off the Asian tiger model. With Australia, Ireland and the Scandinavian economies emerging as 'Western tigers', it seemed that the West (in the narrow Western Europe–American axial sense) had triumphed over all others. It seemed to many that, in *The End of History and the Last Man* (1992), Francis Fukuyama was right: perhaps liberal democracy and market society were the end-points of political history.

It has become fashionable in some conservative circles to extol anew the virtues of imperialism. Historian Niall Ferguson is a key figure in this development. He has built a stellar career by first writing a glowing account of the British Empire, and then arguing that the US political leadership should accept its own role as the new imperial power. These two books by Ferguson have become best-sellers, and both have been made into television documentaries, and in turn have made the Scots-born, Oxford-educated Ferguson a high-profile public intellectual in the United States, where he spends part of the year. As Stephen Howe pointed out in a lengthy review, Ferguson's success is due as much to his flattery of the narcissism of western elites as to his prodigious scholarship.[31]

Against Ferguson's celebrations of the good that the British Empire brought to the conquered, and related calls for the United States to realise its true imperial vocation for the good of all humankind, James's work should sound a cautionary note. While James would have had little time for the Anglo-ethnocentrism of Ferguson, it was James nonetheless who insisted that western European modernity benefited all of humankind. Colonisation, exploitation and forced labour represent the dark side of modernity in James's writings, but they were an inescapable part of the making of the present. Where James's *Black Jacobins* departs from Ferguson's analyses of empire is in the central role assigned to Black and Brown Haitians in releasing the promise of modern citizenship held up by the French Revolution. For James, what the Paris masses began in 1789, the masses of San Domingue would complete.

TOWARDS A CONCLUSION

Colonial society was the context in which insurgent intellectuals emerged from dominated social groups. Educated to serve as functionaries in the service of colonial power, some of these would turn their elite education towards radical ends. James's critical humanism emerged from the immanent critique of colonial society that arose out of his schooling, reflection and writing in Trinidad in the 1920s. One of the ways in which the colonial subject was constructed, and in which colonialism sought to justify itself, was in the production of texts that offered accounts of the respective places of both the colonised and the coloniser in the overall scheme of things. Such texts sought to elaborate and justify a world-view in which Europeans were in every way superior to and destined to rule over non-Europeans. Colonialist texts moved with the accepted frontiers of European bourgeois knowledge. As Europeans came to learn more of the world and bring that world under their sway, increasingly elaborate textual constructions were produced which provided ideological support for European colonialism.[32]

One example from the history of British colonialism will suffice. The Oxford historian James Anthony Froude aroused intense passions when he published, in 1887, his *Travels in the West Indies*. Froude based his book on a trip through the Caribbean in 1886. His aim was to show that the Caribbean territories were not fit to govern themselves because the black majority were insufficiently civilised. John Jacob Thomas, an obscure schoolmaster from rural Trinidad, who had recently published *The Theory and Practice of Creole Grammar* (1869), the first study of Creole linguistics, wrote a scathing reply. *Froudacity: West Indian Fables by James Anthony Froude* (1889) is one of the earliest instances of Caribbean people employing the textual medium to counter colonial discourses. James wrote the introduction to the edition of *Froudacity* that was published in 1969 by John La Rose and Sarah White of New Beacon Books in London.[33]

Learning to use the language and intellectual disciplines of the coloniser is a crucial move on the part of the colonial. In so doing, she begins to equip herself with the tools to counter the colonialist narratives that relegate her to a subordinate status. After learning the language of the coloniser, the next move in building up a strategy of discursive resistance to colonialism is to acquire facility in the intellectual disciplines of the colonisers. This is important because a crucial element of the colonial enterprise is to make the intellectual disciplines of the colonisers the dominant ones while, at the same time, devaluing the knowledge of the colonised, and even denying its very status as knowledge, often dismissing it as superstition. The colonial enterprise works partly by asserting the cultural values of the coloniser; under such conditions it seems to the colonised that if her voice is to be heard she must speak in the language and the disciplines of the coloniser.

In the case of the colonial relationship between the Caribbean and Europe, the disciplines of the colonisers were *modern* ones. They facilitated the construction of a human subject with history and agency even though that subject was in fact exclusively the colonial elite, which in constituting its own subjectivity, simultaneously denied such subjectivity to the colonised. James would break with this colonial elite, though he was schooled to be a member of it. James's appropriation of ideas of the modern human subject, and his discomfort that these ideas were deemed not to apply to the mass of colonised people, would shape much of his work. A drive to vindication, to show that the colonised were also modern subjects, is one of the main motivations behind his works on the Haitian revolution and on cricket and colonialism. Their brutal encounter with modernity, exemplified in plantation slavery, would lead colonised people in the Caribbean to a dream of equality on a humanist basis. Such ideas sometimes opened up the possibility of the construction of a revolutionary subject within the discourses of the coloniser's intellectual disciplines. Taken together, the languages and intellectual disciplines of the coloniser are a large part of the culture of the coloniser: colonial domination is, inter alia, about struggle between cultures and struggle within culture.[34]

In *American Civilization*, James tried to work through what was special about US modernity. His fascination with US space and freedom, compared to the supposed confines of the 'Old World' of Europe, was in keeping with some currents of the liberal left in the middle decades of the twentieth century. James welcomed the imminent end of the European empires, and saw in US liberal democracy and technological prowess the promise of a new era in human civilisation. At the start of the twenty-first century, we know that James got it partly wrong – US hegemony offers little new to the world's majority peoples when compared to British (and French) colonialism. As many Iraqis and Afghans have learned since 9/11, US freedom is for US citizens and the friends of the US only. James was no apologist for US power, and I think he would have been one of the critics of the New World Order had he been alive and active today. He would condemn the abuses of Guantanamo Bay and the authoritarian attack on civil liberties in the United States.

James's humanism arose out of his multidisciplinary approach to the analysis of society and culture; it arose too from a life that spanned almost nine decades and three continents. He consistently argued that cultural criticism and political activity were closely related, and that we would understand both only if we were grounded in the material circumstances of real people. In his work on anticolonialism, on cricket and social change, on popular culture, on revolutionary history and practice, he maintained a commitment to the centrality of the knowing and experiencing subject. He insisted on the importance for leftist praxis of seeing the individual life as a project, and not subsuming individual goals to a Central Committee. These elements are all humanist in their focus on the individual subject, but James developed them along with a critical dimension that was acutely aware of the social and historical constraints on human agency. James's critical humanism harnessed history in the service of a politics of freedom.

NOTES

1. C. Wright Mills, *The Sociological Imagination* (Oxford: Oxford University Press, 1959), pp. 5–10.
2. C.L.R. James, *Beyond a Boundary* (London: Serpent's Tail, 1994), p. 28.
3. There are substantial published and unpublished sources on James's life and work. James offers rich insights into his own life in *Beyond a Boundary*. See also Paul Buhle, *C.L.R. James: The Artist as Revolutionary* (London: Verso, 1989); Paul Buhle and Paget Henry, *C.L.R. James's Caribbean* (Durham: Duke University Press, 1992); William E. Cain and Selwyn R. Cudjoe (eds), *C.L.R. James: His Intellectual Legacy* (Amherst: University of Massachusetts Press, 1995); Farrukh Dhondy, *C.L.R. James: Cricket, the Caribbean, and World Revolution* (London: Weidenfeld & Nicolson, 2001); Keith Hart, 'Anna Grimshaw and C.L.R. James', *The C.L.R. James Journal* 3 (1992), pp. 74–8; Nicole King, *C.L.R. James and Creolization: Circles of Influence* (Jackson: University Press of Mississippi, 2001); Scott McLemee, *C.L.R. James on the 'Negro Question'* (Jackson: University Press of Mississippi, 1996); Aldon Lynn Nielsen, *C.L.R. James: A Critical Introduction* (Jackson: University Press of Mississippi, 1997); Kent Worcester, *C.L.R. James: A Political Biography* (Albany: State University of New York, 1996).
4. See Morroe Berger, *Real and Imagined Worlds: The Novel and Social Science* (Cambridge, Mass.: Harvard University Press, 1977), p. 6.
5. See Alan Swingewood, *The Novel and Revolution* (London: Macmillan, 1975), p. 48.
6. See Anna Grimshaw and Keith Hart, *Anthropology and the Crisis of the Intellectuals* (Cambridge: Prickly Pear Pamphlets, 1993), p. 16.
7. See Paul Atkinson, *The Ethnographic Imagination: Textual Constructions of Reality* (London: Routledge, 1990), pp. 54–6.
8. Kenneth Ramchand, *The West Indian Novel and Its Background* (London: Heinemann, 1983), p. 5.
9. S.R. Cudjoe, *Resistance and Caribbean Literature* (Athens, OH: Ohio University Press, 1980), p. 267.

10. Reinhard Sander, *The Trinidad Awakening: West Indian Literature of the Nineteen Thirties* (New York: Greenwood, 1988), p 148; C.L.R. James, *The Case for West Indian Self-Government* (London: Hogarth Press, 1933).
11. A barrack yard was a collection of dwellings for the urban poor; it was a common feature of the capital of colonial Trinidad. The yard comprised a central open area, often unpaved, with communal washing and bathing facilities. Around this area was a group of one- or two-room wooden dwellings, in which lived single people, couples or even families. A major achievement of postcolonial administrations was the clearance of these yards. Barrack yards featured prominently in many early novels on Trinidad and Jamaica.
12. From a 1973 lecture delivered at Rutgers University (quote from page 10); transcript in James archive; www.clrjamesinstitute.org
13. *Beyond a Boundary*, pp. 29–30.
14. Angus Calder, 'An Audience with C.L.R. James', *Third World Book Review* 1 (1984), p. 21.
15. Avery F. Gordon, 'Globalism and the Prison Industrial Complex: An Interview With Angela Davis', *Race and Class* 40 (1998), pp. 145–57.
16. See Cederic Robinson, *Black Marxism* (London: Zed, 1983).
17. See Anthony Bogues, *Caliban's Freedom: The Early Political Thought of C.L.R. James* (London: Pluto Press, 1997).
18. It may not perhaps have been all that far-fetched to compare Ancient Greece and the modern Caribbean as 'hothouse' culture areas, as is suggested by anthropologist Sidney Mintz. See Sidney Wilfred Mintz, 'Enduring Substances, Trying Theories: The Caribbean Region as Oikumenê', *Journal of the Royal Anthropological Institute* 2:2 (1996), pp. 289–311.
19. See articles by Maurice St Pierre, L. O'Brien Thompson, Hilary McD. Beckles and Brian Stoddart in Beckles and Stoddart (eds), *Liberation Cricket: West Indies Cricket Culture* (Manchester: Manchester University Press, 1995).
20. *Beyond a Boundary*, p. 66.
21. James, *Cricket*, ed. Anna Grimshaw (London: Allison and Busby, 1989), pp. 199–200.
22. See Walter Rodney, *A History of the Guyanese Working People* (Baltimore: Johns Hopkins University Press, 1981); Kelvin Singh, *Race and Class Struggles in a Colonial State: Trinidad 1917–1945* (Calgary and Mona, Kingston: University of Calgary Press and The Press-University of the West Indies, 1994).
23. For James's vivid account of these events see *Beyond a Boundary*, Chapter 18. For the views of a key participant in the movement for West Indian federation and independence, see Eric Williams, *Inward Hunger: The Education of a Prime Minister* (London: Andre Deutsch, 1969).
24. *Beyond a Boundary*, pp. 260–1.
25. See Carl C. Campbell, *The Young Colonials: A Social History of Education in Trinidad and Tobago 1834–1939* (Barbados, Jamaica, Trinidad and Tobago: University Press of the West Indies, 1996), Chapter 1.
26. See James M. Harding, 'Adorno, Ellison, and the Critique of Jazz', *Cultural Critique* 31 (Fall 1995), pp. 129–58.

27. Paul Gilroy, *The Black Atlantic: Modernity and Double Consciousness* (Cambridge, Mass.: Harvard University Press, 1993), p. 4.
28. See McLemee (ed.), *C.L.R. James on the 'Negro Question'*, pp. 74–6.
29. I use 'American' here to mean 'of the United States'. This is in keeping with James's usage, but is of course not ideal in that it excludes half of the continent.
30. See Andrew Ross, 'Civilization in one country', in *Rethinking C.L.R. James: A Critical Reader*, ed. Grant Farred (Cambridge, Mass. & Oxford: Blackwell, 1996), pp. 103–30.
31. Stephen Howe, 'An Oxford Scot at King Dubya's Court: Niall Ferguson's Colossus', http://www.opendemocracy.net/content/articles/PDF/2021.pdf?redirect2=/debates/article-3-77-2021.jsp. *openDemocracy*, 22 July 2004.
32. See Peter Hulme, *Colonial Encounters: Europe and the Native Caribbean, 1492–1797* (London: Routledge, 1992); Ashis Nandy, *Intimate Enemy: Loss and Recovery of Self Under Colonialism* (New York: Oxford University Press, 1983); Edward Said, *Representations of the Intellectual: The 1993 Reith Lectures* (London: Vintage, 1994).
33. For an account of the work of La Rose, White and their associates, see Brian.W. Alleyne, *Radicals Against Race: Black Activism and Cultural Politics* (Oxford: Berg, 2002), especially Chapters 1 and 2.
34. See Cudjoe, *Resistance and Caribbean Literature*; Frantz Fanon, *The Wretched of the Earth* (London: Penguin, 1967), and *Black Skin, White Masks* (New York: Grove, 1967); Amon Saba Saakana, *The Colonial Legacy in Caribbean Literature* (London: Karnak House, 1987); Said, *Representations of the Intellectual*.

Contributors

Brian Alleyne teaches sociology at Goldsmiths College, London. He is the author of *Radicals Against Race: Black Activism and Cultural Politics* (2002). His interests are: globalisation; sociology and political economy of information technologies; new media and interactive environments; ethnography; biography and narrative.

Anthony Bogues is professor and chair of the Africana Studies Department at Brown University. He is the author of *Caliban's Freedom: The Early Political Thought of C.L.R. James* (1997), *Black Heretics, Black Prophets: Radical Political Intellectuals* (2003) and *Empire, Imperial Desire and the Politics of Ways of Life* (2004).

Christopher Gair is Senior Lecturer in the Department of American and Canadian Studies, University of Birmingham. He is the author of *Complicity and Resistance in Jack London's Novels: From Naturalism to Nature* (1997), of *The American Counterculture* (forthcoming), and of numerous essays on American literature and culture.

Nicole King is Associate Professor of Literature at the University of California at San Diego. She is the author of *C.L.R. James and Creolization: Circles of Influence* (2001). Her areas of research expertise include twentieth-century US and Caribbean literature and culture, and she is currently at work on a book that explores American representations of black authenticity at the turn of the twenty-first century.

Richard King is Professor of American Intellectual History at the University of Nottingham. He is the author of *The Party of Eros: Radical Social Thought and the Realm of Freedom* (1972), *A Southern Renaissance: The Cultural Awakening of the American South, 1930–1955* (1980), *Civil Rights and the Idea of Freedom* (1992), *Dixie Debates: Perspective on Southern Cultures* (ed. with Helen Taylor, 1996) and *From Universalism to Particularism: Shifting Ideas of Race and Culture, 1940–1975* (2004).

Donald E. Pease is Avalon Foundation Chair of the Humanities, professor of English and American Literature, Chair of the Master of Arts in Liberal Studies Program, and Director of the Institute on the Future of American Studies at Dartmouth. He is the general editor of the New Americanists Series at Duke University Press.

Eric Porter is Associate Professor of American Studies at the University of California, Santa Cruz. He is the author of *What is this Thing Called Jazz? African American Musicians as Artists, Critics, and Activists* (2002).

Bill Schwarz teaches in the School of English and Drama, Queen Mary, University of London. Most recently he has edited *West Indian Intellectuals in Britain*, and (with Richard Drayton) written the introduction to the Pluto Classic reprint of George Lamming's *The Pleasures of Exile*.

Index

Compiled by Sue Carlton

abolitionism 45, 146
Abyssinia 18, 20, 22, 23, 24, 32
Adorno, Theodor 46, 47, 48, 132, 147, 176, 187–8, 189
Agamben, Giorgio 70
Allen, Gubby 94, 95, 97, 101, 102
American Civilization (James) 39, 40–56, 103, 131, 133, 137, 138–9, 193
 and black activism 43, 45, 47, 145–7
 and popular culture 41–2, 46, 47–9, 51–2, 54–5, 103, 132, 140, 141–3, 163–4, 188, 189
 and US imperialism 46–7, 166–7, 190
 usefulness in twenty-first century 49–51
American Studies
 implications of *American Civilization* 40–56
 and national identity 74–7
 postnational 89–92, 100, 102, 105–6
 transnational 78–84
 and US exceptionalism 66–8, 72, 73, 82–3, 102
American Studies Institute 66
Anderson, Fred 166
anticolonialism 18, 20, 28, 168, 175, 178
Arendt, Hannah 108–24
 and human rights 118–19
 and revolution 121–2
 source of political ideas 109, 122–3
 and totalitarianism 110–12, 114–17
assimilation 77

Bakhtin, M.M. 168
Barnes, S.F. 97–8
Benjamin, Walter 47, 64, 109
Bevan, Aneurin 98
Beyond a Boundary (James) 22, 78, 128–9, 132, 140, 151, 176, 182–3
 and bodyline crisis 90, 96, 98–100, 105
 and rejection of Trotskyism 130–1
 understanding human society 157, 159, 167, 168–71
biopower 52–3, 54
black activism 43, 45, 47, 144, 145–7
The Black Jacobins: Toussaint L'Ouverture and the San Domingo Revolution (James) 13–15, 17, 21, 25, 32, 124, 181–2, 191
Black Marxism 181–2
Black Reconstruction (Du Bois) 13, 166, 182
Blucher, Heinrich 109
bodyline crisis 1932–33 90, 92–7, 98–100, 105
Bonaparte, Napoleon 189
Bondman, Matthew 169–70
Boorstin, Daniel 66
Bourne, Randolph 67
Bradman, Donald 92, 93, 95, 98–9, 105
Brathwaite, Kamau 16
Brecht, Bertolt 109, 116
Buhle, Paul 20
Burnham, James 42
Bush Doctrine 166
Butler, Judith 160

Carby, Hazel V. 98
Cardus, Neville 92
The Case for West-Indian Self-Government (James) 22, 178
Cayton, Andrew 166
Chaplin, Charlie 138–9, 142, 145
Chase, Richard 61, 67–8

Chauliu, Pierre 120
Cherokees 165–6
Childs, Lydia Marie 67
Christophe, Henri 21, 24, 30
Cipriani, Captain 91, 94, 105
clash of civilisations 176, 187
The C.L.R. James Reader 26–7
Cold War 44, 65, 66, 68–9, 71, 78, 80
and American society 67, 103–6
colonialism 53, 72–4, 191–3
Communism 15, 18, 19, 45, 109
see also Marxism; socialism; Trotskyism
Constantine, Learie 91, 96, 100, 130
consumerism 40, 41, 54
cricket 89, 91, 103, 128–9, 130, 131, 140
bodyline crisis 1932–33 90, 92–7, 98–100, 105
and social change in West Indies 176, 182–7
and Taylorisation 98, 100
see also Beyond a Boundary
Croce, Benedetto 148
cultural imperialism 74–7
culture 157–8

Davis, Angela 181
Dayan, Joan 33–4
Deleuze, Gilles 160
Denning, Michael 42
Dessalines, Jean Jacques 16, 17, 21, 24, 25, 30–1
'Dialectical Materialism and the Fate of Humanity' (James) 43, 160
Douglass, Frederick 67
Du Bois, W.E.B. 13, 109, 166, 179
Duberman, Martin 20–1, 24
Dubois, Laurent 31
Dunayevskaya, Raya 43, 150–1

Economic and Philosophic Manuscripts of 1844 (Marx) 150–1
Edwards, Jonathan 165
Eichmann in Jerusalem (Arendt) 117
Eliot, T.S. 140
Ellis Island 59, 62, 64, 68, 71, 72, 74, 78–9, 80–4, 90

Ellison, Ralph 144
Engels, Friedrich 179
enlightenment 180, 188

Facing Reality (James, Lee and Chauliu) 120, 123
Fanon, Franz 152, 162
Fascism 19, 111, 115
Ferguson, Niall 191
Fingleton, Jack 105
Fordism 41, 137, 150
Foucault, Michel 52, 54, 83, 157, 164
Frankfurt School 47, 109, 114, 151
free association 131–2, 137, 151
freedom 42–3, 45, 48, 158, 159, 160–1
America and 50, 53, 164–7
and hegemony 162–4
and popular culture 163–4
French Revolution 1789 189, 191
Freud, Sigmund 159
Froude, James Anthony 192
Fukuyama, Francis 191

Garvey, Amy Ashwood 22
Geggus, David 31
Ghana 128
Gilroy, Paul 129, 188
Glaberman, Martin 43, 150
Gold Coast Revolution 1956 119–20, 122
governmentality 54
Gramsci, Antonio 47, 49, 141, 158, 162, 166
Greece 140, 170, 180, 182
Greek polis 109, 122–3
Green, Michael 165
Griffith, D.W. 142, 145, 146
Grimshaw, Anna 26–7, 42, 45
Guattari, Felix 160

Hall, Stuart 16, 49, 62–3, 157–8, 164
Hart, Keith 42, 45
Hartz, Louis 66, 67
Hegel, G.W.F. 147–8, 159
hegemony
and freedom 162–4
role of language 161–2
US 165–6, 187–91, 193

Heideggar, Martin 116
Hemingway, Ernest 140
heterotopia 83–4
Hicks, Granville 67
Hill, Robert A. 22, 23, 24
A History of Negro Revolt (James) 21, 43
Hitler, Adolf 116
Horkheimer, Max 46, 47, 132, 147
Howe, Stephen 191
human beings
   and culture 157–8
   and desire 159–61
   self-realisation 48, 151–2, 158, 161, 164
   study of human society 168, 170
The Human Condition (Arendt) 122–3
human rights 118–19
humanism 175–94
   critical 175, 188, 191
   Marxist 151–2, 179
Hummer sports utility vehicle 39–40, 54
Humphreys, David 165
Hungarian Revolution 1956 109, 110, 119–22, 158

Immediate Theatre Involvement 32
Immigration and Naturalization Service (INS) 59, 62, 63, 68, 73, 76–7, 79, 82, 119, 133
imperialism 191
   American 46–7, 166–7, 190
   cultural 74–7
individualism 41, 45, 112, 117–18, 131–2
intellectuals 141
International African Friends of Abyssinia (IAFA) 22
International African Opinion 22
International African Service Bureau (IASB) 22, 26

James, C.L.R.
   deportation 42, 67, 119
   detention 59, 68, 71, 74, 80–3, 90
   and Hannah Arendt 108–24
   importance of 123–4
   and Marxism 18, 20, 25, 43–4, 123, 124, 133, 147–52, 158, 175, 188
   partnership with Robeson 18–23, 32
   source of political ideas 109, 122–3
   and Trotskyism 18, 19, 20, 109
   rejection of 130–1, 133, 139–40, 147, 148
   and US citizenship 59, 60–4, 72–3, 79, 92, 104–5, 106, 119
   visit to US 129–30
   and Western culture 176, 180–2
Jardine, Douglas 92, 93–5, 96, 99, 100, 101, 102, 103, 104, 105
Johnson–Forest Tendency 43, 45, 150, 151

Kadar, Janos 122
Kelley, Robin D.G. 22, 27–8
Kenyatta, Jomo 22

labour activism 41, 42, 45–8, 50, 189
Lacan, Jacques 160
Laclau, Ernesto 160
Lamming, George 162
language
   and colonialism 192–3
   and hegemony 161–2
Larwood, Harold 93, 94, 95, 96–7, 101, 103
Lee, Grace 43, 120, 150–1
The Life of Captain Cipriani (James) 19
Lipsitz, George 44
Little Caesar (Burnett) 103
Luxemburg, Rosa 109
Lyndersay, Dexter 32
Lyotard, Jean-François 60

McCarran-Walter Act 59–61, 63, 64, 65–6, 67–8, 71–2, 80, 104, 119
McCarthyism 112, 119
Mahabir, Joy 29
Mailer, Norman 141
Marcuse, Herbert 151

Mariners, Renegades and Castaways (James) 131, 135, 167–8, 188
  and bodyline crisis 97, 100–2, 104, 105
  and Cold War American society 103
  and James's case for citizenship 59, 61–4, 79–80, 83–4, 119
  and postnational American Studies 90, 91, 106
  and totalitarianism 110, 112–13, 117, 137
Marti, Jose 67, 167
Marx, Karl 150–1, 158, 161, 184
Marxism 18, 20, 25, 43–4, 123, 124, 133, 147–52, 158, 175, 188
  see also Communism; socialism; Trotskyism
Mbembe, Achille 41, 52–3, 54
Melville, Herman 44–5, 59, 67, 100, 133–7
  world-historical reading of 136, 138–9, 167–8, 189
  see also Moby-Dick
Mendes, Alfred 179
militarism 40, 41, 54, 55
Mill, John Stuart 118
Mills, C. Wright 175–6
Minty Alley (James) 19, 27, 91, 179
Moby-Dick (Melville) 61–4, 68–77, 110, 112–15, 116–18, 133–7, 138, 168, 170, 188
  and transnational American Studies 78–9, 81–4
  see also Mariners, Renegades and Castaways
Modern Politics (James) 123, 159, 161
Moise 24
Montgomery revolt 1956 119–20, 122

nation-state 119
National Security Strategy 166
necropolitics 41, 52, 54–5
Nielsen, Aldon 49
Nkrumah, Kwame 128
Notes on American Civilization (James) 131, 133
Notes on Dialectics (James) 148, 150

Oldfield, Bert 95–6
The Origins of Totalitarianism (Arendt) 110, 112, 116, 117, 118, 123, 124

Padmore, George 22
pan-Africanism 15, 17, 18–19, 22, 28, 128, 144, 145, 180
Pataudi, Nawab of 94, 101, 105
Pease, Donald E. 89–91, 100, 119, 167–8
Perdue, Theda 165
Philadelphia Negro (Du Bois) 179
Phillips, Wendell 45
Plato 122
popular culture 41–2, 140, 141–3, 168, 188, 189, 190
  and freedom 48, 163–4
  and popular desire 46, 47–8, 51–2, 132
  and violence 41, 53–5, 103
postnational American Studies 89–92, 100, 102, 105–6
power 164–5
  see also hegemony
productivism 148–50

race/racism 115, 143–7, 181–2
Radway, Janice 66
Ramchand, Ken 178
Redburn (Melville) 134
revolts, workers' 119–22, 158, 189
Robeson, Essie 21, 23
Robeson, Paul 13, 15, 17, 24, 28, 109
  Communism 18, 19–20, 33
  partnership with James 18–23, 32, 108
Robinson, Cederic 181
Rolphe-Trouillot, Michel 31
Ross, Andrew 46
Russian Revolution 1917 160

Saint-Domingue Revolution (Haitian Revolution) 14, 16–17, 18, 20, 22, 24, 189, 191
  and voudou 29, 31
  see also The Black Jacobins; Toussaint L'Ouverture

Sander, Reinhard 25, 178
Schlesinger, Arthur 66
Shachtman, Max 42
slavery 53, 71, 146, 163, 181–2
   see also *The Black Jacobins*;
      Saint-Domingue Revolution;
      Toussaint L'Ouverture
social realism 176–9
socialism 18, 41, 52, 109
sovereign will of the people 65–6
Stage Society 23–4
state of emergency 65, 66, 67, 70, 72
   and colonial state 72–4

Thomas, John Jacob 192
Thompson, E.P. 91, 103, 128, 186
Tocqueville, Alexis de 66, 132, 162, 167
totalitarianism 109–12, 114–17, 123, 137–41, 158
   America and 50, 112
   in *American Civilization* 43, 44, 45, 46
   and bodyline crisis 92, 100, 101–2, 105
   Haiti 24
   and human rights 118–19
   importance of leader 116–17
   and *Moby-Dick* 68, 70–1
   and popular culture 46, 52, 55
   and revolution 43, 44, 45, 119–22
   rise of 19
   use of term 110–12
Toussaint L'Ouverture, François Dominique 16, 17, 21, 24, 25, 30, 189
Toussaint L'Ouverture (James) 13–15
   1936 production of 13, 23–4
   Abyssinian context 18, 20, 22, 23, 24, 32
   creolisation 14, 15–18, 29, 31, 33
   lack of aesthetic value 15, 25–8, 32

   post-1967 productions 28, 32
   revised version (1967) 13, 26–7
   and Robeson-James partnership 18–23, 32
   and voudou 28–31, 32, 33–4
Trotsky, Leon 43, 129, 139–40, 189
Trotskyism 18, 19, 20, 109
   James's rejection of 130–1, 133, 139–40, 147, 148
Trotskyist Worker's Party 43
Tubman, Harriet 136

United States
   citizenship 41, 59–64, 72–3, 77, 79, 92, 104–5, 106, 119
   Constitution 104–5
   exceptionalism 44, 50, 53, 64–72, 73, 76, 77–8, 80, 82–3, 90, 102
   and free association 131–2, 137
   and freedom 164–7
   imperialism 46–7, 166–7, 190
   and power/hegemony 165–6, 187–91, 193
   and socialism 67
   and totalitarianism 50, 112

violence, and popular culture 41, 53–5, 103
Voce, Bill 93, 94, 97
voudou 15, 28–31, 32, 33–4

Walcott, Derek 141
Warner, Pelham ('Plum') 94–5, 96, 102
Webb, Constance 144
Weber, Max 114
Wesker, Arnold 25–6, 32
Williams, Raymond 161–2
Wittgenstein, Ludwig 162
Woodfull, Bill 95, 96
Worrell, Frank 186–7
Wright, Richard 67, 144
Wyatt, Bob 95, 101
Wynter, Sylvia 72, 157, 164, 168